Seeing the Child in Child Protection Soci

C000070669

Seeing the Child in Child Protection Social Work

SUE KENNEDY

© Sue Kennedy, under exclusive licence to Springer Nature Limited 2020

All rights reserved. No reproduction, copy or transmission of this publication may be made without written permission.

No portion of this publication may be reproduced, copied or transmitted save with written permission or in accordance with the provisions of the Copyright, Designs and Patents Act 1988, or under the terms of any licence permitting limited copying issued by the Copyright Licensing Agency, Saffron House, 6–10 Kirby Street, London EC1N 8TS.

Any person who does any unauthorized act in relation to this publication may be liable to criminal prosecution and civil claims for damages.

The author has asserted her right to be identified as the author of this work in accordance with the Copyright, Designs and Patents Act 1988.

First published 2020 by
RED GLOBE PRESS

Red Globe Press in the UK is an imprint of Springer Nature Limited, registered in England, company number 785998, of 4 Crinan Street, London, N1 9XW.

Red Globe Press® is a registered trademark in the United States, the United Kingdom, Europe and other countries.

ISBN 978-1-137-50214-8 paperback

This book is printed on paper suitable for recycling and made from fully managed and sustained forest sources. Logging, pulping and manufacturing processes are expected to conform to the environmental regulations of the country of origin.

A catalogue record for this book is available from the British Library.

A catalogue record for this book is available from the Library of Congress.

*In memory
of my parents – Elsie and Stan*

Acknowledgements

This journey has been some time in the making. It began with discussions between family and friends about the state of child protection social work. I had many discussions with my good friend and colleague Dr Angie Bartoli about child protection practice and they usually ended with our saying to each other 'It's all over', an acknowledgement that we were concerned about the direction of politics and practice in children's social work. However, from our musings came questions about past and present practice – our own and others' – and I became motivated to tell the story of some of the children I worked with over the years. My hope was that their testimonies would bring about a shift that means the child is seen in child protection social work.

The children in this book have been a constant reminder to me of why we need to step back and look at what it means to do child protection social work. The future will be a challenge, and if there was ever a time when children need to be seen in child protection social work, it is now. The landscape looks bleak, and cash-strapped Children's Services will be caught up in political ideologies and budget-led decisions that will mean children who need support and protection face powerful adult narratives that again will increase the potential for them to be unseen, unprotected and unknown.

Throughout this journey, I have been, as ever, thankful for the support of my husband, who has tirelessly listened to my struggles and supported me to keep going – a job he has done for so many years. His love and strength have been constants and I am what I am only because of him. I am also indebted to my wonderful friends Bren and Angie for their support and confidence in me to get the book finished. My daughter, as ever, has been a great source of support and wisdom, and without my grandchildren, I am sure I would have lost perspective and stayed in a place that says it's all over.

The support and guidance from the staff at Red Globe Press have been wonderful. Their patience, encouragement and belief in the project are immeasurable. I am thankful for all their help.

Contents

Introduction

Have social workers lost sight of the child in child protection?

Buster Keaton grew up in America around the turn of the 19th century. His childhood has been examined by Miller (1990), who calls attention to the abuse the actor was subjected to by his father and mother on stage in front of an audience.

Buster Keaton started appearing on stage with his parents, who were vaudeville performers, and helped to make them famous by taking severe abuse in front of an audience without batting an eyelash ... *if I should chance a smile, the next hit would be a good deal harder ... I could not even whimper ...* The audience would squeal with delight. (Miller, 1990:39)

This vignette offers a demonstration of how an audience became so focussed on the performance that they failed to see what was really taking place. I use this vignette as a challenge to raise the question of why the audience did not see what was happening to the child. This very question is reminiscent of those asked by the media and politicians several decades later in high-profile child deaths in England where social workers who were known to the child and who had been visiting over a period of time failed to see the risks or make sense of the situation for the child.

The story of Buster Keaton resonates with me as a social worker who remembers times in my practice when I too had to question what I had seen or not seen during home visits and direct work with children. On planned and unplanned home visits, I would be faced with a carer or parent or parents who made every effort to assure me that everything was as it should be. On a good day, the child or children would slip into view. I would see a tableau of people and children locked together in a highly charged situation where emotions were heightened and behaviours extreme. In that moment, I would gather my thoughts, drawing upon all that I had learned, and acknowledge the knot in my stomach, hoping that what I was feeling was not visible or able to imprison me in professional paralysis. There are few social workers who have not experienced such a moment or remember how they responded when faced with such emotions and physical reactions. Equally, there are many social workers who remember what they did at that time and what they did afterwards – to whom they spoke, and how they recorded this. When I think back to those times, the question I ask is – did I see the child and did I get it right for them?

Protecting children from abuse has always been controversial. As the quote above highlights, the general public in the case of Buster Keaton were happy to look on as he was physically abused. They believed that this was entertainment or that no one would dare intervene. However, there is an expectation that those employed and therefore responsible for protecting children will not stand in the margins and look on when a child is being abused or at risk of being abused. Unfortunately, social workers have achieved the dubious distinction of becoming very familiar to the media for not doing their job and not protecting children from abuse. The general public supported by government ministers have shared their sense of incredulity when a child has died from abuse and it was reported that they were known to social workers who had been either visiting them or trying to gain access to their home. The general view from the media discourse is that protecting children from abuse should be straightforward – it can be predicted and mitigated against and professional social workers should be able to do this – they should not stand in the margins. If only it were that easy.

High-profile child abuse investigations and child deaths such as those of Peter Connelly (Baby P) and Victoria Climbié have placed the discipline of social work firmly at the centre of media criticisms and government responses that have seen the production of legislation and policy guidance aimed at ensuring that social workers working in child protection do not fail children. However, the underlying tone of blame that focussed on the inactions and failures of individual social workers has produced more procedural approaches. Social work researchers and commentators argue that these approaches have constrained social work thinking and direct practice (Munro, 2008; Ferguson, 2011; Featherstone *et al.*, 2014) and instead of keeping the child firmly at the centre of practice have drawn social work attention away from the child as a result of the demands of the organisation, systems and adults (Brandon *et al.*, 2012).

Many social workers work extremely hard to ensure this does not happen and are successful in protecting children. However, social workers also say that high caseloads, organisational restructuring, staffing constraints, timescales, limited budgets and performance targets have contributed to child protection's becoming child-blind. In this climate, a proactive and provocative question is, how can social workers reposition their attention and practice to ensure that the child who is the reason for their involvement is seen – really seen – their identity, ethnicity, attributes, abilities, gender and situation – and remains at the heart of social work interventions that seek better outcomes for the child, their parents/carers and the social workers?

Locally and nationally, child protection social workers will be responding to the many questions being asked of them by the general public, media and politicians and more immediately their own organisations. They will also be aware that the political and social work literature has produced a discourse of change that promotes transforming how child protection is delivered. In this climate of change, it is hard to see how social workers can find any sense of stability. If child protection social work as a professional discipline is to emerge recycled from the media and political waste that has tried to dispose of it over the decades, social workers are going to have to find their professional 'one-of-a-kind voice' (Estes, 2010:1) that speaks not only for the child but for themselves.

It may be some years since I was in direct practice. However, the fundamental basics that are involved in carrying out child protection social work have not changed. The introduction of technology to the administration processes has produced a range of challenges alongside ongoing restructuring of service provision. When all is stripped away, what is left are those interpersonal skills and abilities of observation, listening, thinking and understanding which are the tools that, when used well, help social workers 'see beyond the obvious' (Estes, 2010:1). I argue that it is time for social workers to reclaim these skills and abilities and ensure that they are the foundations of a tool kit they develop and add to. The importance of revisiting what many social workers and academics may refer to as basic social work skills is that, by doing so, insights are developed and practice reclaimed. I do not think this is a new way of thinking about social work practice in child protection. The skills of observation, listening, thinking and understanding are the foundations of social work practice and, many newly qualified social workers argue, are stolen by the organisations that demand an industrial approach to responding and intervening in children's lives. If this is the case and there is increasing evidence to support what newly qualified social workers are saying about feeling overwhelmed by the complexity and numbers of child protection cases they are being allocated, it is time to find ways of engaging social workers, whether they are newly qualified or post-qualified, in finding and re-examining their skills and abilities so they can position themselves solidly as the profession that knows and sees children in child protection social work.

Aims and purpose of this book

This book aims to reposition the child by developing child-focussed social work practice that extracts the child from the messiness created by the adults, placing them firmly at the centre of their lived experience. I will argue that, thereby, the needs and behaviour of the adults can be better understood and the outcome for the child is situated within the possibilities for change. I will do this using real-world case studies that draw upon events that took place during my 20 years of social work practice in Children's Services. The words, language and events used will be those of the children I have had the privilege of working with as a social worker and who have let me into their lived experience with little or no real expectations. Using the lives of the children who were known to social work services presents a range of ethical dilemmas, not the least of which is whether I could interpret and represent their experiences for others to learn from without distorting for effect or sounding patronising. I am mindful of the fact that globally children have little or no power over the adult world they live in and this book is an example of that at many levels. The children whose lives are presented in this book did not agree to participate and will be unaware that their experiences have been used to produce ways of learning for those mandated to protect them. For this reason, their names have been changed to ensure they remain anonymous.

The children presented in the case studies have been with me for many years and are the motivation for writing this book. Importantly, I learned from them and my social work practice was enhanced. Therefore, while there are many aims to this book, the central tenet is my intention to present the lived experiences of the children as a testimony to their skills, humour, resilience and childhood in such a way that their interests are served by influencing practitioner practice.

An overall aim of the book is to engage those working with children in the sphere of child protection in an accessible publication grounded in practice experience. The child will be at the centre, and throughout the book, research will be explored and practice developments discussed that should inform planning and interventions in child protection. As part of this process, the tensions and dilemmas that social workers and other professionals may face will be critically considered and I will suggest some creative ways for working with children and the adults in their lives.

Each chapter will draw upon detailed practice experiences using case studies and examples from serious case reviews (SCRs) with references to research, policy and practice. It is important to stress that SCRs occur after a child death or when a child has suffered serious injury and are not representative of the range of child protection and child care practice that takes place across the UK. Indeed, UK child protection social work and its systems and procedures are considered to be the most protective in the Western world (Parton, 2014). Although there have been suggestions that good child protection practice and outcomes should provide the focus for learning lessons, it remains the case that the statutory nature of the SCR continues to provide a formal gathering of information that provides insights into practice that we can learn from, albeit from a position of hindsight. For this reason, I have chosen to draw upon specific SCRs to illustrate how the children in question became invisible to those responsible for providing services to protect them and then pose questions that aim to support new thinking and practice about how to see the child.

I suggested earlier that I will offer creative ways for working with children and the adults in their lives. One of these creative ways will be the introduction of a feminist-informed model (FIM) for practice. I have chosen the FIM as a model to use in child protection practice because it is underpinned by feminist principles that challenge inequality and power. What the FIM brings to child protection practice is its capacity to 'rustle the culture' (Campbell, 2013:7) in such a way that events and situations are viewed from a different perspective. I argue that the FIM achieves this by challenging practitioners to examine the child's experience from the perspectives of:

> The child

> The political

> The critical

> The power

The FIM is offered as a foundational model for practice to be used on its own or to support existing models where social workers are called upon to make a decision about a child's needs or the risks posed to them. The FIM will be explained in Chapter 2 and there will be opportunities to explore how the FIM can be applied in practice by using some of the case studies presented in the book.

Each chapter will provide a distinctive case study that sets out the reason for social work intervention. What is distinctive about each case study is that the words of the child – their story – are used to help practitioners gain some insight into their lived experiences. Each case study has been chosen to reflect a wide range of child protection experiences such as neglect, violence and sexual abuse. In each child's story, I focus on specific aspects – parental capacity, child development and behaviour, and inter-professional working. I argue that these different aspects bring additional complexities to the experiences of all those involved and therefore need to be examined by paying attention to the narratives of the children and the adults.

The book is ambitious in its aspirations to reposition the child and practice in child protection social work. On reflection, this is a huge task for one book and what I hope is that my enthusiasm will inspire students and post-qualified practitioners to rethink how they approach working with children and the adults in their lives.

1

Keeping the Child in Mind

So often it is the media that present pictures of a child who has died as a result of abuse by their parents or carers. The pictures peer out from social media and have come to define child protection in the UK. In the reporting of child deaths, the shocking details of how they were abused tend to overshadow who the children were. The children become defined by the abuse and adult behaviour.

These images are created and presented to ensure the maximum impact in a consumer transaction aimed at selling news. Unfortunately, the images fade in the wake of other news and over time tend to be forgotten in the memory of the general public. For social workers and other professionals, the names and images of the children are captured in time by government policies and legislation introduced to raise the quality of social work practice and reassure the voting public that measures have been taken to manage the risks of child abuse and child deaths.

However, although high-profile child deaths have changed the political and practice landscape of child protection social work, analysis of serious case reviews (Brandon *et al.*, 2012) highlights that children who become involved with Children's Services remain faceless, little understood and invisible. The reason offered by Brandon *et al.* (2012) for this situation is that social workers either distance themselves from getting to know the children or fail to see them as they run straight ahead, summoned to deal with the complexity and anxieties that surround child protection social work. This finding is supported by Ferguson (2003:10), who states:

> The overwhelming response by welfare states to child deaths ... has been to seek bureaucratic solutions by introducing more and more laws, procedures and guidelines. The more risk and uncertainty has been exposed, the greater the attempts to close the gaps through administration changes. While these are valid concerns the problems surround the one-dimensionality of the approach and the relentless focus on new forms of organising child welfare work. The space between organisations and ... the child ... continue to be elusive as ever as all those solid laws and guidelines melt into air.

This chapter is about bringing to the forefront those children who come to the notice of social workers as a result of abuse and is set within an examination of the Children Act 1989 and the Children Act 2004. Both of these acts were considered to be child-centred and ambitious in their intentions to bring about a different social and cultural relationship with children in England and Wales who needed support and protection. An important focus of this chapter will be to question whether the lives of children who are considered likely to suffer significant harm have become more complex in this time frame and, if so, what this means for the child and social work practice in child protection now.

Before we set the scene of this chapter, it is worth being reminded what the definition of a child is in the context of child protection.

A child is anyone who has not yet reached their 18th birthday. Child protection guidance highlights that under-18s who are

➤ aged 16 or over

➤ living independently

➤ in further education

➤ a member of the armed forces

➤ in hospital or

➤ in custody or the secure estate

are still legally children and should be given the same protection and entitlements as any other child.

(HM Government, 2015a, 2015b)

I have chosen a case that is representative of those that many social workers and professionals will be working with now. Although events take place before the introduction of the Children Act 1989, the tragic case of Heidi Koseda is a strong reminder that, whatever the political and policy landscape of the time, some children's lived experiences of living with adults who abuse them and those professionals who are mandated to protect them have a tendency to tell a similar story.

Heidi Koseda – A child not seen

The case of Heidi Koseda, a five-year-old child who died of starvation, raises a number of important points for reflection. Heidi was one of a number of children who died as a result of abuse by their parents and carers and whose death was widely reported by the media during the 1980s. Because Heidi's name did not appear on a child abuse register, the then–Secretary of State decided not to instigate a statutory inquiry. However, because Heidi and her family had been known to a range of professionals the year prior to her death, a study of the case was undertaken by a review panel that presented their findings to the Area Review Committee, which considered the findings and recommendations (London Borough of Hillingdon, 1986).

What the review identified was a catalogue of critical moments in which professionals could have prevented Heidi's death. Owing to the exceptional circumstances of the case, a number of changes to systems, professional relationships, legislation and procedures were recommended. Importantly, the recommendations also identified that, when allegations of child abuse are made about a child, every attempt should be made by professionals to 'see' the child and ensure that all of the children in the household are seen and spoken to.

The recommendation of ensuring that children are seen and spoken to when allegations of abuse are being investigated refers to what the review called the exceptional circumstances of Heidi's case. The exceptional circumstances of the case refer to how Heidi became 'lost' in procedural, practice and legal failures that meant she was not seen by professionals involved with the family. The failures identified by the review were associated with the following:

➤ Referrals expressing concerns about Heidi were not acted upon.

➤ Poor record keeping

➤ Poor or no communications between professionals about concerns for Heidi and her siblings

➤ Policies and procedures not followed

➤ Parents' explanations for Heidi's absence were accepted at 'face value'.

➤ Heidi was not seen.

➤ Poor understanding and interpretation of child care legislation

➤ Professionals perceived that the risks to all of the children were low on the basis of an assumption that Heidi's siblings, when they were seen at health clinics, appeared clean and tidy.

(London Borough of Hillingdon, 1986)

The inquiry reported that, when Heidi was eventually found in a bedroom in the family home, she had probably been dead for at least six to eight weeks and that during this period there had been several visits by health professionals, police officers and social workers to the family home (London Borough of Hillingdon, 1986).

A number of factors in the Heidi Koseda case provide more depth of understanding about the context of her life and the family circumstances that led to professional interventions. The review identified how a change in family circumstances soon caused Mrs Koseda to become isolated from her family and community and how the controlling and violent behaviour of Mr Price, her partner, meant that her and her children's life chances became significantly reduced. Moreover, the review showed how difficult it was for professionals to make sense of or indeed keep pace with the changes that were taking place within the family home as different professionals visited and came away with different perspectives about what the risks to the children were.

For example, the review found that Heidi's parents separated when she was two years old. Before this separation, the family, Mr and Mrs Koseda and their daughter Heidi, were described as being open and friendly and living in a well-kept home. Extended family members, such as the maternal grandmother and an aunt, were supportive and regular visitors to the home. This account is in stark contrast to the review report that shows that, from 1982 to 1984, the home conditions changed rapidly when the mother's new partner, Mr Price, moved in. The home was described as squalid and impoverished. Extended family members, specifically the maternal grandmother, had been denied access and said that Mrs Koseda and Mr Price appeared to 'metaphorically raise the drawbridge' (London Borough of Hillingdon, 1986:1.9) to their home.

For Heidi, the raising of the drawbridge meant that those professionals who stepped into this controlled environment did not see her as she was not part of the adult projection of *the family*. To those professionals who visited, the projected family was Mrs Koseda, Mr Price, James and Lisa. Not only had Heidi been physically removed from the family, this absence contributed to a blurring of her image, meaning that professionals were unable to focus their attention, policies and procedures on finding or protecting her. Instead, they focussed on those children they could see – James and Lisa. This starting point led them elsewhere and failed to prepare them for or make them realise the concerns they had for Heidi.

These critical events came to a conclusion when social workers remained concerned that Heidi had not been seen by professionals for some time. While discussions took place to organise a child protection conference, Heidi's maternal grandmother contacted social services to express concerns about the girl's whereabouts. As a result of mounting concerns for Heidi, a child protection conference was held and the names of all the children – Heidi, James and Lisa – were placed on the child abuse register with recommendations that police visit the home immediately to establish where Heidi was. It was during this visit that Heidi's body was found in the bedroom (London Borough of Hillingdon, 1986).

What became clear from the report of the review panel into Heidi's death were the failures at the beginning of the child protection process when the referral to the local authority Children's Services was not acted upon. This particular inquiry finding in 1986 continues to feature in social work debates about how social workers respond to referrals that express concerns about a child. The debates have focussed on the judgements and decision-making processes that decide which child is at risk and in need of protection (Featherstone *et al.*, 2014). These debates have raised concerns that 'a screen and intervene' approach to referrals which Featherstone *et al.* (2014) argue is driven by time frames and budget-led criteria that are unlikely to identify those children in need of protective services. While these debates continue, it remains the case that a referral to Children's Services is a critical moment in the life of the child and ultimately sets the pace of any social work intervention and indeed influences the decision about whether or not there will be any such intervention.

In the case of Heidi, a number of factors were cited to explain why the initial referral was not acted upon. These included staffing shortages, poor recording of the concerns and sadly the initial referral's ultimately being lost in a system that relied on individual social workers to process incoming referrals and place them in the appropriate box (London Borough of Hillingdon, 1986). Although the referral process in Children's Services has moved on from a paper system, there continue to be ways in which the system can lose sight of the child. For example, in the concluding inquiry report about Heidi, she was described as polite, somewhat nervous, hungry and poorly dressed (London Borough of Hillingdon, 1986). Although this description of Heidi paints a picture of a neglected child, there is nothing in the report about her ethnicity, abilities, religion, culture or a description of what she looked like.

It would be easy to suggest that a lack of description of a child would not happen now. After all, current child care law sets out principles aimed at ensuring that the child and their identity are at the heart of practice by providing a checklist of relevant factors – *'physical, emotional and educational needs ... age, sex, background and any characteristics'* (Children Act 1989, section 1.15 (a)(c)(d)). However, although legislation has drawn attention to important factors for making decisions about the child (such as paying attention to their race, culture and religion), research evidence highlights that many children who come into contact with Children's Services, specifically those from Black, Asian and minority ethnic backgrounds, continue to be failed across the spectrum of Children's Services by practice that ignores principles introduced to ensure that the needs and welfare of the child are paramount (Bernard and Harris, 2016).

For Heidi, the lack of attention paid to her identity – her race, ethnicity, culture and religion – in the initial referral and final report ensured that she remained unseen and unheard and remained unknown.

The child-in-focus years

During the 1980s, Heidi was one of several children who died as a result of abuse and neglect by their parents or carers. The deaths of Jasmine Beckford, Tyra Henry and Kimberley Carlile between 1984 and 1986 resulted in public inquiries that asked questions about the skills and abilities of social workers and other professionals to protect children known to them. Among the questions were, should the social workers have seen the risks posed by the children's parents and carers and could social workers have been more authoritative in ensuring that they gained access to the homes to see the children? Each inquiry highlighted how social workers had failed to physically and emotionally get past the adults to see the children. These findings caused Louis Blom-Cooper (1985), who carried out the Jasmine Beckford inquiry, to comment:

> Thou shalt not, not intervene. Proactive protective services were to be wrapped around children and child welfare professionals were to be clear: the children – not the adults – were their clients; they had to seek out endangered children and discover what they might have to say about their lives.
>
> (Blom-Cooper, 1985)

The message to social workers at this time was to seek out and save children from abusive parents. The timing of these inquiries is important. They took place in the mid-1980s, when the state appeared to take the side of the child by producing a range of recommendations to support social work practice that was more focussed on the rights of the child than those of the parents (Lonne et al., 2009). Children became the focus of intense political attention about how to protect their innocence from those adults – their parents and the state – which were responsible for protecting them. This was a time when the focus on children was framed in a rights-based discourse that promoted giving them a voice in an adult world (Baird, 2009).

The centralising of children in the debates and inquiries led to recommendations that dismantled the generic social services in favour of child-centred services (now understood as Children's Services) and the drafting of new legislation under the Children Act 1989, which was aimed at cementing the figure of the child as central to policy and practice. However, as the final touches were being made to the act and services for children were being transformed, events in Cleveland led to an about-turn and rethink about rights of the child and the role of the state to intervene to protect those rights over those of the parents (Parton, 2014).

In 1987, Middlesex General Hospital witnessed an increase in diagnoses of child sexual abuse on the basis of the research of Dr Marietta Higgs, a paediatrician who suggested that anal dilatation found in children was a factor in sexual abuse (Featherstone *et al.*, 2014). An outcome of this research was that over 121 children from Cleveland were removed from their parents and families by police and social workers while an investigation was carried out. During this protracted investigation over a period of months and years, many of the parents were denied access to their children. This led to a political outcry about the rights of parents and specifically the role of the state to intervene in the private lives of families (Parton, 2014). As a consequence, the introduction of the Children Act 1989 was delayed while the legislation was re-written around principles that acknowledged the rights of parents and children to be fully consulted and involved in the child protection processes. The accompanying guidance and regulation of the legislation encouraged all professionals and specifically social workers to work in partnership with parents, children and young people to ensure that the welfare of the child was paramount and at the centre of interventions and outcomes (White *et al.*, 1990).

The Children Act 1989 is the most significant piece of child care legislation to be introduced in the last three decades. Although the introduction of the act coincided with high-profile child deaths and the Cleveland investigation, it was developed over years and was informed by research (*Review of Child Care Law*, DHSS, 1985) and the Short Report (Social Services Committee, 1984). Both the research and the report highlighted how legislation could be used to support the state in their duties to provide care and protection for children (Parton, 2014). As a consequence, the act was the first legislative attempt to bring about significant changes in the way the state intervened in the lives of children and their families where concerns were being expressed about their care and protection.

There was an acknowledgement in the act that many children in need and their families needed early support that could prevent further problems and reduce emergency interventions and care proceedings (Lonne *et al.*, 2009). Through the specific use of section 17, local authorities were encouraged to work closely with each other and parents to keep children deemed as in need within their immediate and extended family networks and, where possible, minimise the use of investigations under section 47. This approach was considered to be a refocusing of child protection services and a move away from the more intrusive and often stigmatising interventions that focussed on finding out which parent or carer had abused the child (Ferguson, 2011).

However, this approach relied heavily on the interpretation by different local authorities and their respective agencies about what the term 'in need' meant. This situation brought many professionals into conflict with each other about how 'in need' was being interpreted, and questions were asked about whether a child was in need of protection because they were at risk of harm or in need of supportive services to aid their life chances (Rogowski, 2013). In this context, the term 'in need' became polarised and the impact on children and families who came to the attention of professionals and local authority social

workers was significant. The significance was in the response from local authority social workers who were under increasing pressure to get the balance right
between *family support* and *child protection* (Parton, 2014). It became more
complex to make an early analysis and judgement of the needs of children in
an environment where demand for services increased as a result of legislative
changes that demanded that they safeguard and promote the welfare of the
child considered to be in need (Cleaver *et al.*, 2004).

The complexities lay in the unpredictable nature of child abuse and the
introduction of eligibility criteria for Children's Services. Although the introduction of eligibility criteria was aimed at reducing complexity and aiding professionals to make a distinction between a child in need and a child in need of
protection, this action served to increase the barriers that were beginning to be
erected between a range of professionals as they all tried to become proficient
in gaining a working knowledge of the 1989 Children Act (Parton, 2014).
Eligibility criteria became understood as a gate-keeping process employed by
child protection social workers to legitimise using section 17 to signpost children and families to other services, mainly health and education (Rogowski,
2013). As a result, there was growing unease among professionals and social
workers about how section 17 was being interpreted by local authorities and
specifically the way in which the political climate was shaping social work and
public services by using business models of competition, efficiency, procedure
and performance management systems (Parton, 2014).

It is important to note that the Children Act 1989 was considered to be a
progressive piece of legislation in its approach to working with children and
families. While the central principles focussed on working in partnership with
all those who became involved with local authority Children's Services to bring
about the best outcomes for children deemed to be in need, the act also set out
specific principles for working in partnership with children:

➢ The views and wishes of children should be sought about what is happening
   to them.

➢ Support should be appropriate to the child's race, culture, religion and
   language.

➢ The child's physical, educational and emotional needs; age, sex and circumstances should be taken into account.

➢ The likely effect of change on the child.

➢ Delays in the child protection processes can have a detrimental effect on a
   child's welfare.

(White *et al.*, 1990)

These specific principles acknowledge that children can and should be consulted and included in decision-making that affects their lives. The principles also tend to the issue of difference by identifying that children will have a different world view, a different way of communicating, and different status and rights in a process that is essentially about them. However, while many social workers and practitioners have long acknowledged and understood difference and found creative ways of engaging and working directly with children, the effectiveness of the act to place children at the heart of practice appears to have become undermined by a complex set of values, attitudes and behaviours by adults (Petr, 1990).

The growing unease about how services for children were being shaped and the use of legislation to rationalise protective services appeared to be upheld when the death of Victoria Climbié followed closely by the death of Peter Connelly (Baby P) was reported and, through a flurry of media attention and subsequent inquiries, produced recommendations and questions about social work practice that echoed those of previous child deaths: How had the risks to both children been missed by an array of professionals involved with them? It appeared that, even with progressive child-centred legislation, children continued to be unprotected from adults who abused them and from professional practice failures.

The political and public outcry that followed both child deaths produced a new state response to children. Again, politicians focussed on the child, framing legislation, policies and practice around the figure of the child as the future and the projection of the family image onto the consciousness of society as the place for societal progress through the nurturing and protection of the child (Burman and Stacey, 2010). The culmination of political intervention and subsequent inquiries produced the Children Act 2004. This act was set alongside the Children Act 1989 with key themes of partnership working and greater professional accountability (Parton, 2014). It was considered a significant piece of legislation for putting all children at the centre of policies and services. Under a national framework of *Every Child Matters*, Children's Services were to be transformed into targeted interventions whereby professionals worked together to improve the life chances of children under five designated outcomes:

➢ being healthy

➢ staying safe

➢ enjoying and achieving

➢ making a positive contribution

➢ achieving economic well-being

More importantly, the act mobilised a language around children and parents via a range of government policies and procedures constructed to promote the child as a social investment through education (Fawcett et al., 2000). Education in this sense was broad with plans for introducing a range of targeted early years and parenting support services aimed at tackling social exclusion (Parton, 2014). The focus on the child as a social investment intensified during the political term of New Labour. Their ambitions to end child poverty led to a range of new services for children and their families, most notably the opening of Sure Start centres across the UK (Melhuish et al., 2010).

The Sure Start programmes were introduced to meet the needs of pre-school children and their families living in the most deprived areas of the UK (Melhuish et al., 2010). Many of the Sure Start centres were staffed by a range of professionals from health, education and social services in a multi-agency approach to providing holistic services aimed at preventing crisis in families that lead to referrals to social services. While many children and their families benefitted from Sure Start, referrals to social services increased and the number of children placed on child protection registers was not reduced (Jordan and Drakeford, 2012). Importantly, the political aims for ending child poverty in the UK were not realised, and in a bid to refocus Sure Start programmes, New Labour transferred the service to the control of local authorities with a specific set of guidelines that focussed on health and education (Melhuish et al., 2010).

The child-centred years that span the introduction of the Children Acts of 1989 and 2004 whereby the focus of legislation, policies and practice was on children through the promotion of their rights and as a social investment did change the way in which services to children were provided. Whether this was by recognising that the child should be spoken to and their thoughts and views heard in investigations of child abuse or acknowledging that some children during the early stages of their lives may need further support to achieve better life outcomes, the child became the centre of attention. Indeed, the current HM Government (2018) guidance *Working Together to Safeguard Children: A Guide to Inter-agency Working to Safeguard and Promote the Welfare of Children* clearly sets out a child-centred approach by acknowledging that '*A child-centred approach means keeping the child in focus when making decisions about their lives*' (p. 8) and specifies the legislation that social workers should use to support a child-centred approach (p. 9):

➤ the Children Act 1989

➤ the Equality Act 2010

➤ the United Nations Convention on the Rights of the Child

However, while there has been considerable government and policy attention aimed at promoting child-centred practice, the outcomes have been fraught by problems associated with adult themes and ideologies. These themes and ideologies are encapsulated in actions promoting cost-effective services and approaches to providing services to children who are in need or at risk (Parton, 2014). Such an approach is steeped in historical political thinking and ideas about providing state services to those who can prove they deserve them. In this political approach, those seeking services are blamed because they have complex needs or because they have failed to increase or develop the life skills needed to navigate poverty, abuse, discrimination and oppression (Jordon, 2010). As a result, this ideological shift has been blamed for accelerating the levels of complexity in the lives of those children who may need services, such as increasing complex health needs, complex family circumstances, complex educational needs and the complexity associated with the conflict and equality of access to services where racism, class and discrimination continue to determine who is eligible for services (Bernard and Harris, 2016).

As a society, we now appear to have moved into a political period that is in direct conflict with the child-centred legislation and policies introduced over two decades ago. Indeed, blaming children and families for creating and producing problems considered so complex that the state has to ration and target services to those deemed to be the most problematic or dangerous has now effectively increased the gap between children and the legislation and policies introduced to protect them. As a result, the child-centred frameworks and policies introduced to improve life chances and outcomes for children appear to be melting away in a world of conflict that has become more complex and which marginalises children and, according to Campbell (2013), makes children unsafe.

Responding to complexity

Child protection social work is complex, and complexity is an accepted heritage of the work. The term 'complex' and its meaning in social work has evolved and been used to explain why services to children are rationalised, why risk in child protection is unpredictable and why social workers fail to 'see risk to a child' (Munro, 2005:376). Although there appears to be an acceptance of the term within social work discourse, the concept itself also appears to have become more complex as the social constructs of childhood and a child's vulnerability to abuse develop in a world where responses to the figure of the child change rapidly (Burman and Stacey, 2010).

The rapid changes and responses to children tend to take place in the maelstrom of media and political attention that produces a hierarchy of theoretical frameworks leaned on with the aim of producing a child-focussed approach. The different frameworks move along a continuum that swings between the rights of the child and children as an investment for the future (Featherstone et al., 2014). It is these frameworks and approaches to children that frame how child protection social work is practiced. However, the social world of the child in child protection is tricky and is overlaid with adult behaviour that creates a territory filled with complexity (Petr, 1990). As a result, it has become more difficult to find solutions using legislation and policies to respond to the complexity.

What this complexity is remains unclear. This apparent acceptance in social work literature that child protection social work is complex is worth examining (Munro, 2008; Parton, 2014; Featherstone et al., 2014). What is it that is so complex? Can the complexity be deconstructed into bite-sized issues that help us understand what is meant when the term 'complex' is used to explain the multiple ingredients – the obvious and not so obvious – that result in children being vulnerable and at risk of adult violence and neglect? Evidence suggests that social work has become more complex as a result of societal and political changes that have witnessed increased levels of poverty, a widening of child protection concerns such as child trafficking and a reduction in resources that have placed increasing demands on child protection social work (Clapton et al., 2013). Research also suggests that child protection social work has become complex as a result of performance management and IT systems that now place the focus on predicting and managing risks to children as opposed to providing preventative support services (Ferguson, 2011; Houston, 2016).

Finding a way through the evidence and findings to an answer that helps to explain the concept of complexity without becoming reductionist is a challenge. However, according to Stevens and Cox (2007), understanding complex theory in the context of child protection social work can expand our thinking about the hidden orders situated within the politics, behaviours and systems that create complexity and subsequently bring about chaos or order.

Stevens and Cox (2007) argue that, when considering the current discourse being used to explain complexity in child protection social work, we need to bear in mind that some of the component parts – the child, the institution, the systems, the budget, the adults, the nexus of ways in which a child can be abused, the media and the politics – will take precedence over others and, as a consequence, how they are perceived and acted upon will be different. These differences lead to confusion, unpredictability and surprising responses as a result of interactions and relationships with each other. The consequences of these interactions and relationships are summed up by Walby (2007), who points out that issues of inequality bound in age, gender, class, race, sexuality and religion can produce additional disadvantages and inequalities when these component parts interact with each other within or as part of a system.

To explore these arguments, I now draw attention to the case of Ainlee Labonte and the many component parts that came together during her very short life to produce a level of complexity and chaos.

Case study – Ainlee Labonte – A child in mind

In 2002, the death of Ainlee Labonte (age 3) was reported when she was found dead at her parents' home by paramedics. A post-mortem revealed over 60 injuries, including cigarette burns, and a body weight well below that expected of a child her age. The independent review into her death came shortly after that of Victoria Climbié and once again the agencies mandated to protect children were faced with criticisms of failing to respond to protect a child. At the time of Ainlee's death, the 1989 Children Act had been the working legislation for social workers for 11 years, and the case highlights how the component issues increased, producing a complex system that meant the professionals involved were unable to meet the central principle of the act: *the welfare of the child is paramount;* according to the independent review, this was because they became locked into a form of practice paralysis (Kenward, 2002).

Ainlee was the second child born to Leanne Labonte. Leanne was 14 years old when she gave birth to her first child (a boy). Before she became pregnant, her name was placed on the child protection register under the category of physical abuse and the records state she was living in a very violent environment. Leanne and her baby son became homeless and Children's Services supported her to secure temporary accommodation. For a lengthy period, a range of services, social workers, health visitors and housing officers tried to engage with Leanne. The focus of this work was to prepare for a child protection conference where the aim appears to have been de-registering Leanne: taking her name off the child protection register. The independent review highlights this as a critical event in the agency response 'despite there being a case conference to de-register Leanne, there is no risk assessment on her or her baby son when factors of her age, homelessness, isolation and with no financial or appropriate family support were known' (Kenward, 2002:21). This evidence suggests that a child was not being seen. The child at this point is Leanne, who was outside the professional's field of vision and not seen as a child known to have experienced violence and sexual abuse from the adults in her life.

Pause and consider:

Why do you think Leanne was not seen as a child deemed vulnerable and at risk of significant harm?

A number of components referred to in the review act as indicators to a discourse that effectively placed Leanne (the child) behind it. The discourse about Leanne is underpinned by a range of emotions and feelings that interact with each other, producing images that influenced how she was perceived and responded to. These feelings became negative and blaming towards Leanne and as a consequence they supported the construction of a moral discourse that focussed on her as a mother first with all the responsibilities attributed to the role.

> Leanne was manipulative, aggressive and ambivalent towards the caring agencies ... she became pregnant a third time ... she had an abortion ... and had a record for shoplifting ... Leanne's relationship with her son was lost in a power struggle with the agencies.
>
> (Kenward, 2002:7)

The mention of a power struggle assumes a level of equality in the relationship between Leanne and the agencies. She was considered an adult who, according to the review report, 'set the boundaries for working with social services' (Kenward, 2002:28). The statement highlights the tensions that were emerging as a result of an approach that focussed on Leanne as an adult and mother first. As a result of this thinking that focussed on Leanne as an adult, all of the professional energies were bound in adult themes of parental responsibility and actions aimed at getting Leanne to 'mother' appropriately and protectively. The fact that she was unable to do this was not understood or examined by the agencies or adults trying to engage with her at that time.

Leanne's behaviour became more risky:

➤ forming a relationship at 15 with Dennis Henry (age 35), who had a history of homelessness, violence and criminal behaviour

➤ giving birth to Ainlee

➤ becoming pregnant with a third child

➤ failing to attend health appointments for herself and her children

➤ failing to provide care and supervision to her children

➤ failing to comply with a residential parenting assessment

A heightened sense of panic and despair emerged. Because the risky behaviour was often accompanied by acts of physical violence and verbal abuse towards professionals, health visitors and social workers became frightened of Leanne and, according to Kenward (2002), this fear created an emotional and physical distancing that prevented the attention from being directed towards the children:

> 'The professionals knew that the family had no support mechanisms, Leanne's mother did not look after her grandchildren, there was a war of attrition with

neighbours, the children were refused nursery placements as not meeting the criteria', so the inevitable answer has to be that she was alone. Ainlee was alone for most of her life and no one appeared to ask the question – 'where was Ainlee?'

(Kenward, 2002:23)

The life of Ainlee featured a number of components that created a complex layer of adult themes, actions and inactions that had tragic consequences for Ainlee and all those involved. To help illuminate these components, I have produced a Complexity Component diagram (Figure 2.1). This diagram is offered to provide a visual aid to help us understand and see the range of component parts that built up around Ainlee.

As we examine each component and begin to make links between them, we see how it is easy in practice to lose sight of the child. For example, when the components increase, they can become co-constructed in a powerful relationship that can lead to the child's being obscured. There was

Figure 2.1 Complexity Components

compelling evidence of this being the case in the review report (Kenward, 2002) on the death of Ainlee Labonte:

> **Violence:** Leanne and Dennis were threatening, violent and abusive towards professionals and members of the public.

> **Fear:** Professionals stated that they were frightened of Leanne and Dennis and feared for their own safety.

> **Access:** Health visitors, GPs, social workers and housing staff felt intimidated and therefore would not visit the home. Leanne and Dennis were barred from the Housing Office. Staff at health clinics and hospitals refused to meet with Leanne and Dennis unless they were supervised or accompanied by other professionals.

> **Isolation:** The children were living in an environment that professionals were not prepared to visit. The children did not meet the criteria for nursery provision. Family and community networks had broken down.

> **Parental skills:** A social worker who did visit the family home observed the children being subjected to verbal abuse and inappropriate punishments – Ainlee (age 1) being strapped into a high chair that was turned towards a wall – but failed to challenge what they saw. Instead, they appeared to accept the mother's explanation that the punishment was because Ainlee was 'throwing food around' (Kenward, 2002:10).

> **Practice:** Police were called to several reports of domestic violence and did not report these to social services. Social services closed the case and informed the agencies and parents that any future concerns about the children would be dealt with via the duty social worker.

> **Legislation:** The local authority used section 20 of the 1989 Children's Act to accommodate Leanne's older son on the premise of working together to understand his needs. This legislative approach set the direction of practice that focussed on needs versus risk. A legislative approach that the review (Kenward, 2002:29) argued meant the 'local authority avoided going to court to apply for a Care Order on all the children ... even, when the risk factors increased and parents failed to keep to a service contract allowing access to the children'.

> **Ethnicity/race:** Records make no reference to the ethnicity or race of the children. However, the review states that Leanne claimed she was the subject of 'racial abuse' from people living in her community (p. 20).

The review identified how the relationship between the components of violence and fear became so powerful that professionals focussed on their own self-protection and, as a result, how they became caught in a complex web of emotions that led to the manipulation of the available systems to the benefit of the adults (Kenward, 2002). The review does not suggest that this was deliberate, but it does highlight how professional fears caused the children to become isolated from those people who could have protected them (Kenward, 2002).

The evidence from the Ainlee Labonte case highlights how complexity is constructed around the child and through adult behaviours, systems and practice approaches and how these contributed to Ainlee's becoming invisible. Stevens and Cox (2007) suggest that being able to identify the separate components and how they, separately and together, can create a complex set of circumstances can help professionals see the child in the child protection process.

At this point, it is worth taking time to examine the particular legislative component of the Ainlee Labonte case in more detail by considering the following question.

Pause and consider:

Why do you think the local authority chose to use section 20 rather than apply to the courts for a section 31 Care Order?

The failure to gain access to Ainlee and her siblings was identified by the review as one of the factors that made it possible for the children to be overlooked by professionals (Kenward, 2002). All of the spaces and places available to the social workers and professionals involved with Ainlee were either controlled or secured by adults. This meant that, to gain any access to the children, the adults had to negotiate a range of professional and personal challenges in the spaces and places that Ferguson (2011) refers to as being an important component of practicing child protection. For example, Ferguson (2011) highlights how social work practice in child protection takes place in the intimate spaces of family life – the bedroom, kitchen, living room – and how reviews have failed to discuss the issue and its relation to practice. This crucial point was reflected in the case of Heidi Koseda, where professionals who visited the family home were criticised for failing to ask parents if they could see around the home. This was a critical event in the life of Heidi and her siblings; the very fact of not gaining access to the intimate spaces meant that she remained vulnerable and at risk.

Social workers visit and see children in a range of settings other than their home and this means they will be going into other adults' 'territory'. The home visit is the most often highlighted in reviews as the place that social workers failed to access. I have very vivid recollections of going into hospitals and schools where the values, beliefs and anxieties of these environments in relation to the child, which were often exacerbated by parents' behaviour, made it very difficult for me to gain access to the child. In both environments, I was met with a range of mixed emotions and expectations that had been exacerbated by the behaviours of the parents. Whereas one teacher was clearly pleased to see me, saying 'thank goodness you are here, you can sort the mother out, and let them know that we (the school) had no choice but to send for you', a consultant paediatrician was less pleased, expressing his anger that I had not 'done what he wanted me to do' and had the mother arrested.

Although my presence in both environments was about responding to the needs of the children, I became caught up in the emotional needs of the adults – including my own. This emotional connection itself is complex and linked to a range of complex components. For me, in both situations, being a woman, my professional identity, my professional reputation, my culture and my ethnicity all came together to influence the dynamics of my practice. In both situations, I did see both children but not without some lengthy and forceful negotiations. I managed to get into a classroom that the children had barricaded themselves into and I listened to them tell me they did not want to be with their foster carers; the child wanted to go home to look after their mum and attend to a small baby receiving treatment for drug-induced withdrawal symptoms.

In both situations, being able to see the children gave me a wealth of information that supported later interventions – the baby did go home with its mother and both thrived with a network of maternal family support. The child at school never went home to her mother, whose alcoholism gravely impacted on her own health. This is a description of how the adult behaviour and environment together had an impact on practice. As Ferguson (2011) argues, trying to ensure that you see the child in tense adult environments where you are the 'visitor' brings with it extra emotional and psychological complexities and to be able to deal with them in such situations the social worker has to 'move purposefully towards the child' (p. 120).

Conclusion: Finding a way through

Finding a way through to children like Ainlee and Heidi continues to perplex governments and policy-makers, although there have been significant changes to legislation and policies as a result of inquiries and research that recommends that child protection should be child-centred (HM Government, 2015a, 2015b). Transforming the language of legislation, policy and research into practice continues to elude the most skilled and competent social worker. Even with the most sophisticated systems in place, children continue to be abused and killed by those adults responsible for caring for them. As the first two chapters have highlighted, keeping the child in view is fraught with difficulties, and although policy guidance recommends that it is important to 'put the needs of the children first' (HM Government, 2018), achieving this in an adult world continues to be contentious.

Social workers strive to ensure that they do get past the adults to see the child and capture their words and expressions to make the best decisions for them. This is not easily achieved in an uncertain practice environment where social workers and their allied professionals face continual changes to where and how they practice. These changes also contribute to the complex nature of child protection through the creation of components that individually and together obscure the child, their experience, their needs and the risks.

The aim must be to identify these components of complexity and make sense of them so that we can find a way into the world of the child. I argue that finding a way through and into the world of the child will require looking and seeing the child from a different perspective. I know it will not be easy and will not provide all the answers. In fact, it will raise more questions and more thinking and will challenge you. But I believe that those social workers working in child protection will want to take the challenge.

2

A Child-Centred Model for Practice

There are many child-centred models currently available for social workers. The most influential has been the assessment framework that formalises information about the child around three domains of child development, parental capacity, and family and environment (Department of Health, 2000). The assessment framework is now embedded in child protection practice. It provides social workers with a conceptual map that places the child at the centre of thinking and analysis.

How this is used in practice has been a cause for some concern, specifically where the emphasis of one domain is unequal to that of others and as a result can cloud social workers' decision-making, an issue that was identified in the serious case review of Peter Connelly (Baby P). The serious case review identified that the emphasis of the assessment had focussed on parental capacity and whether or not Peter's mother was coping rather than on his needs or the risks to him (Barlow *et al.*, 2012).

Over the years, a range of models, frameworks and instruments have been introduced to help social workers analyse risk and need under the terms of the legal phrase 'significant harm' (Littlechild, 2008). The growth in their development has been triggered by subsequent government policy-makers' and researchers' beliefs that structuring and formalising social workers' thinking can reduce complexity, standardise practice, and predict and manage risk (Houston and Griffiths, 2000). Within this belief is the contested argument that these models, frameworks and instruments are more effective than clinical judgement commonly understood as tacit knowledge, professional wisdom and 'gut feelings' (Munro, 2008). While the debate about clinical judgement versus formalised technical approaches has raged on in the academic literature, government policy-makers have remained steadfastly resolved to hold onto checklists and instrumental assessments to ensure quality control of child protection practice and services (Parton, 2014).

However, all of the methods have their limitations, and evidence from an analysis of serious case reviews continues to highlight how children become missed in assessments, analysis, judgements and decision-making as a result of a lack of rigour and an inability to critically analyse information as opposed to gathering it and completing forms (Department for Education, 2016).

With this less-than-positive outcome, the question is posed, is it possible to develop a child-centred model that works for the child? I have no doubts that social workers working in child protection teams in the UK will be carrying out excellent work that places the child at the centre of practice. They will be carrying out assessments, making judgements and decisions with existing models and frameworks, and finding creative ways to use them. Unfortunately, the celebration of good practice is more than likely to take place within local teams and many of the creative ideas either stay or move with the creator or creators. Equally, where good practice is identified in serious case reviews, it is often overshadowed in recommendations aimed at changing the systems that led to a child death (Brandon *et al.*, 2012).

For example, there was evidence of good practice identified by the independent reviewer in the Ainlee Labonte case: *'There were, however, individuals trying to respond to the needs of the children, a duty social worker who completed an exemplary piece of work then handed on, what was, however, not followed up'* (Kenward, 2002:23). Without any details, it is not clear why the reviewer identified the practice as exemplary. While this evidence confirms that good child-centred practice took place in a case surrounded by adult behaviour that drew attention away from the child, it also confirms that little or no further attention was paid to the good practice or how this could be used to inform future social work practice. This outcome supports the view of Sumner (1906), who defined approaches that overlook the child as similar to ethnocentrism where 'a view of things in which one's own group is the centre of everything, and all others are scaled and rated to it' (p. 112). In the case of Ainlee Labonte, the exemplary individual practice that placed the child at the centre of thinking became the outsider in a world where the insiders, the adults, their behaviour, agencies, roles and responsibilities became more important and superior in terms of scrutiny.

Research and serious case reviews have identified common themes that led to the child's being overshadowed and made invisible. It may be helpful to look closely at those themes and consider them in the context of developing a child-centred model for practice. Evidence from research (Brandon *et al.*, 2012) suggests that the key themes can be grouped around the direct (human) and indirect (non-human) work with children and are linked to how social workers gather, prioritise and assess information.

The assessment framework provides the structure and a bridge between the human and non-human elements of assessment. Chapter 1 of *Working Together to Safeguard Children: A Guide to Inter-agency Working to Safeguard and Promote the Welfare of Children* (HM Government, 2015a, 2015b) sets out the purpose

➢ of gathering information about the child and family

➢ of analysing their needs and the nature and level of risk and harm being suffered by the child

➤ of deciding whether the child is in need (section 17) or is suffering significant harm (section 47) (or both)

➤ of providing support to address those needs to improve the child's outcomes to make them safe.

How social workers carry out the practice of gathering information about the
child will include the following:

➤ checking whether or not the child and their family are already known to the
local authority

➤ seeking information about the child and their family from other
professionals

➤ directly observing the child and their parents in a range of different
settings

➤ interviewing the child alone

➤ working directly with the child

➤ talking to extended family members and in some cases people from their
community

Gathering information will be carried out within a mandated period of time.
For example, front-line social workers will be under pressure to gather as much
information as possible within one working day. Although policy changes by
HM Government (2015a, 2015b) have introduced more flexible time frames to
complete assessments, it is the initial response to referrals that sets the pace
and direction of judgements. What this means in terms of practice is that social
workers are most likely to be making sense of a child's circumstances with little
information available to them (Wilkins, 2013). At this point, social workers will
be speculating, hypothesising and making an early analysis about what is going
on in the family and specifically what risks are posed to the child.

This early analysis based on the information available is considered to be the
action that is taken before making a judgement about the risks posed to the
child and before making a decision about which social work intervention should
take place (Platt, 2006). This early analysis about risk has received much government and research attention. The findings suggest that while social workers
are good at gathering a range of information, they appear to lack the confidence to make sense of it or indeed make an accurate analysis of a child's needs
or the risks posed to them (Barlow et al., 2012). The analysis cites a range of
factors responsible for influencing and impacting on social workers' skills and
abilities to analyse information. These include practicing critical and reflective

thinking, lack of supervision, time pressures, workload, organisational and political pressures, fear of making mistakes, blaming service users for their own lives, and the emotional toll of having to listen and respond to reports of child abuse (Barlow et al., 2012).

The power of these factors to influence and dictate the pace and focus of practice is well documented in the social work literature (Ferguson, 2011; Featherstone et al., 2014; Warner, 2015). These powerful factors are complex and difficult to negotiate, making it very difficult for social workers to keep the child at the centre of practice. This situation was made very real in the Ainlee Labonte case when health professionals reported that her mother, Leanne, was pregnant. Even with all the background information available to social workers, a pre-birth assessment was not carried out to consider the risks to Ainlee.

Pause and consider:

Factors of workload pressures, fears of making a mistake and organisational pressures. How do you think, individually or collectively, they can make it difficult for social workers to stay focussed on the child?

Making an accurate analysis of information about the child and using that analysis to inform judgements and decision-making have generated a number of developments that have introduced a range of assessment tools to address the issue (Barlow et al., 2012). These new developments can be broadly classified as (a) consensus-based (Baumann et al., 2011) or (b) statistically based (Shlonsky and Wagner, 2005). The appeal of these risk assessment tools was in their potential to guide the direction of analysis and support the classification and rationalisation of risk (Barlow et al., 2012). However, the use of predictive instrumental approaches to guiding clinical judgement about risk failed to understand that, within a competency framework, there will be a range of what Macdonald and Macdonald (2010) refer to as false positives (non-dangerous families are assessed as high-risk) and false negatives (a dangerous family is judged to be safe). This means it is unlikely that a mathematical solution to formalising risk will help social workers to detect or predict who will abuse children and how.

As Munro (2005) has pointed out, 75 per cent of inquiries into child abuse deaths concluded that professional error was a factor in failures to 'see risk to a child' (p. 376). The context from which this conclusion was drawn needs to be considered. Serious case reviews are focussed principally on learning lessons and are based on principles of hindsight theory that support a narrative that an accurate judgement of probable risk was predictable (Wood et al., 2010).

However, evidence from analysis of serious case reviews concluded that, even with more detailed information, predicting whether child abuse will occur is largely impossible (Brandon *et al.*, 2012).

What is emerging from research is an acknowledgement that social workers in child protection continue to face a critical vocabulary about their skills and abilities to predict which child is at risk that has resounded for the past two decades. If the existing models are not able to harness the skills and abilities of social workers, it is time to examine the assessment process and whether this can be enhanced by introducing a child-centred model that draws social workers' attention towards the child by helping them to negotiate and understand the factors that may be causing them to look elsewhere.

The issue has become how to reach child protection social workers in ways that bring about a change in practice to ensure the child doesn't get lost and that engage them in critical thinking with the aim of enhancing their skills and abilities to make a confident analysis of the child's needs or the risks (or both). To bring about change requires a provocative approach that unsettles current thinking by posing questions that may raise the possibilities of a different truth. Indeed, Barlow *et al.* (2012:21) suggest that there needs to be a 'third generation approach' to assessment that supports the clinical and technical aspects of current assessment models.

The model I am proposing is a feminist-informed model (FIM) set within feminist theoretical thinking and ideas that take into account the current climate in which practice takes place. The FIM aims to 'undo' child protection policies and practice that have caused the child to go unnoticed. The approach of the FIM is reflective, critical and politically attuned to the current environment in which child protection policies are practiced in England and Wales. It uses four specific themes to do this and is designed to emphasise their interrelatedness in such a way that the child and their needs remain a constant.

Why use a feminist approach? Feminist thinking and ideas maintain that gender significantly influences how we experience and interpret the world around us. Feminists acknowledge how the child and child protection are mutually implicated at every turn: the child is the focus yet is denied its central image and is propelled into being the lynchpin of the family (Burman and Stacey, 2010). Using an FIM emphasises these relationships and their emotional, political and personal context, raising important questions about society, power and the provision of care. Using a feminist perspective provides a framework to examine the relational aspects of child protection policy and practice and, through critical examination, helps to provide a clearer picture of the child within a power field dominated by the needs, desires and behaviours of adults, represented in (Figure 3.1).

The FIM can be used as a stand-alone model or alongside other models for assessing the needs of or risks to children.

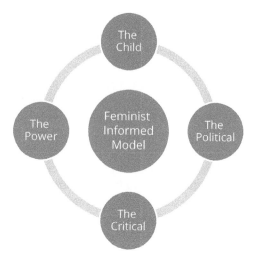

Figure 3.1 Feminist-Informed Model

The child

The common thread of so many child deaths is the lack of focus on the child (Cosser *et al.,* 2013). We know this and yet finding a way to undo what we know appears to have eluded adults. We can change this situation by doing two things. First, we can listen to children who have told researchers what they need from those mandated to protect them. In research carried out by Cosser *et al.* (2013), children who had been involved with child protection services said they wanted

> ➤ adults to be vigilant and to notice when things are troubling them

> ➤ to be heard and understood and to have that understanding acted upon

> ➤ to be able to develop an ongoing stable relationship of trust with those helping them

> ➤ to be treated with the expectation that they are competent rather than not

> ➤ to be informed about and involved in procedures, decisions, concerns and plans

> ➤ to be informed of the outcome of assessments and decisions and reasons when their views have not met with a positive response

> ➤ to be provided with support in their own right

> ➤ to be provided with advocacy to assist them in putting forward their views.

Second, we can become more inquisitive and less accepting of information that offers an overly simplistic presentation of the child. It is not enough to state their age, ethnicity, culture, gender or disability. This information can provide only a silhouette of the child. Although they are important factors, they all need to be either deconstructed or developed so that the child is recognised as a colourful and filled-out identity that is more difficult to lose sight of.

For example, take the factor of age. The age of a child is often used to signal to others what to expect or not, what services are due or not, and what is legally required or not. The age of the child provides a hook on which we hang our understanding about what their age means in relation to their lived circumstances and experiences. An analysis of serious case reviews in England identified 'that the highest risks of maltreatment related deaths are in infancy and the first five years of life' (Brandon, 2008). The findings acknowledge that babies and young children have very specific needs and, because of their age, are reliant on adults for their health, safety and well-being. This is not to suggest that it is only babies and young children who are reliant on adults. Children of all ages will be dependent on adults, even those teenagers and young adults who present as sorted and streetwise and able to handle an adult world (Cosser et al., 2013).

Recognising the child in child protection goes beyond the literal. The social worker's roles as communicator, advocate and supporter are pivotal to making the child visible. The importance of this role cannot be stated strongly enough and carries with it the responsibility of those working in child protection to ensure that they have the communication and advocacy skills to recognise the child, to notice their needs and to act.

The political

Being aware of the political nature of child protection is important to understanding the child-in-context. The external political landscape will define the way services are provided and to which child. Being politically and policy-aware enables social workers to gain a deeper knowledge and understanding about how they and others practice. The political element of the FIM can appear overwhelming, especially when the term 'politics' is heavily laden with a narrative that is closely linked to polemic political positioning. However, politics is about ideas, principles and values that through challenge and discussion can lead to new ways of thinking. Essentially, politics becomes about 'imagining a better future' (Gray and Webb, 2013). The desire of the political element is to spark a critical engagement with debates in order to develop a deeper understanding about the political and ideological structures that surround the child and importantly how individually and together they can become a louder voice than that of the child.

Many political and ideological strands weave in and out of child protection. They can be grouped around attitudes towards class, gender, race and family and have been used to shape social work policies and practice. As social work tries to operate in an environment of professional disadvantage, especially among those facing public-sector austerity measures, politically informed social work is a new form of resistance on behalf of children (Gray and Webb, 2013). It is a child-focussed resistance that social workers can use to remind ourselves and challenge others when child-centred principles are forgotten.

Understanding external politics and how these shape society and subsequent social work policies and practice is a step towards confronting the political situation in child protection. Being a political social worker can be achieved by taking personal responsibility for developing a skill set that is practical and steeped in social work values. It is about being in tune with the needs of others – in child protection this is the child – and finding the best possible ways to help them.

The critical

The critical element of the FIM raises important questions about the needs of the child within the context of interconnecting and significant relationships. It is an approach that draws upon critical and feminist theory to promote change. Both critical and feminist theoretical approaches emphasise the use of reflection in practice and how this can be used to develop knowledge and different ways of knowing and direct attention to new possibilities. Central to the critical approach is learning about the self and how we practice. Although both (practice and the self) will be surrounded by different discourses, there will be similar mental activities that tend to focus on

➢ feelings

➢ past and present actions

➢ the future.

The mental activity of reflection is described as a cycle of *action-reflection-action* (Gray and Webb, 2013) and is understood mostly as a process of thinking and learning from events that take place in practice. Although there has been some criticism that the processes involved in reflection are somewhat vague and little is understood about how they are applied in practice (Taylor, 2013), it is accepted that when reflection is done well practice can be transformative.

Within the FIM, it is acknowledged that reflection is complex and that the processes involved are influenced by external and internal world views. The FIM sets out practical ways of developing and increasing the practice of reflection by highlighting the importance of recording, supervising, talking to peers, observing and listening with the aim of harnessing the process of looking inwards and outwards to seek clarity and self-awareness. This critical approach is a challenge and the challenges are made clear in the words of Cixous (2008):

> when plumbing the depths of the "I"... it will take you deep down ... to the heart... with however many characters there are, and with their various roles, functions destinies. That's what allows you to make observations at various degrees of remove... ...from there you can see something tiny or huge, but always human nature playing itself out (p. 4).

The critical asks you to engage with the past and present, the 'I' and others, and the possibilities and the future through a critical interrogation of many contradictions and take a hard look at how they construct practice and relationships.

The power

Addressing power in child protection requires us to acknowledge that within 'the triad of social worker, parents and child' (Cossar et al., 2014), the child tends to sit in the least powerful position. The relational aspects of this triad are tied together by emotional relationships between children and their parents and social workers striking the balance between the child's right to protection and working in partnership with parents to achieve this. It is of little surprise to find how the child is overlooked when those involved in this relationship face one another with suspicion, despair, fears and anger.

The aim is to use this element of the FIM to examine power in relation to the child so that we recognise how conflicts can cause power imbalances and what this means for the child. The approach promotes a 'child zone of engagement' for social workers to enable them to develop and increase their knowledge and skills to capture the essence of the child and who they are. This can be done only by gaining the trust of the child and from practice that seeks to redress power imbalances by ensuring that the child's thoughts and views about what is happening to them are valued by hearing and understanding them.

Practice that seeks to challenge injustice and power imbalances is not straightforward. Even when we understand the position of children in child protection and have worked closely with them to find out what they want for their future, the pressures and demands of the organisation will be factors in how we go about challenging issues of power in relation to protecting the child.

Conclusion: The child in focus

This chapter has highlighted the debates surrounding the current child-centred models for practice. It has also introduced an FIM for practice that aims to keep the child in focus. The four key inter-related elements focus on the child and are designed to support reflection and the processes of looking inwards and out-wards. It is also useful to think of the model as a way of challenging narratives that lead us away from the child. However, no model on its own can bring about a refocusing on the child. This can be achieved only by social workers taking responsibility for equipping themselves with the knowledge and skills to be effective critical thinkers and practitioners.

A critical approach requires social workers to be actively vigilant of the adult world and how this frames thinking and ideas about children. It is always worth taking the time to remind ourselves of the child at the centre of the work and the one that may reside in us and remember that neither the child nor the social worker can really anticipate or prepare for the event of revelation (Cixous, 1998). Tuning in to see, hear and understand the child calls upon social work-ers to invest in a renewed commitment to a child-centred agenda, an approach that accepts the many challenges they will face. To close this chapter, I have included a poem by Trudy Allen (1991:177), age 12, that I believe sums up how children feel living in an adult world.

> *The teachers and the children*
> *Went on a sponsored walk*
> *The teachers led the children*
> *And wouldn't let them talk*
> *Up and down the hillside*
> *Along the sandy beach*
> *The teachers taking great strides*
> *I wish they'd only teach.*

3

Life with a Violent Mother

The role of fear and the many emotions it can produce in the practice of child protection social work is only now being fully understood and acknowledged. Social workers going about the business of protecting children can find themselves in dangerous situations. They face hostility and threats of violence from service users and may well be going out to visit children and their families living in communities where local services and resources are non-existent. These can be built-up urban or rural communities and there is nothing more frightening than finding yourself being threatened in a family home on an estate where you know that getting support or help will be difficult. The dangers are often exacerbated when this takes place late in the evening, when it always appears that the hostility and fear are somehow heightened by the darkness.

This chapter aims to explore the role of fear in child protection. It considers the challenges and tensions that exist in child protection when social workers are faced with aggressive parents who create a multi-layered environment of unnerving hostility that produces a miasma of fear. There will be a focus on how this fear impacts on social workers' practice and capacity to balance the needs of the child when they are faced with behaviour that swings from seductive co-operation to threats and acts of violence towards them.

The feminist-informed model (FIM) will be used to bring to life important debates about practice with the aim of developing a solid base for understanding the relational aspects of the FIM and their influence on Simon, his family and professionals. Simon's story takes place in the 1970s, predating the Children Act 1989. At the time, Simon was little understood, and although agencies noticed that things were troubling him, their attempts to intervene were thwarted by his mother's verbal and physical aggression towards them. Simon's story has been included in this book because it raises important practice issues relevant for today's social workers.

Simon's story

Simon lived with his mother (Shirley), father (Ron) and younger sibling (Sally). He was white British and lived in a terraced house owned by his parents. The home was well kept. Internally and externally, it was decorated to a high standard, it was clean and the home interiors suggested comfort, warmth and a sense of pride. Both parents were employed. Shirley was employed part-time at a local shop and his father worked shifts at a local factory. Outwardly, the family appeared to be ordinary and to meet societal expectations through its acceptance of social norms. However, when Simon began to attend school (age 5), his violent and aggressive outbursts drew attention from a range of agencies. The school found it increasingly difficult to contain his behaviour or understand what the triggers were. Staff struggled to connect the child they saw – who was attractive, creative, bright, and well dressed and could smile and be attentive to staff – with the child who could explode into a ball of verbal and physical aggression. When school staff tried to engage with his parents, it was always his mother they met with because, according to Shirley, his father was on the wrong shift. When staff met with Shirley, she would deny his behaviour (he was not like this at home), resort to blame (the school was picking on Simon) and use animosity with the aim of humiliating staff (teachers were useless). When Simon attacked another child (boy), pushing him to the floor and punching him, and while lashing out hit a member of staff trying to stop him, the school felt they had no option but to exclude him. He was 6 years old.

Because he was excluded from school, social workers became a staple professional involved with Simon and his family. He was made the subject of a Care Order under the Children and Young Persons Act 1969 under section (d) being beyond the control of his parents and section (e) not receiving education. As was most common during this period, he was placed in a therapeutic children's home miles away from his home. He returned to live with his parents after his mother and father 'helped him to break out' during a visit. He subsequently remained at home. Social workers continued to try to engage with both parents to meet Simon's needs. However, Shirley's behaviour towards them was erratic, volatile and violent. This included slapping and punching two women social workers, following a social worker in his car and attempting to drive him off the road, making verbally abusive phone calls to social workers and threatening them with violence should they attempt to visit. As a result, contact with child care social workers effectively tailed off. It wasn't until Simon's criminal behaviour brought him to the attention of the youth justice system that social workers again became involved with him and his family.

In the above vignette, Shirley's aggressive, hostile and violent behaviour is all too clear. Social workers and other professionals distanced themselves from the family as a result of her behaviour. This outcome has been identified in serious case reviews where the aggressive, threatening and intimidating behaviour of parents has seriously impacted social work decisions and interventions (Laird, 2013). However, this is not the full story for Simon and the social workers. Although social work intervention became limited as a result of his mother's behaviour, it was the skills of social workers over time that helped youth justice social workers to develop a relationship with Simon and his family. This relationship provided information that helped to engage and support Simon in his own right.

The child: Living with fear, aggression and violence

The FIM requires social workers to place the child at the forefront of practice. It requires an approach that seeks out who the child is by identifying important factors that help to focus on the child and, in doing so, begin the process of examining their lived experiences. Although current guidance on achieving a child-centred approach directs practitioners to the principles of the Children Acts 1989 and 2004 and offers advice about seeing and talking to children (HM Government, 2018), the details on how to achieve this remain unclear. For example, the legislative and policy guidance refers to

- keeping the child in focus
- noticing when things are troubling children
- seeing the child.

But there is little detail attached to the advice about how to do all of the above. Instead, there appears to be an assumption that the practices of seeing, focussing and noticing are straightforward and rooted in the skill of *'observing children in their environment'* (Department for Education, 2018:4). However, whereas the skill of child observation is accepted as an important practice skill in child protection social work, how it is developed and employed in practice has become a case for debate. The social work literature expresses concerns that the skill of child observation is often overlooked in social work education (Horwath, 2016). Research suggests that when social workers employ the skill of child observation, they do so without any critical analysis of the task and that, as a result, the outcomes for children have become meaningless (Nutbrown and Carter, 2010).

While both issues continue to be contested, evidence from serious case reviews suggests that when social workers are carrying out the task of observing a child in environments controlled by adults, whether this is the home or school, they face challenging situations that can hijack their professional skills and abilities (Brandon *et al.*, 2012). As Laird (2013) points out, trying to get past parents to see the child is fraught with personal danger for social workers. So it is understandable that when individual social workers are faced with open hostility or the threat of violence, they are unable to carry out a meaningful observation of the child.

What this means for the child is that, although they may be *seen*, their experience is not fully understood. This is because the social worker or practitioner is unable to make sense of what they are seeing since they are trying to deal with a wealth of emotions associated with fear. In this context, their senses and feelings have been effectively paralysed by fear. This professional paralysis was identified as a factor in the Ainlee Labonte review (Kenward, 2002:24) when, during home visits, social workers reported that they observed '*Ainlee strapped into a high chair which was turned to face the wall. She was quiet'*. Unfortunately, social workers failed to challenge Ainlee's mother about what they were seeing or take the time to go and see how the child was. According to the review, this professional oversight was believed to have occurred because social workers were fearful of the mother's reaction towards them.

This professional paralysis brought on by fear of violence was also a factor in the life of Simon. For example, it is difficult to offer any authentic descriptions of Simon's lived experience because these are not known. His own story, which should include his wishes and feelings, remains unsaid and unclear. Although social workers were involved with Simon and his family for many years, there is little about him in the case records. Because social workers found it difficult to get past his mother's behaviour, there is little in the records that tells anyone what it was like for a small child to live with a mother who was outwardly hostile and aggressive.

How would using the FIM in the practice of child observation help? How do we seek out the child by identifying important factors, and how do we decide what factors are important? The post-qualifying statement that sets out the knowledge and skill standards for child and family practitioners (Department for Education, 2018) provides three areas for practice:

➤ relationships

➤ communication

➤ child development

The statement makes it clear that practitioners should be able to carry out all three areas effectively and underline the importance of focussing on the child by understanding their needs in relation to their age, culture, behaviour, environment and parents. While the FIM supports the statement, it offers an additional lens to examine and bring the child into focus. This lens helps to magnify the child within the context of their environment and heighten our awareness of their situation. It does this by emphasising the activities taking place and asks us to look closely at how they interact with each other to bring about meaning and actions. For example, if we examined the report that Ainlee was strapped into a high chair which was turned to face the wall, the FIM approach would be to centralise the child by asking the following:

> **Pause and consider:**
>
> What does it mean for Ainlee to be strapped into a high chair that has been turned to face a wall? How would we expect Ainlee to communicate how she feels in this situation? Would we expect a baby of about 18 to 24 months to be quiet? What do these actions tell us about the relationship between Ainlee and her mother? How do we feel about what we are observing? What actions should we take and what will this mean for Ainlee?

Social workers knew that Simon witnessed his mother using aggressive behaviour from which she gained and achieved some form of benefit. The benefits were keeping social workers from being able to do their job, an outcome that meant they only ever understood Simon in relation to his behaviour. Social workers believed it was this behaviour, and not the risk his mother posed to him, that was now impacting on his education and the family unit.

It is worth being reminded of the time in which the social work intervention took place. This was the 1970s, a time of social and political change that influenced social work practice. Politics and social policy were heavily influenced by social attitudes that placed the family at the centre of policies that emphasised the importance of the family unit to prepare children for taking their place in society as good citizens (Madge, 2006). It was a time when social work practice was steeped in therapeutic/psychodynamic theories that supported identifying individual problems within the family and finding ways to resolve them (Garrett, 2013). The focus of this approach was not necessarily on the child as an individual in need or at risk (or both). The focus was the family and in particular the mother as the primary carer to ensure that the family functioned as society expected it to (White, 2006).

Social workers believed that Simon's behaviour was casting a shadow over the family functioning. This belief was not uncommon of its time. Social workers reasoned that to change the family functioning, Simon should be separated and insulated from the influences of his mother. This approach was based on therapeutic theories that argued this was the best way forward for children displaying difficult or challenging behaviour. It was an intervention that considered that *difficult* children needed therapeutic support to help them develop the skills and behaviours to deal with the outside world (Whittaker *et al.*, 2015).

Taking Simon out of the family home was a monumental life experience that had ongoing consequences for him. He was 10 when he was taken into care and placed in a therapeutic children's home miles away from his family. When his parents took him out of the home, their actions set the scene and tone for future social work interventions. Simon aligned himself against social workers, and as he grew into an adolescent, his behaviour became more challenging and aggressive. Simon's response is not unusual. According to Cossar *et al.* (2013), when children feel let down by social workers or believe that they have gone unnoticed, they will become uncooperative, and they will rationalise whatever fears they may have about their family since they believe the alternatives are no better.

Pause and consider:

How might using a FIM have helped social workers to see Simon? For example, consider what it must have meant for Simon to live with a violent mother. What are the risks? Was his behaviour his way of communicating how frightened and confused he was? What was his relationship with his sister? How could social workers have engaged Simon, described by his school as creative and bright? How would we find out how his mother describes him?

Simon's lived experience will be familiar to social workers. Although Simon was a child of the 1970s, there will be social workers across the UK trying to engage with violent, aggressive and hostile parents in order to assess or investigate the needs of and risks to the child. They will also be faced with children whose aggressive behaviour has become a well-developed script which is modelled on violent behaviour they have witnessed and which they will use to respond physically or verbally to conflict (Laird, 2013). In both of these engagements, social workers will be expected to see the child and take actions that bring about changes. However, the reality is that many social workers and practitioners in this position find it stressful and challenging. How this situation is being addressed by governments and the profession is worth examining.

The politics of fear

The FIM asks social workers to be aware of the political context of their practice. While the politicisation of child protection has been well documented in terms of the changes to organisations and practice, the political issues that surround working with service users who pose a threat to social workers have been given little or no attention by subsequent governments and policy-makers (Warner, 2015).

All the social workers involved with Simon and his family were subjected to verbal abuse and threats of violence, and some social workers were physically assaulted. Although the time of this experience was in the late 1970s, the threat and experience of violence towards social workers, particularly child protection social workers, have remained constant. While findings from research carried out internationally and nationally reveal that child protection social workers have been verbally and physically assaulted as they try to do their job (Littlechild, 2008; Laird, 2013; Schraer, 2014) and that this experience is a factor influencing practice (Brandon *et al.*, 2012), the political response has been poor.

When government and policy-makers have responded to research findings, they have done so by promoting a discourse that suggests that social workers need to become more authoritative and challenging with service users by being strong, objective and resolute in their approach (Featherstone *et al.*, 2014). Underpinning this discourse is a belief that those social workers who fail to be authoritative and challenging should not be in child protection social work. This belief was made clear to me during my own practice when a middle manager in Children's Services told those working in child protection that 'if they couldn't stand the heat' they should get out.

This discourse takes no account of fear and those things which social workers may fear in their day-to-day practice. This approach ultimately promotes a perspective that fear in its place can be managed and controlled. This perspective is pervasive and, for social workers and the profession of social work, offers a strong assertion about the context of fear in practice. This assertion promotes the view that the perceived lack of control over the behaviour of others is evidence of weakness in the individual social worker and that this weakness has led to failures in practice and the worst outcomes for children (Laird, 2013).

Featherstone *et al.* (2014) argues that this perspective has gained ground because it is overlaid with language associated with masculine attributes that promote strength and the skills to face down any threat of violence from service users. The language is equally suggestive in its promotion of a practitioner who will not shy away from conflict with colleagues or other professionals in their determination to protect children. As a result of this narrative, a concerning image emerges that implies that to be anything less is to be too emotional, too subjective, too timid and too feminine, a position that reflects what is considered by politicians and the media to be all that is wrong with social work (Warner, 2015).

The implications of this narrative are manifested in an environment where the experience of fear – the fear of violence from service users, the fear of getting decisions wrong, the fear of challenging others, the fear of individual colleagues, the fear of complaints – has created a working environment that social workers say is not safe for them or service users because they '*do not feel protected*' or able to '*talk about how they feel*'. This response to fear, according to Altheide (2002), will only create and promote new fears.

The social work response to research findings has been to call for more training to help social workers deal with conflict and hostility (Laird, 2013). However, the response nationally and locally to providing training has been slow. According to Bibby (2017), this is because there is some reluctance to acknowledge the risks that social workers face from service users. Certainly, my own social work training offered little in the way of advice or strategies for dealing with hostility or conflict. Indeed, the approach was to rely on the experience of practice educators and the placement experience to provide on-the-job training. This approach of its time assumed that practice educators and the placement could provide the experience and training needed. I was fortunate to have very experienced practice educators in social work and probation who understood the importance of training to respond to threats of violence by parents and clients. Equally, once qualified, I had managers who provided support and training. However, it does need to be made clear that, even with all the training, support and access to experienced colleagues, when you come face to face with an angry and threatening parent, particularly in their 'place' of home, all the training and strategies can leave you in an instant as the emotions of fright or flight take over.

> **Pause and consider:**
>
> An incident or event that caused you feelings of fear. Think carefully about where this took place, who was involved and the range of feelings you experienced as a result.

Fear of violence from service users is also infused with contradictions and tensions. Enshrined in UK legislation for England, Scotland and Northern Ireland are requirements for partnership working between the state and parents and carers. Partnership working is set out in the Department of Health's (2000:12–13) *Framework for the Assessment of Children in Need and Their Families*, whose principles make clear what is expected between social workers working on behalf of the state and parents:

➤ 'Partnership between the State and the family, lies at the heart of child care legislation'

➤ 'It will be critical to develop a co-operative working relationship, so that parents or caregivers feel respected and informed, that staff are being open and honest with them'.

➤ 'Developing a working relationship with children and family members will not always be easy to achieve and can be difficult ... However resistant the family or difficult the circumstances, it remains important to continue to try to find ways of engaging the family'.

Partnership working with parents, families and children is a constant in policy, professional standards and competencies for social workers. The emphasis in partnership working is on building effective relationships through good communication whereby social workers:

> Act respectfully even when people are angry, hostile and resistant to change. Be able to manage tensions between parents, carers and family members, in ways that shows persistence, determination and professional confidence.

> (Department for Education, 2018:3)

However, as Laird (2013) points out, achieving these exacting expectations while dealing with a range of challenging behaviours in difficult circumstances places social workers in an impossible position, especially when they are being shouted at and verbally threatened and are in fear of being physically attacked. It is difficult to maintain persistence, determination and professional confidence in such stressful situations.

For those who try and those who have been verbally abused or physically attacked, the impact is profound. Research by Littlechild (2005) identified depression, high anxiety and debilitating health as common outcomes for social workers who have experienced a range of violent behaviour, including ongoing threats of violence towards them and their families and physical attacks that have led to poor retention in the area of child protection social work.

There is a growing acknowledgement that social workers in all settings and fields are facing hostility and experiencing a range of violent behaviours directly and now via internet sources (British Association of Social Workers, 2018). Support, training and advice remain inconsistent and few provisions are made available to social workers in the shape of policy guidance that acknowledges the risk of violence at work (Bibby, 2017).

For those working in a range of other agencies (for example, the Fire and Rescue Service in consultation with practitioners published *Tackling Violence at Work: Good Practice Guidance Document for Fire and Rescue Services* (Department for Communities and Local Government, 2006)), there is an acknowledgement that guidance for those working in protective services is much needed. Equally, such documents and guidance acknowledge that violence towards staff exists. For the profession of social work, the lack of government and professional attention to the issue appears to support the corrosive thinking and ideology that social workers, specifically child protection social workers, are expected to accept a level of aggression and hostility as they carry out their daily work (Littlechild, 2005).

As highlighted by Littlechild (2005), the government guidance in the 1999 edition of *Working Together to Safeguard Children* makes only a brief reference to the violence that social workers working in child protection may face and some even briefer guidance about how to avoid it. However, this advice appears to have been removed from the updated edition of *Working Together to Safeguard Children* (2018) policy guidance with no acknowledgement that child protection social work is a risky business for individual social workers. The failure of government guidance to acknowledge the risks of violence from service users to social workers sends a strong message to the profession. The message singles social workers out as being somehow different from other professionals by implying that social work is the 'other' profession that is excluded from being protected.

This reluctance by the profession and government policy-makers to recognise the risks to social workers of violence and what this means for the individual social worker fails to acknowledge the impact on children who need protection. If social workers feel unprotected and unheard, it follows that they will not have the emotional resources to tune in to those children who are living in fear of violence. What social work and individual social workers need now, alongside clear policy recognition about fear of violence, are strategies and tactics for actively engaging with these important issues.

In the case of Simon, social workers responded to Shirley's hostility and violence by distancing themselves emotionally and physically from the family. This distancing was a strategy that was influenced by the fears and anxieties of individual social workers to working directly with Shirley. This strategy was reflected in the case recordings that focussed on decisions about who should respond to the needs of the *family* and how this would be carried out. As a consequence, social workers could not engage Simon in any effective relationship, listen to his views and wishes and feelings or observe and talk to him and subsequently could not write him into the case records. Fear directed practice that obscured Simon.

It would be easy to criticise the practice of social workers in the 1970s. However, they were dealing with a situation that was difficult to cope with. It feels a perfectly normal response to want to run away from this situation and take a position of standing on the sidelines in the hope that the situation resolves itself or there is a shift in relationships that presents a different way to practice with the family.

Social workers did not have to wait too long on the sidelines before they became involved with Simon and his family. Simon's aggressive behaviour was channelled into offending, which brought him to the attention of the youth courts and youth justice social workers. Simon's life once again featured social workers who were expected to try to make sense of his behaviour within the context of his social and parental background.

Using the critical element of the FIM to make sense of Simon's lived experience

The critical element of the FIM highlights the importance of using reflection as a way of developing knowledge. In this section, I want to raise the profile of social work recording as a reflective tool for practice and highlight how case records can be used to support critical thinking and analysis.

Using social work records as a tool for reflection is not new. Many social workers have been doing this to good effect over the years. Though accepted as an important skill and tool in social work, it appears to have been overlooked as a response to meeting the demands of performance management systems and subsequently it has not been given enough prominence in the social work literature (Timms, 2018). As a consequence, social workers have failed to grasp its importance to their practice, and evidence suggests that the skill of record-ing and how this is used to inform practice have become a cause for concern (Timms, 2018).

Social workers argue that recording has become an inconvenient prac-tice because of time-limited processes that mean they have to 'spend too much time at their desks and computers and not enough time with service users' (Ferguson, 2011:38). Although I do have some sympathy with what social workers are saying and I am well aware of the stresses associated with recording in a pressurised environment, this lamenting discourse has evolved from a 'desk-bound' narrative that has lost sight of the importance of recording in the lives of children. While the debates about performance management systems and workload pressures are all valid, they suggest that these pressures carry more importance than the practice of recording. Ferguson (2011:35) has warned against this outcome by arguing that there needs to be a greater understanding of what the 'doing of practice' means for children.

Raising the importance of recording in practice, first as a document of practice and second as a reflective tool, appears to be well overdue. Although social work recording appears to have become a contentious practice because of workload and time pressures, there is also the issue about how and what to record. For example, when recordings are vague, lack clarity or misrepresent what has taken place, they can become meaningless and, more concerning, they can lead to poor outcomes for children (Ames, 2014). As Rennison (1962:67) despairs:

> Social workers rarely re-read their words, but apparently are satisfied to commit them to paper and leave them for posterity.

Pause and consider:

Have you recently read through a case file and used the recordings to reflect on deci-sions about risk and need? Did the recordings help you make sense of practice? What challenges did you encounter?

Child care social workers working with Simon had left a wealth of recorded information for posterity. What youth justice social workers found in the child care records were answers to questions about Shirley's mental health. The recordings showed the following:

> Shirley (age 17) was diagnosed as having a 'sociopathic personality'. This diagnosis was made in 1973 and the term 'sociopathic personality' is now better understood as an anti-social personality disorder (Latalova and Prasko, 2010).

> Between the ages of 17 and 20, Shirley was made the subject of mental health legislation that placed her in a local mental health hospital for treatment.

Although the psychiatric assessment and diagnosis of Shirley were held on Simon's case file, there was little information to say how or if this was used to inform social work interventions. For example, did Shirley's mental health pose a risk to Simon and his sister? This is not an assumption that adults with mental health problems pose a risk to their children. However, Shirley's mental health was characterised by her violent and aggressive behaviour, and analysis of serious case reviews found that the mental health of a parent can pose a risk to children (Department for Education, 2016).

There are some important factors that may explain why Shirley's mental health diagnosis took a back seat in social work decision-making and interventions. The factors are those that have emerged from serious case reviews (Brandon et al., 2012).

> The constant change of social worker in response to Shirley's behaviour meant that the psychiatric report became 'buried' underneath a wealth of recordings about events and social workers' fears of being verbally or physically abused.

> Recordings minimised her behaviour.

> When confronted by social workers about her mental health needs, Shirley denied them and acted aggressively.

However, while the information about Shirley's mental health appears to have lain on the file as a marker, it helped youth justice social workers understand what they were dealing with. By consulting with colleagues from mental health, they now understood the many 'faces' of Shirley. Although they were often frustrated by the 'head' games she employed to distract and block out what they were trying to confront her with (for example, during a home visit, she insisted on singing to social workers using a new karaoke machine she had bought), they did manage to develop a relationship with her that supported their work with Simon. This relationship was always fragile and finely balanced. It was never partnership working in the true sense. As Laird (2013:184) comments, when social workers are faced with 'deep-seated aggressive behaviours' linked to mental health problems, it is highly unlikely that social workers will be able to engage constructively with service users.

While the documented practice of social workers in 1970s provided insight into Shirley's mental health, it also offered glimpses of what Simon's life had been like growing up with a violent mother. The records of social workers' interpretations suggested that Simon and his sister were

> ➢ well cared for by both parents

> ➢ comfortable in their mother's presence

> ➢ close to their father

> ➢ bright and creative.

These interpretations of what social workers observed could easily be questioned. Given that these recordings were made at a time when social workers were recording their fears and anxieties about trying to engage with Shirley and her husband, they stand out as an oasis of good parental capacity in what was otherwise a landscape of fear, aggression and hostility. What these recordings suggest is that even when Shirley's behaviour was erratic and volatile, there appeared to be some strong bonds between the children and their parents.

The suggestion that Simon had a strong bond with his parents went some way to explain why he would not engage with social workers who wanted to talk about his relationship with his mother. He refused to engage in discussions about his family background, being very protective of his mother, and would challenge those who suggested his mother was 'a problem'. His relationship with his mother was complex and important to him. By acknowledging this, youth justice social workers took a different approach to engaging Simon and his family.

The power of fear

What emerges from the testimony of Simon is the power of fear to trigger a set of feelings that, when they collide, can influence actions and decision-making. Not all feelings will be equal in their power to influence social workers' practice. For example, social workers feeling angry and sad about the situation of a child can help them to focus their thinking and analysis (Munro, 2008). However, when any of these feelings is accompanied by fear, it is fear that will win out, and the power of fear will always affect how we look at and respond to situations (Altheide, 2002).

For Simon, fear created a range of conflicts between the adults who should have been protecting him. As a result, there was an imbalance of power as social workers tried to respond to the needs of his mother. This imbalance of power effectively reduced how social workers were able to make sense of or meet the needs of Simon. In the case of Simon fear became a dominant factor that influenced social work decision-making and practice . As a result, Simon became invisible to all those involved.

Evidence of fear dominating in child protection has been documented in the analysis of serious case reviews, highlighting how the power of fear has framed the following:

Social workers' responses and practice: It is possible that fear of the father's aggression towards staff and the threat he posed clouded professional judgement in this case (Children's Services Network, Coventry Local Safeguarding Children Board, Serious Case Review, Daniel Pelka, 2013).

Policy responses: You must be careful of parents who intimidate and lie and you must find ways to deal with such behaviours (Department of Health, 2002).

Parents and families: Parents may be fearful and mistrustful of child protection services, especially if the parents have had previous negative experiences (Department for Education, 2016).

Although youth justice social workers experienced violence, aggression and hostility from Simon's mother, there was a subtle change to this relationship over time. The change was located in how Simon and his parents viewed the involvement of youth justice social workers. While some of the tensions remained, youth justice social workers were accepted because Simon and his parents believed their interventions were to support Simon against the state, specifically the police. This subtle shift in the relationship between Shirley, Simon and youth justice social workers could be attributed to a different perspective about the fears associated with the role of child care social workers and their mandated powers. What this shift allowed youth justice workers to do was refocus on Simon. They used the opportunity to look at the here-and-now and avoided looking back at his childhood and how this related to his offending behaviour.

This approach supported a different type of relationship. It created some balance between social workers and Simon. He was taken seriously and supported in his own right. He was 'held in mind' by social workers (Ferguson, 2017:108), who focussed on advocacy and ensuring he had all the information he needed to support him through the criminal justice processes.

Conclusion

The miasma of fear that surrounded Simon became a critical factor in how social workers saw him and it shaped their interventions. Simon was viewed as an extension of his mother and his behaviour became the focus of social workers' interventions. Although this focus appeared child-centred and resulted in Simon's being removed from the home, it only served to confirm to him that social workers had not been able to see or understand him.

The impact on Simon and his cognitive development, reasoning and decision-making were defined by growing up with a mother who was able to create fear in others. There is no doubt that his relationship with his mother was complex, and whether or not his gradual involvement in offending is an outcome of this relationship remains an outstanding question. Evidence suggests that this may well be the case. Outcomes for children living with parental mental health highlight that children experience behavioural or emotional problems or both (Cleaver *et al.*, 2011). There is no doubt that Simon's lived experience shaped his perceptions of the world around him.

Social workers trying to engage with Shirley's aggressive, unreasonable and violent behaviour led to interventions that did not fully pay attention to her mental health. Even if this had been understood and the early psychological assessments had been given greater weight, they would have needed an acknowledgement from Shirley that her mental health was impacting on her parenting capacity. For Shirley to concede that she had a mental health need or indeed that this was contributing to her violent behaviour was the 'Pandora's box' she was determined to keep the lid on. She did so using and creating a barrier of fear that effectively 'disabled' social work skills, strategies and policies for partnership working.

The issue of violent behaviour towards social workers trying to do their job needs to be acknowledged by the profession and government and steps need to be taken to ensure that the current culture of policy acceptance is challenged. However, there is a place in practice for acknowledging and talking about fear in all its forms in a way that ensures that the inherent risks that come with the work of child protection social work are rationally appreciated and understood. Such an approach will have an impact on social workers' practice and might be summarised as the following:

> Acknowledge that the foundations of child protection social work are steeped in conflict. Evidence suggests that this conflict can and does produce fear. Understand that fear is a critical life experience and, when acknowledged, can help us to understand the relationships of the here, now and close by.

➤ Understand the political context that legislates and guides state interventions; the critical roles and responsibilities of practice and interventions; the needs of the child, their parents and family networks; and the power inequalities and tensions that bind them all together.

➤ Acknowledge how these relationships create conflicts, barriers and events that produce a narrative of fear.

➤ Pay attention to how a narrative of fear succeeds in narrowing thinking and practice and can result in practice that fails to keep the child fully in focus. Understand how fear affects partnership working and influences how we engage with children and adults.

➤ Be aware that losing sight of the child in the context of fear can have long-term implications for the child and practice. The implications have been well documented in analysis of serious case reviews and these highlight how social workers' professional skills and abilities are hijacked, leaving children vulnerable to poor decision-making.

➤ Acknowledge the importance of social work recording and how it can be used as a reflective tool to critically interrogate past and present practice.

➤ Increase professional awareness of the impact of parental mental health needs on children and the range of behaviours this can produce in adults and their children.

Simon's childhood was influenced by the behaviour of the adults who were his main carers and those professionals who tried to intervene. Fear was a significant factor in Simon's childhood, his adolescence and his adulthood. It created a framework for relationships, practice and outcomes. This framework of fear kept Simon firmly in the background. When he tried to communicate with adults – teachers and social workers – in the only way he knew how, by being aggressive, the adults did not fully notice or understand what was happening to him. Instead, social workers acted within a legal framework of its time that meant taking him out of the family home. By doing so, they were unable to develop a relationship him with because he had learned not to trust those trying to help him.

It would be a neat conclusion to say that Simon found a way to engage with youth justice social workers in a way that changed his life chances. While his relationship with youth justice social workers was different and he did come to trust some of them to advise him and provide practical support, it was always interwoven with his relationship with his mother. To gain Simon's trust, youth justice social workers acknowledged that they had to gain his mother's trust. This acknowledgement helped social workers to understand her mental health needs and subsequently supported them to gain insight into family relationships. However, fear had shaped Simon's life and it continued to shape his future. In his words:

> Look I know that you are trying to help, but you don't know my world and trying to get me to fit into yours is … well … just shit really. So don't mess with my head. You have to understand that this is it … I can make a lot of money quickly – look I was paid three thousand pound last night for a car – it's easy. See what I mean – this is what I do – I just can't do the other stuff … like be an apprentice or do that, that's what others do … not me.

4

The Child's Voice in Sexual Abuse. Katy's Story: Learning to Scream

In the wake of the #MeToo campaign where women around the world have mobilised into calling to account their sexual abusers, there has been an acknowledgement that for women to speak out publicly about their abuse takes time and courage. While the actions by these women are providing a wider platform to discuss and debate the issues, questions emerged about why women take so long to speak out about being sexually abused or do not speak out at all. This has led to further questions about why children, specifically girls, are socially constructed to accept unwanted male sexual attentions and what this says about a society that continues to emphasise the physical attributes of girls as part of their social and educational development and achievement.

Speaking out about sexual abuse is fraught with challenges. For children and adults, the challenges are wrapped in two dominant and interconnected feelings of fear and being believed. For children, telling another adult is filled with paradox – how do children tell an adult that another adult is sexually abusing them? How do children tell their mother that their father, their mother's lover or another close member of the family is sexually abusing them and what happens to the child, their family and their existing world when they do tell? Such questions are not easily answered, and for many children their childhood and adulthood will be scarred by their experience of sexual abuse, leaving them with their constant memories and testimonies. From the wave of media reports about the sexual abuse of young boys by Barry Bennell, a professional football coach, over a period of thirty years, it is the testimony of Andy Woodward, now 45, that helped to shine a light on the impact of sexual abuse on childhood and adulthood:

> This massive horrible burden … has shaped my life. Panic attacks … suicidal thoughts, depression and … living with fear. I was frightened to death because he had complete power over me and my family … I also had to endure the hellish ordeal of seeing the man who had exploited and abused me marry my sister … it was torture.
>
> (*Guardian*, 2018a, 2018b, 2018c)

Social workers are the ones who are mandated to make those enquiries necessary to determine whether a child has suffered significant harm or is likely to suffer significant harm. This may mean carrying out an interview with a child who has alleged that they have been sexually abused or provide follow-up support services. In both situations, social workers will be faced with working with vulnerable children who will be experiencing a range of feelings and living with the knowledge and fear that adults cannot be trusted and may pose a risk to them. How do social workers meet the needs of this specific group of children who have had the courage to speak out about the sexual abuse they have been or are being subjected to? How do they provide support services in a profession where direct work with children is increasingly becoming a practice that other agencies are being asked to do?

For those social workers who are carrying out direct work with children as part of a child-in-need or protection plan, this chapter will look at the role of the social worker providing this type of service using the case study of Katy. The case study will provide the legislative and policy context in which allegations of sexual abuse are jointly investigated by social workers and police officers and consider what happens next. Through the story of Katy, this chapter will examine how social workers engage with children in a way that does not place the burden of responsibility for keeping safe on the child. The chapter will focus on communication and listening skills, drawing upon current models of good practice and research that looks at children's experiences of direct contact with social workers. At key points in Katy's story, critical questions will be posed to the reader about what is taking place and responses made. The reader will also be asked to consider how Katy and all children can be fully involved in the decision-making processes that determine outcomes. In this chapter, attention will be paid to the context in which direct work with children who have been sexually abused takes place and how social workers ensure that they effectively communicate, listen to and interpret what is being told to them while taking into consideration child development.

Katy's story

Katy (age 4) was attending a local authority-funded nursery part-time when she told a nursery worker that 'Freddie had put his finger in her flower'. Freddie was her mother's partner and father of her two younger brothers, Daniel and Dylan. Police and social workers carried out an investigation under the codes and guidance of the *Memorandum of Good Practice* implemented through the Criminal Justice Act 1991. Katy was video-interviewed by a trained social worker and police officer in a social services specialist video suite. During the video interview,

▶

> ◀
>
> Katy repeated what she had told the nursery worker that, while her mother was 'next door' and she was 'in bed', Freddie came into her bedroom and got into her bed, told her to take off her pyjamas and then put his finger in her 'flower', which she explained was her 'front bottom'.
>
> Police carried out an investigation and interviewed Freddie, who denied Katy's claims. The social worker and police officer who video-recorded their interview with Katy believed what she had told them. However, the video was not submitted to the Crown Prosecution Service as a result of Katy's age and concerns about her memory – that is, her ability to provide a clear date and time when the alleged abuse took place. Although the allegations were deemed by the police investigation to be unsubstantiated, social services proceeded with a child protection conference and Katy's name was placed on the child protection register under sexual abuse. Freddie left the family home, refusing to work with social workers. Katy's mother (Sharon) was devastated and said she didn't know what or whom to believe. The social worker allocated the case worked closely with Sharon and Katy, and the direct work with Katy focussed on developing protective strategies.

Sexual abuse of children

While the nexus of ways in which children can be abused by adults is widening – internet and child sexual exploitation/trafficking – and societal, government and media responses have been those of incredulity and horror as reports and inquiries presented information about the scale and the appalling nature of the abuse suffered by children and young people, the very notion that an adult would sexually abuse a child continues to defy ideas of societal rationality. Indeed, the sexual abuse of children continues to be an area of abuse loaded with anxieties and alarm around gender, sex and sexuality. Current statistics for England and Wales identify that girls are more likely to suffer child sexual abuse than boys and are between four and six years old when the abuse first occurs (National Statistics, 2016). So it is little wonder that the area of sexual abuse presents child protection social workers with special problems.

Although this chapter focusses on the sexual abuse of Katy, it does not neglect the issues that surround the sexual abuse of boys. It was acknowledged earlier that speaking out about being sexually abused is located within a paradigm of fear, belief and uncertainty. With the additional spheres of gender, sex and sexuality, the paradigm becomes murky and somewhat contentiously steeped in rigid cultural and societal thinking about gender (Featherstone, 2006). Hooper and Warwick (2006) argue that constructions of masculinity place restrictions on boys to report sexual abuse and a level of reluctance by some professionals to understand or believe such reports. This argument poses a range of questions about the statistical 'evidence' and estimates that girls are overly represented in reports of sexual abuse (Featherstone, 2006). As reports about the sexual abuse of boys emerge from the masculinised world of football, the knowledge and understanding about gendered patterns of sexual abuse may need to be reviewed.

The sexual abuse and exploitation of children are not new phenomena. Research into child sexual abuse from incest and stranger to organised networks, institutional abuse and the involvement of families (making pornographic films) has been carried out since the late 1970s (Burgess and Clark, 1984; Gallagher, 1994; Nelson, 2016; Kelly and Karsna, 2017). The changing landscape of child sexual abuse has meant that different forms and contexts of abuse are now being recognised and, according to Kelly and Karsna (2017), has provided a welcome public platform for survivors to tell about their experiences to professionals and society. This widening context in which child sexual abuse is now being framed would suggest that there is developing knowledge and understanding about the scale and scope of child sexual abuse in England and Wales and new ways of attending to them (Kelly and Karsna, 2017). However, while research and the testimonies of adult survivors are being used to challenge state responses and interventions in the lives of children who have been sexually abused, there remains a level of societal ambiguity and restlessness about child sexual abuse, which sits within a discourse of hierarchical ordering of the problem and suffering.

This ambiguity and restlessness are best understood through literature and art and their history of presenting and framing children within the constructive language and images of sexuality and sexual desires where the word 'Lolita' has come to be understood as a child's sexual awakening as opposed to the grooming and rape of a child (Carroll, 2012). As a result, understanding and attending to child sexual abuse continue to be fraught with attitudes and beliefs that silence victims or see them as the protagonist and criminal (or that do both). An example of these attitudes and beliefs were laid bare in the findings from the Independent Inquiry into Child Sexual Exploitation in Rotherham (1997–2013), when it was reported that girls of 11 were not seen by professionals, police and social workers as children but as architects of their own victimisation with some children when they were found drunk and partially clothed in rooms and cars with adult males being 'arrested for offences such as drunk and disorderly, with no action taken against the perpetrators of rape and sexual assault' (Jay, 2014:36).

In the *Working Together* (2010) guidance, sexual abuse of children involves

forcing or enticing a child or young person to take part in sexual activities, not necessarily involving a high level of violence, whether or not the child is aware of what is happening. The activities may involve physical contact, including assault by penetration (for example, rape or oral sex) or non-penetrative acts such as masturbation, kissing, rubbing and toughing outside of clothing. They may also include non-contact activities, such as involving children in looking at, or in the production of, sexual images, watching sexual activities, encouraging children to behave in sexually inappropriate ways, or grooming a child in preparation for abuse (including via the internet). Sexual abuse is not solely perpetrated by adult males. Women can also commit acts of sexual abuse, as can other children.

(HM Government, 2010:93)

While working definitions of sexual abuse of children are useful and necessary, there is the issue of connecting with this specific type of abuse that brings with it a range of special problems. It needs to be acknowledged that, for many adults, being confronted by sex, sexuality and sexual activity is guilt-ridden, embarrassing and up against the morality within us (Haug, 1987). This is a set of feelings and emotions that are not easily discussed and that, for many professional social workers, are filled with painful memories. Alongside the adultness of sexual heuristics – feelings and emotions – child sexual abuse is often an act of violence committed within an overlapping sequence of other forms of abuse, such as neglect and emotional, physical and domestic violence (Pritchard, 2004). With the developing knowledge about child sexual exploitation in England and Wales, the boundaries between child sexual abuse and child sexual exploitation have become merged, adding further challenges and complications to those already faced by social workers working in child protection (Melrose and Pearce, 2013). For children, these special problems that pose challenges and complications for adults have become detrimental, producing barriers to reporting and finding the right services to meet their needs.

Research has shown that sexual abusers of children are most likely to be an adult who is known to them. Overall, the vast majority of sexual abusers are male, and although women do feature in research findings, the numbers are much smaller and are concentrated within women as mothers (Kelly and Karsna, 2017). Although research findings suggest there is little doubt that men are more likely to be reported to the police for the sexual abuse of children, producing the definitive notion of the male within the field of child sexual abuse (Pritchard, 2004), this outcome has tended to obscure the role that women play in the sexual abuse of children.

For Mulkeen (2013), this obscuring has meant that women are less likely to be recognised or even considered by social workers and safeguarding agencies to be the perpetrators of sexual abuse of children. This lack of recognition has meant that many children reporting being sexually abused by their mothers either have not been believed or have been left in homes to be further sexually abused while social workers considered the needs of the women or other areas of abuse, such as neglect (Mulkeen, 2013).

Whatever the challenges and overlapping features, the scale and nature of child sexual abuse in England and Wales continue to tax those agencies mandated to investigate and provide services to those children who allege they have been sexually abused. For those cases that enter the criminal justice and child protection systems, the layers of complexity are added to by processes of investigation and assessment. As discussed earlier, this complexity is contained in the value system of the police officer or social worker, who may or may not wish to believe that a mother can sexually abuse their child or who may have feelings of discomfort as they try to find a language that helps them talk to a four-year-old about an assault by penetration. Whatever the area of adult complexity, the child will become aware of this and will sense and understand that what they are trying to tell adults is unpalatable to them and something they do not want to hear.

When children have found a way of expressing their needs to adults, it is through a perspective filled with a set of compromises as they negotiate the adult world of feelings and emotions often on their behalf. Katy, the little girl in this chapter, would only tell someone who was not going to look sad or cross because she said that when she told the nursery worker 'she began to cry and then her voice got loud and she told me to sit still and wait while she went to get someone'. Katy had observed and sensed that what she was saying to the nursery worker had upset and worried her and as a result she was clear that she didn't want the same thing to happen again.

Katy was a brave and perceptive little girl who found the words to express her experience of being sexually abused. However, the weight placed on her words in this specific case was not strong enough to substantiate the allegations and, as a result, social workers had to find a way to intervene that offered Katy ongoing protection.

Legislation and interventions

The investigation of child sexual abuse rests on the alleged victim's speaking out and being able to provide details of the abuse, the abuser, dates, times and place. When a child does speak out, the investigation is undertaken by police and social workers jointly using section 47 1(b) of the 1989 Children Act, which states:

> Where a local authority have reasonable cause to suspect that a child who lives, or is found, in their area is suffering, or likely to suffer significant harm, the authority shall make, or cause to be made, such enquiries as they consider necessary to enable them to decide whether they should take any action to safeguard or promote the child's welfare.

> (White *et al.*, 1990)

It is widely accepted that carrying out joint police and social work investigations into allegations of child sexual abuse is good practice (Sternberg *et al.*,

2001). This approach was driven by the introduction of the *Memorandum of Good Practice* in 1992. The publication was guidance for police officers and social workers responsible for undertaking video-recorded interviews with child victims or witnesses. The publication provided core principles for conducting video-recorded interviews with children which could be used in court as opposed to the child having to appear publicly and give a live 'examination-in-chief' (Davies and Wescott, 1999:iii). However, despite the clarity and specificity of the publication, its implementation across England and Wales was not as effective as hoped in terms of subsequent prosecutions. The poor implementation of the guidance was considered to have been effected by a range of issues connected to staff shortages (police and social workers), variable training opportunities, a range of different interviewing styles and varied interpretations of the guidance. As a result, the details of the children's evidence was often lost because those interviewing the children found themselves grappling with competing styles of interviewing, one that is investigative and questioning and another that is fluid and supports the child to tell their story (Davies and Wescott, 1999).

The difficulty surrounding the forensic interview approach is the focus on gathering evidence that can stand up to the adversarial cross-examination in a judicial system where the emphasis is on assisting the legal advisors (lawyers and barristers) to present their opposing cases rather than meeting the needs of the child (Lamb *et al.*, 2011). This situation has presented the police and social workers responsible for carrying out interviews with a range of difficulties. They have to balance the needs of the child and be sympathetic to their situation while trying to ensure that the information provided by the child is clear and can stand up to legal scrutiny and challenge. As a result of legal reforms that acknowledged the vulnerability of adult and child witnesses in providing and giving evidence via video-recorded interviews, the *Memorandum of Good Practice* was replaced by the *Achieving Best Evidence in Criminal Proceedings* guidance (2002), which was updated in 2007. This guidance acknowledges the context in which allegations of abuse take place with specific reference to the intersections with child protection systems and procedures:

Any video-recorded interview serves two primary purposes:

➢ evidence gathering for use in the investigation and in criminal proceedings
➢ the evidence-in-chief of the witness

In addition, any relevant information gained during the interview can be used to inform inquiries regarding significant harm under section 47 of the Children Act 1989 and any subsequent actions to safeguard and promote the child's welfare and, in some cases, the welfare of other children.

(Ministry of Justice, 2011:2:18)

There has been a range of legislative developments in the use of the *Achieving Best Evidence* guidance and subsequent research about the impact and outcomes of video-recorded interviewing of children (Bull and Corran, 2002; Lamb *et al.*, 2011) (with references to interviewing children with specific needs, child development, children's memory and understanding of truth and lies). But the reality of practice in the 'real world' suggests that police officers and social workers continue to struggle with understanding and meeting the needs of the child during what is an emotional and anxiety-ridden interview process.

The decision to video-record an interview with Katy was taken during a strategy meeting. The purpose of a strategy meeting is described in *Working Together to Safeguard Children* (HM Government, 2010:36):

> to determine the child's welfare and plan rapid action if there is reasonable cause to suspect the child is suffering, or likely to suffer significant harm.

Under section 47 of the Children Act 1989, a strategy meeting was held. The participants included police officers, a nursery worker, a health visitor, a social worker and a team manager who chaired the meeting. At the meeting, information was shared about her physical and emotional development and her communication skills that helped to shape how any interview would be conducted. Before we detail the video-recorded interview of Katy, it is important to consider those issues associated with interviewing a four-year-old.

Pause and consider:

What issues would you need to consider that take into account Katy's age, and how would you gain her 'consent' to conduct a video-recorded interview? How would you explain the purpose of a proposed video-recorded interview to Katy at a level that is age-appropriate?

The decision to interview Katy by way of a video-recording was taken on the basis of information already gathered about the family circumstances: concerns about siblings, the alleged offender remained in the family home, Katy's mother was initially very supportive and Katy had provided a statement that was considered to be a clear allegation of being sexually abused. However, careful consideration was given to the fact that having carried out a video-recorded interview of Katy's story would not exclude her from being called by a judge to give evidence in person to a court. While the idea that a child could be called by a judge to be present in a court sounds unlikely or rather draconian, it remains the case that the 'judge has the final word on whether or not the statement will be admitted' (Ministry of Justice, 2011:13). In light of all the issues, it was agreed that a video-recorded interview would take place with Katy. While the focus was on gathering evidence for use in criminal proceedings, the aim was to determine her welfare and that of her siblings and seek to protect them.

I was the social worker identified to be the lead interviewer. I was supported by a police colleague who communicated with me via an audio ear piece. We had worked and trained together using the *Memorandum of Good Practice* (Home Office, 1992) guidance. The interview took place at Children's Services in a building that had been specially adapted for video-recorded interviews and direct work with children. This meant that Katy did not have to go to a police station. Before the proposed interview, I was able to spend some time with her in a designated play area, getting to know her and explaining to her and her mother what would happen, who I was, and where each adult would be and how she could access her mother whenever she needed to.

As I stated in previous chapters, working with children and finding ways to communicate with them are not easy. My approach with Katy was to try to understand what it must be like for her to go with an adult she has only just met into a room she has never seen before and tell them about something that caused her distress. Although I had some information about Katy and her skills and abilities in terms of meeting appropriate developmental milestones for her age, this information is always one-dimensional and rarely prepares you for that first meeting with the child.

From the information already provided, I knew that Katy liked drawing, talking and running about and that she found it difficult to concentrate on some tasks at nursery and she could be bossy. In my first encounter with Katy and after introductions, I was struck by her sharp awareness of the situation and her ability at the age of four to ask pertinent and important questions before and during the interview and in many ways highlight how as adults we can get caught up in the details of a process without thinking about how they may seem to a child. These are some of Katy's questions and responses:

> Will it be just me and you in the room?

> Where will the man (police officer) be?

> Will he hear what I am saying?

> Can I see the thing in your ear?

> What will he (police officer) say to you?

> Can I play with the toys and talk to you?

> Can my mum hear what I am saying?

> Can I go home with my mum after talking to you?

> Yes, I can tell the truth, I'm not silly.

- ➤ Will Freddie get into trouble?

- ➤ He frightens me – can you take him away?

- ➤ Yes, I know where my flower is, it is here (pointing to her vagina).

- ➤ He did it when I went to bed.

- ➤ He came into my bedroom when I was asleep and woke me up.

- ➤ He told me not to tell my mum or he would hit me.

- ➤ I don't know any more.

- ➤ I am tired and want something to eat.

- ➤ What are the days of the week?

Katy's response about telling the truth and letting me know that she is not silly was in response to my attempt to find out whether she knew the difference between telling the truth and telling lies. At that time, training had advised interviewers to use age-appropriate approaches such as holding up red and blue pens and asking the child to confirm what colour they were. Once the colours had been established, the interviewer was to ask the child what would be happening if I told you that the pens were not red and blue but different colours. To this attempt, Katy looked at me with a sense of 'pity' and said 'you would be very silly and I am not silly'. In further attempts to gain an understanding of whether she could tell the difference between telling a lie and telling the truth, she turned to me clearly exasperated and said 'yes, I can tell the truth'.

This example of my rather clumsy approach to determining Katy's capacity to understand the difference between telling the truth and lies is a salient reminder that using any guidance to interview children should be applied with critical caution and an awareness of the child. However, under the new best evidence guidance, the 'witness should not be asked to demonstrate their understanding of truth and lies during the interview' as a result of previous legal challenges to the way in which police and social workers gathered this specific evidence for criminal proceedings (Ministry of Justice, 2011:2.172).

In my early meeting with Katy and throughout the video-recorded interview, I often found myself lost in observing, listening and conversing with her or trying to 'match' and compare the skills and abilities of this four-year-old with the generalised child development milestones for children her age. What I found was that Katy was full of surprises. I dispensed with any thinking about what she should or should not be doing at this point of the milestones and let her set the pace that supported a narrative telling of her experience.

This approach at the time did not support a forensic interview approach, but it did provide Katy with the opportunity to tell in her words what had happened. At the time, I felt strongly that letting her set the pace was in her best interests and that using a forensic interview style that meant focussing on more details about the day, date and time may cause her unnecessary distress. For example, I became aware that as I was pursuing these details with Katy she became agitated and it was she who brought the interview to an end by telling me she was tired and hungry, which I interpreted as meaning that she had had enough.

This had wider implications for the investigation in terms of being able to pursue criminal proceedings. While the police officer and I believed that Katy had been sexually abused by Freddie, his denial and the decision by the Crown Prosecution Service not to pursue criminal proceedings meant that consideration now needed to be given to how to protect Katy. The information provided by Katy did support the implementation of child protection procedures and helped to shape the social work intervention. Before we consider what this looked like, it is worth examining how issues identified during the interview relate to factors associated with understanding child development.

Child development

During any direct work with children, social workers need to consider a range of factors connected to the child. Although there are checklists available for social workers to refer to when they undertake direct work with children, such as those found in (*Achieving Best Evidence*, 2012) and the assessment framework guidance (Department of Health, 2000) concerns have emerged from findings in serious case reviews about social workers knowledge and understanding of child development that have resulted in recommendations that suggest 'there is scope for improvements in child development training for all professionals' (Brandon *et al.*, 2012:5). However, there is a clear call for professional improvement in the knowledge and understanding of child development and attachment timescales (Department for Education, 2018) and some specific areas to focus on emerge:

➤ understanding normal motor development in childhood

➤ understanding the disabled child beyond their disability

➤ understanding parental capacity

➤ understanding resilience in children

It remains the case that child development is dependent on a number of wide-ranging factors, many that are only just receiving attention and being understood – such as emotional abuse and neglect (Davies and Ward, 2012; Horwath,

2013) and racism (Bernard and Harris, 2016) – for supporting the best outcomes for children.

While recommendations from serious case reviews highlight the gap in social workers' and professionals' knowledge and understanding about child development, frustrations continue to be expressed when a child death or serious injury is reported and the findings ask why social workers failed to recognise a number of indicators around the child's health and development that could suggest abuse was taking place (Brandon *et al.*, 2012). Not all indicators lead to a finding of child abuse, but a number of well-recognised and accepted factors are now associated with the needs of parents and impact on their parental capacity and subsequently the development of their child or children (Davies and Ward, 2012). The key areas that social workers will know and be dealing with are the following:

➢ parental mental health

➢ parental drug and alcohol misuse

➢ parental learning disability

➢ parental domestic violence

These key issues, particularly in combination, have been analysed in a comprehensive body of work by Cleaver *et al.* (2011) in *Children's Needs – Parenting Capacity: The Impact of Parental Mental Illness, Learning Disability, Problem Alcohol and Drug use, and Domestic Violence on Children's Safety*. The overall conclusion drawn from this analysis is that those children living with parents whose parental capacity is influenced by one or more of the key factors are likely to be at risk of harm (Davies and Ward, 2012).

However, although a substantial body of work that helps to understand the key factors that impact on a child's development is emerging, it remains the case that being able to understand how this is manifested in a child's physical, socio-emotional, cognitive, behavioural and sexual development is not always straightforward. While social workers will understand some of the basic tenets associated with the discourse underpinning the nature-versus-nurture debates, whereby the genetic or behavioural influences of the parents are considered in terms of their impact on a child's development and ultimately their life chances, the research findings are argued to be either ambiguous (Featherstone *et al.*, 2014) or substantial in their impact (Horwath, 2013).

These contentious debates about what influences a child's development have produced a wealth of 'fashionable and powerful ideas' that social workers draw upon to make sense of a child's behaviour and that Featherstone *et al.* (2014:57) argue should be approached critically and cautiously. These debates have widened the library of information for social workers to draw upon to make sense of a child's behaviour by categorising it using evidence-based theoretical frameworks such as attachment and neuroscience (Featherstone *et al.,* 2014). But they have also created a fog-like environment in which social workers grope their way forward in the hope of finding the answer to a child's behaviour in the promise and promotion of a new idea. This is not to say that the ideas and thinking generated by the nature-versus-nurture debate should be discarded. Rather, it is a plea on behalf of the children that if a particular model of thinking is adopted, such as attachment theories, social workers should do this in the knowledge and understanding that this 'idea' may well determine the child's life chances (positively and negatively). Before the thinking and ideas are applied, it is worth asking some questions:

> **Pause and consider:**
>
> What has influenced your beliefs about child development? Are these based on knowledge gained through critical investigation of the debates? Do the ideas and thinking you have adopted really capture the essence of the child? What will be the outcome for the child as a result of your interpretation of the information?

Along with Katy's testimony of her experience, there follows an examination of some of the debates about the impact of parental behaviour on a child's universal development and their behaviour.

Parental substance and alcohol misuse

Parental substance and alcohol misuse is now recognised as being a major factor in the lives of 1.3 million children in the UK (Davies and Ward, 2012). For children, the impact of parental substance and alcohol misuse before and after birth is widely accepted as having a detrimental effect on their long-term future and health and well-being (Horwath, 2013). Those parents who misuse substances and alcohol are more likely to become preoccupied with meeting their own needs. As a result, the child's direct needs and their home environment suffer from being neglected (Davies and Ward, 2012).

The misuse of alcohol by Katy's mother (Sharon) was a factor in her early life. Sharon's own childhood had been heavily influenced by her parents' alcohol misuse. Her family history and functioning were characterised by alcohol misuse, domestic violence and neglect, all experienced in the shadow of a town with high unemployment and a cultural history of inherent alcohol and drug misuse. Sharon grew up in a home where using alcohol was understood and used as a 'crutch' or 'celebrant' to deal with the issue of living. The impact on

Sharon was a disrupted education, a nomadic adolescence whereby she moved between her home and living with friends and relatives, and early sexual relations that resulted in pregnancy and limited job choices. From this platform, Sharon moved into a council flat with a newly born Katy, and with social benefits, grit and determination to provide a better beginning and childhood for her daughter, she settled into a life of day-to-day struggle to survive and ensure that Katy was provided for.

During this period, Sharon met Freddie, who was not from the town. His difference in terms of his culture, his self-assured approach to the world, his interest in her and his middle-class aspirations were what Sharon described as highly attractive and a 'godsend'. Freddie moved into the flat and his job at a local factory meant that his financial contribution to the household reduced the levels of struggle for Sharon. For the first time, Sharon believed that she could transcend her childhood legacy. There followed two pregnancies, Dylan and Harris, and the family moved into a three-bedroom council house and what Sharon believed was a stake in a new future.

However, shortly after her pregnancy with Dylan, her relationship with Freddie altered. He became controlling and aggressive and frequently verbally abused and humiliated her. Sharon often fought back physically and verbally and their relationship became a round of aggressive incidents followed by using sex to 'make up'. After the birth of Harris, their relationship 'cooled', and according to Sharon, they settled into a life of living together but leading what Sharon referred to as separate lives: Freddie went to work, he came home; she went out with friends, she came home. As a cloak of depression and anxiety began to envelope her, she turned to alcohol. Somewhere in all of this, the children survived and Katy developed, and universal and statutory services remained on the edges of the children's survival.

What this survival meant for Katy was being alert to the needs and behaviour of her mother and Freddie. She became highly attuned to her surroundings and at an early age knew when to 'disappear' in the house and how to find ways of entertaining and sometimes feeding herself and her brothers – packets of crisps, cereal, soft drinks and bread. Sharon's history and this scenario of Katy's appearing to develop independently with little attention or encouragement from her mother will be familiar to many social workers.

At this point, it would be easy to suggest that Sharon's behaviour (influenced by her use of alcohol) and her relationship with Freddie were symptoms of neglect and, as such, to go down the familiar path of assuming that Sharon was not a good-enough parent providing love, affection, stimulation and safety for Katy. Some of the specifics involved in being a neglectful parent, particularly a mother, are highlighted in research:

➢ being unable to recognise the age-appropriate needs of their children (Cleaver *et al.,* 2011)

➢ being easily upset and angry with their children (Crittenden, 1999)

➢ being unable to set clear and consistent boundaries (Cleaver *et al.,* 2011)

➢ struggling to interpret their children's emotions and actions accurately (Hildyard and Wolfe, 2007)

➢ having difficulty providing verbal and social stimulation (McAllister and Lee, 2016)

➢ being unable to identify risk (Hildyard and Wolfe, 2007)

However, while there is no doubt that Katy was harmed by living in a home where adult needs, specifically Freddie's, were dominant, a number of positives were identified in Katy's behaviour and development. These positives suggested that, in all her struggles as a parent, Sharon had provided some good parenting that included love, affection and stimulation.

For example, Katy had good verbal skills and was able to respond to a new social situation (being video-interviewed) that many children found difficult. She demonstrated during the interview that she could write her name and knew her numbers as she counted out how many small dolls she could find in the toy house. She also talked easily about how she and her mum liked singing. Katy's observed behaviour appeared to support nursery reports that her general development was in line with those expected of a four-year-old, and it was tempting to conclude that somehow her mother's increasing dependency on alcohol was not having a major impact on her. Such a conclusion is not without some merit. Iwaniec *et al.* (2006) suggests that some children can develop a resilience that supports them to achieve against a background of inconsistent and harmful parental behaviours. However, Bentovim *et al.* (2009) is more cautious, positing that we do not fully understand the impact of detrimental parental behaviour on children, a situation that some argue is because research generally continues to focus on the behaviour and needs of the adults (Cleaver *et al.,* 2011).

Burden of responsibility

Because the impact of detrimental parental behaviours on children remains contentious, there is a growing focus on understanding the resilience of 'the individual child' by policy-makers (HM Government, 2015a, 2015b:23). This growing interest in the resilience of the child to survive and overcome parental behaviours has caused some concern amongst social work academics who argue that this approach appears to place the burden of responsibility of staying safe on the child (Featherstone *et al.,* 2014). This argument is somewhat supported by frameworks that draw upon concepts of resilience to shape how social workers carry out direct work with children who are living with parental problems (Newman and Blackburn, 2002).

Research by Newman and Blackburn (2002) examined how resilience frameworks were being operationalised in direct work with children and identified that social workers were more likely to adopt a protective behaviour model that focussed on increasing the child's self-esteem, creating opportunities for cognitive growth and introducing strategies for reducing risk:

> ➤ identifying internal (family) and external (school and community) networks of adults they trust to talk to

> ➤ understanding that their body is a private space

> ➤ saying no and speaking out

> ➤ not keeping a bad secret

These are all valuable strategies, and although they go beyond the stranger/danger advice that permeated UK culture in the early 1950s and 1960s, the onus is still on the child to act or speak out. Without alternative frameworks, how do we ensure that children do not shoulder the burden of responsibility for keeping themselves safe?

Wrench (2017) acknowledges that resources available to social workers undertaking direct work with children who have alleged they have been sexually abused are limited. Although she offers a range of creative strategies for working directly with children who have been sexually abused, she posits that interventions that focus on *keeping safe* may never fully meet the needs of children in the short or long term. This situation can leave us asking, if not protective behaviour models then what? But I argue, from my experience, that the time you give to the child is the most important resource.

It is worth being reminded that speaking out about being sexually abused is part of a process and that, for many children, the time spent with social workers may be the only time they have felt listened to by an adult in a safe environment. In the following, I offer some suggestions based on the work I did with Katy. I include ideas from work with other children to help social workers begin to think through what might be going on for that child.

Planning the work that you intend to do with the child is important for the child and for the social worker. This may sound like an obvious suggestion. But large caseloads and time pressures can mean that planning direct work with children is not always given the priority it needs. There are two main areas to focus on that I believe will help in planning direct work with children. First, take time to consider what you already know about the child in terms of their cognitive and physical development, their likes and dislikes, what they are considered to be good at and any behaviour that may be a challenge. Second, make every effort to match the strategies and activities to what you know about the child. In my work with Katy, I put together a plan of work with her that focussed on five key areas:

1. ***Taking allegations seriously:*** Children rarely lie about being sexually abused and do not have the adult sophistication to maintain a lie. They may also have been threatened with violence and discouraged to speak out by being told that no adult would believe them. By taking Katy's allegation seriously, I shaped and set the tone of the work with her. It was a starting point that showed respect for her. It also meant that the work would not be set around a 'fishing expedition' that placed her under pressure to elaborate on what she had already told me. I avoided putting her under any more pressure to tell more.

2. ***Pacing:*** This is a process that requires being aware of and attentive to the needs of the child. This meant I used her language and if I didn't understand her I asked her to help me out. For example, Katy's cultural background was Scottish, and during a session where she was playing at shopping, she told me she was just going to the shops to get the 'messages'. This is a Scottish colloquial term for buying food such as milk and bread. I knew what she meant and did not have to check this out with her. However, during supervision, my manager said they had no idea what it meant but wondered whether it was some sort of code her mother used when going out to buy something illegal! I reassured them that it was no such thing but I did have to ask a Scottish colleague to confirm that it was not a word for something sinister. While I have used this as an example of understanding a child's language, it is also an important reminder that having a good knowledge of a child's ethnicity and cultural background is essential to being able to engage with them and understand them.

    This approach of pacing can present a range of challenges for social workers working in an environment where time has become the ultimate resource. Children can and will pick up on any feelings of anxiety, unease and frustration. Children need time to work out whether you are the one they can invest their time with. They will do this by moving in and out of the planned work, drip-feeding you information, and testing your listening, observation and interpretative skills. This may mean having to improvise with the work that you had planned or dispensing with it altogether. However, your day is going and whatever the child presents to you on that day, you need to ensure that you are able to keep your own feelings in check in order to meet the needs of working with the child. Remember, work pressures and demands are not the fault of the child.

3. ***Reassurance:*** This is about ensuring that the child knows they are not to blame for the abuse. In the work with Katy, I reassured her at the beginning

that she was not in any trouble with me or the police and that what had happened was not her fault. This reassurance was integral to the work. While the aim was to ensure that any sense of blame she may be feeling was not hers to hold, it was also a way of raising a belief in herself by developing her self-esteem and strength of character to be able to help her understand the messages about how to keep safe now and in the future. I used storytelling with Katy to help explore her feelings and issues of blame. At the time, I used a book about toys in a child's bedroom and how one of them, a teddy bear, had been naughty and touched one of the other toys on their body in place that was private – 'Her flower!', shouted Katy.

You can be creative and make up your own stories or use some of the existing literature available. (See resources and services of the National Society for the Prevention of Cruelty to Children.) However, although this area of literature is growing, there are gaps, particularly for black and ethnic minority children, and I continue to find ways to adapt or make up stories that are age-appropriate for children to deal with a range of issues. At the end of the work with Katy, I gave her the book we had used. This was a gift and reminder of the work she had been doing with me.

4. **Skills:** Skill development was about building Katy's self-esteem and her assertiveness by encouraging her to speak out against any other Freddie who may come into her life. The speaking out was turned into something very practical and came about during some play in a soft room. Katy told me that we had to play hide-and-seek. As I would make a big issue of trying to find her in the soft room, her excitement would boil over and she would scream with anticipation of being found and ultimately let me know where she was. Katy could scream very loud and this became the platform for developing a protective behaviour skill. She liked the freedom and the attention screaming got her. However, screaming during play is a very different intuitive response from one when you are fearful. Helping children to speak out in an adult world remains steeped in social constructions of childhood and narratives that run parallel to those of women as a minority group (Mayall, 2002).

   The purpose of encouraging Katy to scream and to use this when she felt threatened by the unwanted attentions of another Freddie was in a small way aimed at helping her to reclaim her body and space. To change the current societal status quo for children, boys *and* girls, there needs to be an approach, within any protective behaviour model, that acknowledges how gender categorisations that attribute and underpin the feminine and the masculine shape our responses to children.

5. **Adult network team (ANT)** is a conceptual framework that brings together theories from sociology and psychology in a proposal that links the activities

involved in developing and building networks (Bruno, 2007). Simply put, the people or actors involved in the network use their identities, emotions and actions in a network designed to build people's strength and resolve to overcome a problem or difficult situation (Bruno, 2007). The ANT framework was implemented by using an eco-map in the work with Katy. Eco-maps provide a visual means of helping children talk about and identify social networks (Baumgartner *et al.*, 2012). In the work with Katy, we worked together to produce a large cutout of clouds that she gave names to: mummy, social worker (Sue), aunt (Issy), neighbour (Jen), nursery worker (Carly), Freddie, brother (Dylan), brother (Harris) and uncle (Terry). The clouds were Katy's idea as she liked the thought that they floated around her. Katy placed the cutout clouds around her, beginning with those she said she 'liked' and those she didn't. It was an effective way of identifying what networks Katy had and especially which adults she felt she could tell if she was afraid or worried. As the 'game of clouds' developed, Katy was able to provide valuable information about whom she trusted and who she believed could protect her now and in the future. Interestingly, it was her aunt Issy (her mother's sister) whom she wanted close to her as she believed her aunt could protect her because she knew that Freddie was 'scared' of Issy. Using and adapting eco-maps can aid the assessment process and can be used in a range of settings. I have found them to be a fun way of gathering information and providing a visual diagram/picture of a child's social world.

No doubt, the current models available for supporting children who have been sexually abused are based on educational ideas about protection within the general population of children. Not all children will be sexually abused, and providing educational models that focus on self-esteem, being assertive and developing their awareness is a solid aspiration. For those children who have been sexually abused, the focus on protecting themselves from further abuse is magnified because they know through experience that this is a David-and-Goliath situation. Providing Katy with a relatively simple tool – her voice to scream – was a way of actively promoting assertiveness, helping her growth and promoting a useful skill for ensuring that this could stop time, albeit briefly. In the words of Dunmore (1994:49), it was a way of acknowledging that Katy knew who the wolves were and what they were capable of and that her screaming skills could let them know that *'wolves don't frighten (her) much even when they howl in the dark. With wolves, (she) knows where you are'.*

To ensure that the burden of responsibility does not always fall to the child, protective interventions should be carried out with the parent or carer in mind. There is an acknowledgement in the social work literature that working with a non-abusing parent can help the child to understand that they were not to blame, build trust with their parent and create a protective layer that helps them to grow in the future (Daniel *et al.*, 2010; Wrench, 2017).

On two occasions, I worked with Katy and her mother and used the time to reinforce the messages underpinning the five key areas. We all worked together on a simple quiz based on the protective work that mother and daughter had completed. Katy's mother engaged with the work and there were a range of similarities in her responses to those of her daughter. This was a reminder that Sharon's lived experience had impacted on her social, cognitive and emotional development. Sharon's low self-esteem was the result of not experiencing the adult and care-giving response that had supported a childhood development of security. Her own parents' availability was inconsistent and she grew up with little or no parental attention that was attuned to her own needs.

However, bringing together mother and daughter was an opportunity to visit a range of complex emotions that both were experiencing. Through different activities, Sharon was able to understand how events and her own behaviour had placed a disproportionate amount of responsibility on her daughter to become resilient and keep safe. Katy had an opportunity to have her mother to herself in a safe space where she could express and test out her feelings about what had happened. There is no doubt that the feelings were complex and represent the impossible borders which mothers of sexually abused daughter's experience and which social work and society expect them both to transcend through their protective maternal instincts (Warner, 2015) and the development of individual resilience (HM Government, 2015a, 2015b).

Who are you?

This is an important question. I have included a discussion about who we are because it is considered a neglected dimension in direct work with children (Wrench, 2017). Who we are poses a question that seeks to find out what it is – the skill set, values and attitudes – we bring to working directly with children.

It is often assumed that social workers working in Children's Services have arrived in this specialist field because they are a particular type of person who has an affinity with children. So often, student social workers said they saw their future in child protection because they believed they could protect and save children from abuse. The details of what this may look like are rarely fully understood in the classroom setting or developed during practice placements where the focus was often on their own survival – getting through in order that they could qualify and then they would practice 'differently' (Lomax et al., 2010).

However, when faced with undertaking direct work with a child, whether this is short term (duty home visit) or over a contracted period of time (protection plan), many qualified social workers say they feel overwhelmed by the responsibility, accountability and expectations – the organisation's, their own and those of the child. These feelings are heightened by fears of causing further distress to a child who has been or may have been sexually abused (Wrench, 2017).

From my experience, children 'get' adults. It is in their best interests to be attuned to us. They will pick up on our behaviour and feelings and very quickly make a decision about whether or not we are worthy of their trust and time. To help you become attuned to children, it is worth taking the time to consider who you are and what this brings to working directly with children. I offer the following questions to support a reflective process that will aid planning direct work with children:

➣ Do you like children and specifically the child or children you are going to work with? As Madge (2006:86) found from her research, 'not many adults like children enough'. It is worth taking time to honestly explore this question even if it raises issues for you.

➣ Can you suspend your adultness and enter into a child's world of play? Could you happily pretend to be a character of a child's asking? For example, if you are asked to be a dragon, could you do this with abandon without feeling self-conscious?

➣ How attuned are you to a child's signals? Could you pick up quickly that a child is uncomfortable with the activities you have prepared?

➣ Are you comfortable talking with children about private parts of the body?

➣ Do you have fixed thinking about a child's culture? Do you draw upon stereotypes?

➣ Do you have a wide knowledge and understanding about how children communicate with each other and adults? Would you rely solely on a child's being able to use language to communicate with you?

➣ Are you prepared to get dirty using arts and crafts with children? Over the years, I have tried to avoid using glitter with children, but they love it, and I have survived the wrath of caretakers and cleaners by taking time to clean up after sessions with children.

➣ Are the activities you are proposing to use designed around your imagination, skills and abilities? Can you spend time with a child on the floor at their level to engage them in an activity? Can you ensure that the environment is child-friendly with suitable small tables and chairs?

➣ Can you be emotionally strong when you don't feel it? In the words of a young girl who was very clear about the type of social worker she needed, 'I don't want a "flake" – they will have no idea what it's like for me and won't be able to keep it together – that's no good to me'.

I acknowledged earlier in this chapter that there are few formal social work resources available to support direct work with children, whether they have been sexually abused or experienced other forms of abuse. But the work of Wrench (2017) draws attention to children's literature as another source for social workers to use when working with children and refers to *Mr Jelly* by Roger Hargreaves (2007) as a book that can help children use counting and breathing to help them reduce feelings of anxiety – flutters in their body.

Finding an appropriate resource and adapting this means undertaking research and often gathering ideas from other social workers, other disciplines such as education, and web-based materials to help you work with vulnerable children and their families. Putting in the time will help you develop your skills and confidence in working directly with children. There is, of course, the child as a resource as they will also help you identify different ways to work with them. Do not be afraid of letting the child lead you. Katy helped me to identify a resource that could work for her.

Conclusion

Sometimes, we need to acknowledge that there is only so much that social workers can do to 'protect' children, although I concur with Pritchard's (2004:130) argument about 'professional iatrogenesis' whereby social workers inadvertently cause the child further pain and distress by becoming a co-conspirator in a system that, though designed to protect children, conversely leaves them unprotected. Whether this is through the rationing of services, time constraints or a lack of knowledge coupled with a sloppy work ethic that causes further damage, it is worth reminding ourselves and others that the blame for abusing a child often lies with the parent or carer who carried out the abuse, not the social worker.

Who we are as social workers is an important aspect to what we bring to the field of child protection. The social workers 'tool kit' is primarily their lived experiences, practice experiences, training, knowledge and interpersonal skills and how they apply these will be bound up in a range of emotions that feature in child protection practice. Many social workers say they feel anxious about working directly with children because they experience a common confusion about whether or not the work they are doing is therapy or therapeutic (May-Chahal and Coleman, 2003). This common confusion has to some degree been the cause of many social workers' making the case that direct work with children is a specialist field and therefore beyond their own skills and abilities and work that they can 'contract' out to others. This situation is heavily influenced by managerial systems and an ideology that promotes change through performance targets and value-for-money thinking that social work academics argue has led to the demise of relational and humane social work (Ruch *et al.*, 2010; Ferguson, 2011; Featherstone *et al.*, 2014).

Although child care social work demands that social workers have a developed and broad range of skills, working in a therapeutic way is not beyond social workers' skill set. While social workers may not be trained in psychotherapy, they are able to recognise that the significant harming of a child will potentially affect their health, well-being, development and life chances. When working with children across the service fields, it is worth keeping in mind that:

> Those children who come to the attention of child care social workers do so because the adults in their lives are either likely to cause them significant harm or have already caused them significant harm. Thinking therapeutically, relationally, holistically and humanely simply translated means understanding what this lived experience means for the child and their relationship with another adult now and this may be the social worker mandated to provide protective services.
>
> (May-Chahal and Coleman, 2003:63)

Children should not be patronised by adult approaches and narratives that leave them feeling either outside or to blame for their experience. Children will know if they are being tolerated or 'worked' by social workers and this will lead to feelings of distrust and a lack of respect and they will, regardless of their age, ethnicity, class, (dis)ability and gender, withdraw and ultimately 'write you off' as yet another adult who has failed to understand or help them. Investing in children means taking responsibility for your own learning and ensuring that you are critically aware of ideas and thinking about child development. Ultimately, developing your knowledge and understanding shows that you want to find out about children and with this will come respect.

For those children who have been sexually abused, it is always a salient reminder that this experience will change them and introducing any protective behaviour model needs to be done with this in mind. Children who have been sexually abused already know the fear of an adult using and abusing their body for their own needs. Acknowledging the role of the adult in the abuse provides a starting point for work with children. It is a starting point for direct work that helps the child to place the blame with the adult responsible for the abuse, providing opportunities for the child to develop their own resources to respond to those feelings that leave them anxious, sick with fear, anticipation and loss.

Working in collaboration with the child to build adult protective networks can be the detail that helps them understand that they are not to blame for the abuse and may prove to be a turning point in a child's development and future. As Gilligan (2000:37) suggests, do not be distracted over the big questions by losing sight of *'crucial details of what can sustain the ... child now, today and in the future'*. For example, if the focus of work with Katy had agonised over her mother's relationship with Freddie and whether she was a protective parent, I may not have been able to identify her needs within the world of her experience and take actions needed to improve her situation at the time. However, an important detail was the relationship between Katy and her mother, and engaging Sharon in the protective model of working did bring about a change in her relationship, actions and responses to Katy. Importantly, Sharon developed a relationship of trust with me and other professionals that helped us to understand her within the context of her lived childhood experience.

Was the work with Katy effective? Is there a positive conclusion to this chapter? Katy did use her screaming effectively. She alerted her mother to Freddie's returning to the family home. He had let himself into the home via the front door while Sharon was in the kitchen and she told me this during a home visit. Although Katy's actions were a positive outcome for her at that time, it caused Sharon to become anxious about what would happen next. She was fearful that I would take steps to remove the children from her care and for a period of time she became distant. Although she was compliant with the social work processes of core group meetings and agreed to home visits by professionals (health visitor and social worker), there was a veil of secrecy descending around the family and the reason for this was exposed when Sharon telephoned me to say that her youngest child had been hurt by Freddie.

Freddie had returned to the family home. It had been a short period and Sharon had kept his return a secret from Katy because Sharon knew Katy would tell social workers or her sister. How she had managed to do this was by sending Katy to play next door with her neighbour's children or to sleep over at her sister's or by letting Freddie in when all the children were (she said) asleep. However, on an occasion when Katy was at her sister's, Freddie and Sharon had a 'drinking binge' and when Sharon woke in the morning she found her youngest child badly injured in her bed and she had no idea how this had happened.

This outcome will no doubt be one that many social workers will have experienced and there will be those reading this chapter who believe it was also inevitable as a result of the self-interests of the adults, specifically Sharon's as a mother. No doubt, social work is just beginning to acknowledge the complex nature of adult intimate relationships and their power to justify, overlook and explain away behaviours that harm children (Featherstone et al., 2014). If as a profession we continue to promote the protection and nurturing of children within the unachievable concept of mothering, we will fail to notice the details or be attuned to what this may mean for children living in homes where they may face being harmed.

Katy's life was changed as a result of being sexually abused by her mother's lover. Her relationship with her mother changed – she saw and witnessed the child in her mother – and although she initially felt believed by her mother,

Freddie's return to the family home left her unsure and cautious about her mother's capacity to protect her. These feelings impacted on her ongoing development, influencing her sense of self-worth and shaping her levels of resilience. At the age of 15, her education had been disrupted as a result of her mother's decline into alcoholism, and she and her brothers were taken into care and placed in different foster homes. Katy was unable to settle and on a number of occasions, she 'voted with her feet', running away from her foster carers to return to live with her mother.

Although that spark of the bright, insightful and engaging child was present, it was often hidden deeply behind knowing eyes and a rebellious front that she used to protect herself, which she told me many years later included being able to scream like no other.

5

A Child Living with Parents Who Use Drugs. Connie's Story: My Dad Didn't Mean to Kill My Mum

When the media reported that Kate Moss, the model, had been 'caught' using cocaine, the ensuing reporting speculated on the use of drugs in the world of modelling and whether or not she would lose her lucrative financial sponsorship deals. It did not focus on whether or not Kate Moss's using drugs may be impacting on the life of her child. Eventually, the media storm about Kate Moss and her use of cocaine abated when she continued to be successful as a model and businesswoman and secure rich investment and sponsorship deals. What this reporting did was to minimise the use of drugs by promoting a world of fantasy, where the use of illegal drugs is part of the fabric available to those who have money, where their use is easily controlled and where there is little or no impact on the lives of the users, their families or their children. This somewhat romantic image of drug use is not the usual or expected media representation of parental drug use and not one the general public would hold. In fact, the image that many people have of drug users, specifically those who are parents, more often results from the media's use of the 'politics of disgust', whereby they are painted as irresponsible and selfish and worthy of moral condemnation (Warner, 2015:65).

Reports from the Advisory Council on the Misuse of Drugs (2011) identify that there are between 250,000 and 350,000 children of problem drug users – about one child for every problem drug user living in the UK. For those children living with a parent, parents or carer who is considered a problem drug user, the consequences can prove to be detrimental to their health, well-being and development since strong associations have been made between parental problem drug use and child neglect (Horwath, 2013).

> Problem drug use in the UK is characterised by the use of multiple drugs, often by injection, and is strongly associated with socioeconomic deprivation and other factors that may affect parenting capacity.
>
> (The Advisory Council on the Misuse of Drugs, 2011:10)

Parental drug use is described in social work literature as one of the 'toxic three', joining domestic violence and parental mental health in a complex sphere of parental behaviour that has severe consequences for the children living with them (Horwath, 2013). Research nationally and internationally (The Advisory Council on the Misuse of Drugs, 2011; Forrester and Harwin, 2011; National Advisory Committee on Drugs, Annual Report, 2011) and serious case reviews (Brandon et al., 2012) tend to support placing parental behaviour within a hierarchical framework that stresses the adverse consequences to children. But it is also acknowledged that within this hierarchy of factors there will be a range of other causal and driving influences that have led to the drug abuse, domestic violence and mental health issues (Featherstone et al., 2014). It is often these underlying causal factors – a traumatic event most often experienced during childhood – that can set the direction for later adult behaviour and that have been the focus of research aimed at trying to understand the causes, outcomes and impact on parenting.

Whereas there is a range of literature focussed on the adults and their needs, there is little that can help social workers understand what it is like for a child to live with a parent drug user (The Advisory Council on the Misuse of Drugs, 2011; Forrester and Harwin, 2011; Welbourne, 2012). As a result of this inattention to the child, there is little in the literature to help social workers understand what it is like for a child when one of their parents either dies or is killed as a result of their use of drugs.

This chapter explores the complexity of parental needs, behaviour and family histories in the context of drug use and the tragic consequences for a small child called Connie when her father was charged with manslaughter after he had been found guilty of administering a fatal dose of heroin to her mother. The chapter explores how the situation overwhelmed a range of professionals who struggled to focus on meeting her needs as a result of an adult narrative that developed to explain her behaviour and that subsequently marginalised her and left her vulnerable. There will be an explanation about how a systems approach was used to plan and organise a set of child and extended family observations that provided new insight into her behaviour and needs. This chapter provides an opportunity to critically reflect on the use of child observation as a model of practice to gain an understanding of the child in complex traumatic situations where the child's behaviour is understood as a form of communication and how this is interpreted by social workers. This chapter takes a critical look at the detrimental effects an adult narrative can have on the child, specifically on how and why this is constructed. But the aim is to bring this back to Connie and, through her testimony, engage the reader in focussing on the impact of a traumatic event that left Connie alone and trying to defend herself and her father against extended family members and professionals.

Connie's testimony

Connie was the only child of parents Vicky and Danny. Together they lived in council accommodation on a new estate with access to local resources and services. Living nearby in privately owned detached houses were Connie's extended maternal family: maternal aunt and uncle, their three children and maternal grandparents. Her paternal relations – her paternal grandparents and aunts and uncles – also lived in the town. Connie spent much of her early childhood growing up with and being cared for by her maternal family – mostly her aunt and grandmother. The extended family knew that Vicky and Danny abused drugs. This caused tensions because the family blamed Danny for Vicky's drug addiction. Vicky had been a bright girl attending the local grammar school before she met Danny. After she met Danny, they both embarked on a lifestyle of securing casual employment to support their love of music festivals and taking drugs. Because of the extended family support, Connie did not come to the attention of services. Her childhood development and life chances did not appear to be compromised by her parents' drug abuse.

When Connie was seven, emergency services were called to the property in response to a telephone call from Danny. He confirmed that Vicky had injected heroin and Vicky was taken to hospital, where she was confirmed to be dead on arrival. Connie was in the house during these events. She had been woken up by her father's screams of distress, the professional traffic of emergency services including the police, and the anger and accusations levelled at Danny by her grandmother and grandfather before being taken to the home of her maternal aunt. Danny was arrested and initially charged with murder of Vicky. During the ensuring police investigation and her father's conviction of manslaughter and her mother's funeral, Connie stayed with her maternal aunt and uncle and it was agreed that was where she would remain. During these events, Children's Services were not involved. On the surface, the family had did what was expected of them. They did not want and did not seek help from the agencies. They had taken Connie in, providing her with stability and a future.

When Connie was eight, she came to the attention of Children's Services via a referral from Child and Adolescent Mental Health Services (CAMHS) expressing concerns that she may have been sexually abused by multiple men who were known to her father. Although her father was serving a custodial sentence, her maternal family and CAMHS were concerned that he was seeking contact with a view to her returning to his care on his release. The concerns were supported by reports from school, CAMHS and her maternal aunt and uncle that her behaviour was difficult to cope with. According to social workers at CAMHS, she had provided them with a list of names of men her father had taken her to and where she had been told to do naughty things. Adult anxieties, concerns and fears were high, and child protection social workers were under pressure to undertake a joint investigation with police to video-record an interview with Connie. However, after a strategy meeting where Connie was described by teachers and family members as a precocious day dreamer who tells lies about other children stealing from her; who fabricates stories about how she would paint, collect leaves, and dance with her mum and dad; who lacks concentration and is jumpy, rebellious and sexually provocative; and who masturbates

▶

◀

in school and at her aunt and uncle's home, a decision was made not to pursue a video-recorded interview. Instead, it was agreed that a social worker from the child protection team would undertake direct work with Connie. The aim of the work would be to gain some insight and try to make sense of her behaviour in the context of her traumatic loss.

Parental problem drug use

The term 'parental problem drug use' is subjective. There will be many adults who would want to argue that their drug use is not a problem for them and they will minimise how much they use and say they are in control and, for those who are parents, it is something they do when the children are not about. This is the challenge for social workers working with a parent, parents and carers who are in denial about their 'drug problem' and the impact on their children. No parent or carer wants to admit, especially to a social worker, that they are addicted to drugs – for fear of losing their children. Keeping their drug addiction a secret from the 'authorities' by using a range of avoidance tactics and playing on the lack of knowledge that many social workers will have about the type of drug they are using, its effects and how they take it is part of the problem (Ross, 2011).

My own naivety about parental drug use led me to advocate strongly on behalf of a young pregnant woman who convinced me she was not injecting amphetamines. She showed me her arms and legs to prove to me that she was 'clean'. I took advice from colleagues working in drug counselling services, read literature that highlighted the debates about pregnant women using amphetamines and the impact on the unborn child, and felt rather foolish when the child was born with withdrawal symptoms. I questioned my professional skills and abilities and asked myself what had I missed and whether any preconceptions of the young woman, her lifestyle and her engagement with me clouded my thinking and actions. These were all questions that other professionals asked me before and after a child protection conference. The young woman told me that she had been using amphetamines throughout her pregnancy and had been fearful of telling me but had guessed that I had little knowledge about what drugs she was taking or how she used them. Her deception was to ensure that I continued to advocate for her with other professionals and be effective in keeping them out of her life.

I offer this example of my practice as a way of generating reflection about the levels of awareness and range of knowledge that social workers working in child protection need when working with parental problem drug use. Before we resume the discussion about parental problem drug use, it is worth taking time to reflect on the following:

> **Pause and consider:**
>
> What is your experience of working with parents who use drugs? Have your personal attitude and preconceptions of parental drug use changed? How would you describe your thoughts and views on parents who use drugs? How have you developed your working knowledge of working with parents who use drugs?

At this point, it is worth being clear what is meant by the term 'parental problem drug use' in the context of social work. The Advisory Council on the Misuse of Drugs (2011:7) accepts that not all drug use is 'incompatible with being a good parent'. While this statement is helpful for challenging some of the views and personal attitudes that some social workers may have about parents who use drugs, it can also add to feelings of confusion and uncertainty. This confusion and uncertainty are compounded by the range of language used in government policy documents, social work literature and research to refer to adults who misuse/use drugs. As a result, 'umbrella terms' such as 'substance-using parents' have been used as an over-arching reference to refer to the misuse/use of drugs and alcohol by parents. Providing a definitive term of reference that is understood appears to be problematic. For the purposes of this chapter I have adopted the term 'parental problem drug use'. I believe this description is specific about which adults we are talking about and because it pays attention to there being a process; and finally it signals to the reader that drugs and their use are under scrutiny.

To support a greater understanding of the term 'parental problem drug use', I refer to the following description from the Advisory Council on the Misuse of Drugs (2011:7):

> By problem drug use we mean drug use with serious negative consequences of physical, psychological, social and interpersonal, financial or legal nature for users and those around them. Such drug use will be heavy, with features of dependence. In the UK this is typically involves use of one or more of the following: heroin and other opiates, benzodiazepines, cocaine or amphetamines.

While it is accepted that the consequences of parental problem drug use for the user and their children vary, there is little doubt from research and literature that the consequences for the children can be damaging (Ross, 2011). For Connie, the impact was devastating. Overnight, her lived experience changed. In a short period, she suffered the death of her mother and the additional tragedy of being told that her father was to blame. For a seven-year-old child, she had suffered overwhelming traumatic stresses that those adults providing care, education, counselling services and protection appeared not to recognise or understand because they became lost in their own feelings of pain, anger, guilt and fear. The intensity of these adult feelings provided the climate for a narrative to develop about her behaviour. Connie became a vessel for the adults' emotional distress into which they poured

> their fears about her father Danny's future release from prison

> feelings of anger about her father's killing her mother

> their fear and anger about preconceived attitudes and perceptions about her parents' drug use and the lifestyle and people they believed Connie had been exposed to by her father

> feelings of guilt for denying, minimising and supporting parental problem drug use

> their pain of losing someone they loved.

This adult outpouring of feelings exacerbated Connie's already fragile emotional state. Terr (1991) describes how children who have suffered trauma will go to great lengths to protect themselves by creating a world of fantasy that they can withdraw to, cutting themselves off from the present; they will regress to a place in their childhood where they felt safe and they will create powerful images of an adult – a potential superhero, someone to save them – they can invest in emotionally. This description by Terr (1991) closely represents some of Connie's behaviour and there is no doubt that she presented as a child who was lost, dislocated and fearful of her future.

The reasons the adults were slow to recognise Connie's emotional distress and take responsibility for their own feelings that were contributing to her trauma were deeply hidden behind professional ideas and processes, intimate relationships, unrequited love, failure, revenge and loss. Helping Connie to find her voice and be able to express her feelings in this cacophony of adult distress was difficult. It required careful pacing, time, a range of communication and analytical skills, and a level of preparedness to challenge and deal with hidden adult issues. The biggest hurdle was engaging Connie in direct work. She was suspicious and cautious of another adult – someone being involved in her life – and she was not going to make it easy for them.

Someone somewhere has the power to see

According to Cree (2013), the term 'power' is a contested site theoretically and specifically within social work policy and practice. Feminists have challenged the grand narratives of power for failing to address a range of unjust social relations, particularly those that oppress women and children. As a result of evolving discussions and debates about power in social work – the use and misuse – the term itself and how it is applied in practice continue to be somewhat illusory.

Although many social workers will understand the debates and work tirelessly to ensure that service users are not further oppressed, others will assume they are empowering service users by simply not misusing their mandated powers (Dominelli, 2002; Cree, 2013; Featherstone et al., 2014).

Working on behalf of others and recognising the many faces of power are also becoming challenges for social workers working in child protection. According to the social work literature (Ferguson, 2011; Warner, 2015), social workers in child protection are finding it increasingly difficult to see past the many faces of power because their working environment now places too much pressure on them to meet performance targets that are all about outcomes, such as number of cases closed, number of children adopted, number of service user complaints and number of referrals dealt with. In this current working environment, social workers argue that it is difficult to manage their own professional lives, let alone look at what they can do to empower others (Cree, 2013).

What does this emerging situation mean for children involved in child protection services? Where do children, as a group of service users, fit into an environment that is increasingly becoming inward-looking as opposed to looking up and out? Unfortunately, they are not in the foreground. For many children, specifically for Connie, power and how this is exercised by adults leave them feeling out of control without the language to explain how they feel or even be heard. What choices do they have in this adult world that renders them powerless?

According to Cree (2013), adult service users will use every behavioural expression available to them to level the playing field. Children struggling to make sense of what is going on will also find ways to make themselves noticed and heard. Connie expressed her struggles by sabotaging the direct work planned. On arrival at the children's centre, she would run amok. She ran into each room, scattering pens, crayons and paper, hiding behind curtains and under desks, and climbing on tables until she believed the social worker had got the message – 'I am not playing your game'.

I was that social worker trying to make sense of what was going on for Connie. For three weeks, she kept up her resistance to my attempts to undertake direct work with her. At the 'end' of each session, she would appear relieved to be leaving the children's centre and getting into the transport arranged to take her back to her aunt and uncle's home. On the fourth week, Connie's behaviour changed dramatically.

I had dispensed with organising any planned work, and she became agitated that I had not prepared anything for her 'to do'. I followed her as she gathered crayons and paper and put them on the floor. We sat together as she directed me to draw a scary monster – it had to fill the page and be black with a big 'shouty' mouth. As the session came to an end, Connie appeared physically shaken and agitated. She struggled to verbalise what she wanted to tell me and when she did tell me, her words were urgent and pleading. Eventually, she said the following:

- My uncle is coming to collect me.
- He will ask what we have done.
- Don't tell him I was naughty.
- Tell him I was good all the time – tell him.
- He always talks to the other social worker about me. They talk in a room when I am outside. He will talk to you.
- You have to tell him.
- He will shout at me if you don't tell him I am talking to you about things he tells me to say.
- He tells me to say that my dad took me to men who did things to me – he didn't.
- He says my dad was a 'fucking druggy waster'.
- I love my dad.

When I met with her uncle, he did exactly what Connie said he would do. He immediately asked how the sessions were going and asked what Connie had told me and when I would be doing something about it. He asked if he could speak to me in another room and when I said no and explained to him that, before discussing the work I was doing with Connie, I would like to talk to him and his wife and Connie's maternal grandparents and consult my colleagues from CAMHS, he became belligerent and aggressive. I stood my ground and talked him down:

- This must be a difficult time for you.
- You clearly care for Connie and want what is best for her.
- I can see this because you are so upset and angry with me.
- I am also sure that her mother, if she were alive, would want what is best for her daughter.

> I need you, her aunt and her maternal grandparents to help me with this so that together we can decide what is best for her future.

It was the mention of Connie's mother that stopped her uncle metaphorically in his tracks. His demeanour changed and he became visibly upset. He sat down and nodded his head as I talked about working together to secure a settled future for Connie. There may have been other ways to interpret and deal with this situation and I accept that I exercised my professional power over Connie's uncle by sending a message, albeit covertly, that I was looking to the future with all that this implied. However, I believe that, without using my professional authority to challenge Connie's uncle, the adults and (we) the professionals would have continued to pursue an approach that failed to take into consideration what was going on for her within the context of allegations of sexual abuse.

I also acknowledge that something in what Connie had told me about her uncle and how he talked about her father alerted me consciously or unconsciously to the power of adult relationships and their capacity for creating meaning for the adults in order for them to cope with the demands of the situation. Simply put, I tuned in to the relationship between Connie's uncle and her mother and became curious about his anger and distress and how this was influencing his relationship with Connie.

Following on from this very challenging and difficult confrontation with Connie's uncle, I reflected with my supervisor on what Connie had told me, what this may mean in terms of what she had been saying to colleagues in CAMHS, whether or not her uncle posed a sexual risk to her, and the adult narratives around their concerns that she may have been sexually abused and asked the following reflective questions:

1. What was Connie trying to tell us?

2. Has she been sexually abused?

3. Are past and present adult relationships influencing behaviours and responses to Connie?

4. Are perceptions of parental problem drug users influencing thinking and ideas about Connie's life with her parents and fuelling fears about her father?

5. What does Connie want to happen?

What was agreed with my supervisor was that the power of the adult feelings and how these were being exercised over Connie needed to be understood and exposed in order for her health and well-being to be protected and her future secured. What was needed was a better explanation of the current situation. To do this, I worked together with my supervisor, using a systems approach to examine some of the 'theories' and hypothetical questions that were forming.

Knowing from within the situation: A systems approach

Gergen (2001:56) posits that there is a 'kind of knowledge one has within a social situation and which exists only in that situation'. In Connie's situation, which was specific to her, her family and the professionals, there was a wealth of knowledge and experience that had come together in what appeared to be a joint activity of helping Connie when in fact their overlapping histories, differences and intimate relationships were creating conditions that made her feel unsafe and anxious. The many relationships involved in Connie's life appeared to be creating multiple narratives, alliances and interests that needed rethinking from the inside in order for the outside to be understood.

To make sense of what was taking place, a systems model was used. It was anticipated that using a systemic approach based on the work of Bronfenbrenner (1979), who promotes an ecological approach to examine how people develop processes, relationships and narratives within their environment, would help to make sense of what was happening in Connie's life. Using a systems model for making sense of the lives of children and their families is a well-established approach in social work and one that has been developed and used over time to support an analysis of situations that now goes beyond understanding what has happened to understanding why it did (Social Care Institute for Excellence, 2008).

Using a systems model that includes a structured table of thinking is an approach designed to help social workers gather factual information and set out their thinking and ideas as they are being formed from the work taking place (Social Care Institute for Excellence, 2008). It is this structured process that engages social workers in active thinking that can be used to gain a better understanding of what is known about the child and their family. I have used the case and story of Connie to demonstrate how this structured table of thinking is applied to a systems model for practice (Table 5.1).

On its own, the structured table of thinking brings together facts, thinking and ideas about what is taking place for the child. Through this process, themes and systems will begin to emerge, as will areas that need further investigation and explanation. As you can see from the Structured Table of Thinking represented in Table 5.1, a wealth of information about Connie and her circumstances was gathered and this generated a number of ideas and thinking. At the time of working with Connie, I was able to identify what I believed to be key themes and systems. These were presented in what I now refer to as Connie's Circle and shown in (Figure 5.1).

Before we examine the four key themes further, it is helpful to take some time to pause and consider the systems approach and the structured table of thinking and what this could bring to your own practice.

Table 5.1 Structured table of thinking

Summary of the case		
The child and networks	**What is known**	**Thinking and ideas**
Connie	Age: 7	Trauma – loss, sexual abuse, fear and uncertainty
	Children's Services history: Not previously known	
	Ethnicity: White British/Scottish heritage	
	Religion: Church of Scotland	
	Attainments: Meeting expected literacy and numeracy attainments for age	
	Presentation: Precocious, lies, lacks concentration, rebellious, masturbates in school, not sleeping, nightmares, looks tired and haunted	
	Current situation: Has lost her mother as a result of a heroin overdose, was present when emergency services attended. Father was arrested and is now in custody. She now lives with maternal aunt and uncle and their children. She is attending school regularly. She is seeing a social worker from CAMHS. She has alleged she may have been sexually abused by a number of men that her father took her to	
Parents – Vicky and Danny	Mother – Vicky, drug user (heroin)	Danny – loss, uncertainty, drug withdrawal, fear, past and present relationships with his own family and his 'in-laws'
	Father – Danny, drug user (heroin)	
	No reports that either adult came to the attention of police, health or Children's Services	
	Death of mother as a result of fatal heroin overdose allegedly administered by her partner, Connie's father	
	Father now in custody, charged with murder	
Maternal extended family	Maternal aunt and uncle now caring for Connie. They have two children, both boys, ages 12 and 9. Both adults work and live in a privately owned 3-bedroom house. They have been supporting Connie and her parents for many years. While they knew about the drug use, they did not know the extent and believed Vicky had stopped 'using'	Maternal aunt and uncle – loss, past and present relationships with Vicky (as sister) and Danny, substitute parents for Connie, fear, uncertainty, family knowledge about drug use
	Maternal grandparents actively involved in supporting the care of Connie. They have also been supporting their daughter Vicky over the years financially and with child care. They knew about the drug use but believed that Danny was the heavy 'user' and Vicky had stopped taking drugs	Maternal grandparents – loss, uncertainty, fear, past and present relationships with their daughter and Danny, family knowledge about drug use

Table 5.1 *Continued*

Summary of the case		
The child and networks	**What is known**	**Thinking and ideas**
Paternal extended family	Little known about Danny's family. He has brothers and a mother who live in the town. Currently it is not known how much involvement they had with Connie.	Paternal family – loss, uncertainty, fear, marginalised, drug use
CAMHS	Have been undertaking direct work with Connie after receiving a referral from maternal aunt and uncle. Basis of work was bereavement, loss and behaviour. During several sessions and after being told by maternal uncle that he believed she had been sexually abused, a session had explored the concerns with Connie. According to CAMHS social worker, Connie had provided names of multiple men (a list) to the worker and said her father took her to them and she had done 'naughty' things.	Social worker – fears and concerns about allegations of sexual abuse and alleged involvement of father. Frustrated that investigation into allegations is not going ahead.
Police	Had arrested Danny after suspicions were raised by health professionals about the administering and quantity of heroin. He was charged with murder and placed in custody. While there were no official records of police being involved with Vicky and Danny, police intelligence suggested he was a known drug user in the town, alongside his brothers.	Concerned that Connie may have been sexually abused and father's involvement and that this needs further investigation. Frustrated about timing and decision not to proceed with video-recorded interview.
School	Connie has been attending the school since age 5. Her mother or father would bring her and on occasions her maternal aunt/grandparents would collect her. While Connie has always been a little girl who has found it difficult to 'fit in' with other children and accept rules and boundaries, since the recent events her behaviour has escalated and her class teacher, classroom support and head teacher have all had to place sanctions on her – taking her out of class to be in a different classroom. She has good literacy and numeracy skills but has poor concentration and often fails to complete set tasks.	Worried about Connie's ongoing behaviour and the impact on other children in the class. Class teacher and classroom assistant very worried about her masturbating – rubbing herself openly in class.

Table 5.1 *Continued*

Summary of the case		
The child and networks	**What is known**	**Thinking and ideas**
Children's Services social work	Became involved after receiving a referral expressing concerns that Connie may have been sexually abused. Strategy meeting held and decision made not to pursue video-recorded interview. Social work intervention focussing on loss. Connie resisted any attempts to engage her in direct work. However, recently, she has been observed being frightened of her maternal uncle and has suggested that he has told her what to say to CAMHS social worker.	Concerned about the information from Connie that her maternal uncle may have 'scripted' and 'coached' Connie to allege she had been sexually abused. Concerned about the risks he poses to Connie as a result of this and the fact she has demonstrated being frightened of him. Further concerns about family relationships past and present that minimised parental problem drug use. Concerns about Connie's health and well-being and adult/school perceptions of her.

Pause and consider:

How would you use the structured table of thinking with a case that you are currently responsible for or involved with?

Interpreting and analysing a structured table of thinking are challenging. It is often the case that the process will produce more ideas and thinking. For Connie, interpretation and analysis were achieved by using critical reflection. The use of critical reflection is an important element of the FIM, and although I did not use the FIM when working with Connie, I believe it is possible to bring together a systems approach using a table of structured thinking and the principles of the FIM to aid analysis.

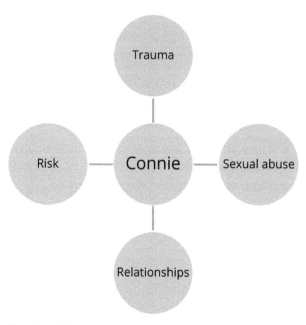

Figure 5.1   Connie's Circle

For example, the critical element of the FIM promotes a reflective approach that draws upon the work of Fook (2002) and Morley (2014), who both promote learning about the 'self' to raise consciousness about language, how this is constructed and used to shape relationships, and how ultimately these relationships are used to exercise power. Morley (2014:69) argues that social workers who develop their reflective skills of looking inwards and outwards are able to 'develop alternative *ways of* thinking'.

Connie's Circle was an alternative way of thinking. It was alternative because it opened up a discussion about four key areas and enabled an examination of them in relation to Connie.

1. **Trauma**

Although as a profession social workers are becoming more aware of the impact of trauma on children, how this is translated into practice remains patchy and, according to Fonagy and Target (2007), over-reliant on theoretical models of attachment that focus on the parent–child relationship and observable behaviours that can be measured. While wider discussions and debates are taking place about the effects of trauma on children from familial abuse, experiences of war, community tragedies such as the fire at Grenfell Tower and the Manchester bombing at a pop concert, it remains the case that the adult world is still on the back foot when it comes to understanding and responding to children who have suffered trauma, specifically post-traumatic stress disorder (PTSD) (Agerholm, 2018).

What is emerging from research (Terr, 1991) and practice is that there are certain symptoms of PTSD which are particularly profound in children where a parent has been imprisoned and have suffered a specific stressful event (Bockneck, Sanderson and Britner, 2009). Connie witnessed stressful events that led to the death of her mother and the arrest of her father. This specific event ultimately meant she suffered the loss of both parents in a short period of time. Her trauma of loss was compounded by seeing the adults around her experiencing distress, instability about where she was going to live and with whom, and the uncertainty of whether she would ever see her father again.

In addition to experiencing these many traumas, Connie was exposed to adult feelings and behaviours that wouldn't have been part of her everyday growing up. For her this was very unsettling and traumatic. Connie was surrounded by the trauma of adults, and the impact of her own trauma was observed in her behaviours and symptoms which are now explained.

Dreaming and memories

Connie struggled to get to sleep and would wake up frequently in the night, making small noises and sounds. According to Terr (1991), children will experience repetitive dreams as they relive the trauma and many children will be frightened to go to bed for fear of reliving the memories. These dreams and memories trigger feelings that the children will express during their sleep, such as screaming, appearing to talk in their sleep, or making sounds and noises not unlike snuffled cries and whimpering as they relive their memories through their dreams (Hendricks et al., 1993).

These noises and sounds were interpreted by her uncle to be those related to Connie's masturbating in her sleep – information that he had passed to CAMHS and that was supported by school reports that Connie was observed masturbating in class.

Dreaming and memories will also be experienced while apparently awake. For example, during school, if the child is bored, they will appear to drift off, losing their concentration when in fact they are reliving the memories and fears of their trauma (Terr, 1991). Some children will also present as tired and wanting to sleep during the day, which, according to Hendricks et al. (1993), is another way that many children respond to the memories and dreams they are experiencing.

Although Connie's teachers knew about the stressful events in her life and the family background, their responses were situated in narratives related to her performance in class (lack of concentration) and her behaviour that adults perceived was disturbing others, the children and classroom assistants, so they removed her from the class. This response failed to understand her behaviour as symptoms of trauma.

Hyper-alert

Connie's exposure to trauma had resulted in her becoming hyper-alert and jumpy. She was hyper-alert around adults at school and home and during the direct social work. She expressed herself at school and home as fidgeting and never sitting still. At the children's centre, she was watchful, tense and jumpy and she expressed this through behaviour that was challenging, repetitive and destructive. For example, her behaviour never led anywhere, it was a fusion of anxiety and fear, and she dispatched these by keeping on the move and trying to remain ahead of adult plans. However, there was no relief and no resolution for Connie from her hyper-alert 'play', which, according to Hendriks *et al.* (1993), is directly associated with new fears the child is experiencing from the traumatic events.

For Connie, these new fears were those linked to the adult behaviour, specifically that of her maternal uncle, who she claimed had introduced a new trauma of sexual abuse that she was trying to make sense of. Terr (1991) points out that, for the traumatised child, their 'future is a landscape filled with crags, pits and monsters' (p. 1543).

Dislocation

Dislocation is a symptom that to the outside world is manifested in a range of behaviours, such as withdrawing from the outside world physically and emotionally (Terr, 1991). Connie's withdrawal was observed when she was with her maternal family at their respective homes and when they came to the children's centre to collect her. Connie would always take up a position that was farthest way from the adults. For example, I observed her in her maternal aunt and uncles' home with her cousins, aunt and uncle and during this meeting she took up a position in the corner of the room that was as far away as she could get from the discussions. What was more interesting was how the adults and the children appeared to forget she was in the room, rarely looking across at her as they became engrossed in wanting to talk about how they were coping with their own grief and now having to care for Connie. Connie's dislocation was a form of protection from the uncertainty and instability she was now suffering as a result of the loss of her parents and her home.

I interpreted this dislocation as not only a form of protection but a silent and powerful message that she did not trust this 'family', especially the adults, to support or protect her. Connie had recognised how powerful the adults had become in expressing their own grief and vulnerabilities and subsequently how vulnerable she now was – she no longer trusted the adults to be good to her. This powerful image of Connie's dislocation summed up the cumulative trauma she was experiencing through her sense of rage and sadness that sat alongside her fears about her future.

2. **Sexual abuse**

The concerns that Connie had been sexually abused were based on allegations made by her maternal uncle, reports that Connie had confirmed to a CAMHS worker that her father had taken her to other men who did naughty things to her and supported by her 'sexualised' masturbatory behaviour.

The relationship made between child masturbation and exposure to sexual abuse and sexual exploitation is not new. Over the years, there has been an accepted belief that childhood 'compulsive masturbation' can be an indicator of sexual abuse (Finkelhor, 1984:106). However, this accepted belief has been challenged (Terr, 1991), and Finkelhor (1984), in his theorising about childhood sexual abuse, expressed caution when using behavioural indicators, such as childhood masturbation, to signal the presence of sexual abuse.

Connie's masturbatory behaviour posed a challenge to all of the adults involved with her. Although there were some strongly held beliefs that her behaviour was a strong indicator of being sexually abused, there was also a keen interest within the adult group to test out what Connie was saying about her maternal uncle.

3. **Relationships**

Connie's relationship with the adults in her life was now overlaid with loss and mistrust. The needs of the adults had become all-consuming. Their fears, anger and anxieties for and about her had left little room to acknowledge or tune in to what might be going on with Connie. Barriers of suspicion, anger and fear grew between the family and professionals. Connie became more isolated within her maternal family and was not sure which professional to trust. Making sense of the adult relationships and how Connie viewed them was important for her future. Connie's future was dependent on adults making decisions about what should happen next.

Connie's relationship with her maternal uncle and the worker from CAMHS became a starting point for examining what she had said about being 'told what to say'. As a starting point, it provided a different perspective about what was going on with Connie. Connie alleged that she was 'coached' by her maternal uncle to tell the CAMHS social worker that she had been sexually abused by several different men known to her father. She described feeling butterflies in her tummy and wasps in her head when she was with both of them. According to Connie, it was the CAMHS social worker and her maternal uncle who suggested 'something naughty' had happened to her, and because 'they both looked happy when I said men's names', she had gone along with it. However, when she could not elaborate or provide more details, her maternal uncle became increasingly angry with her and the CAMHS social worker.

Connie's allegations were 'investigated' and the relationship between her maternal uncle, her father and mother unfolded. A story of unrequited love for

Connie's mother was eventually told through anger, rage and reluctance by her maternal uncle. During the investigation, the maternal uncle spoke about his love for Connie's mother and said he had never understood why she had chosen Connie's father over him. He said her death had left him with unresolved feelings of anger and hatred towards Connie's father. He remained firm in his belief that Connie had been sexually abused and her father had been involved in this. He said his belief was based on her masturbatory behaviour and her father's being a 'druggy'. For him this was 'proof' that Connie had been sexually abused. However, he failed to provide any other information to support his belief, and when he was asked whether he had 'told her what to say', he blamed the CAMHS social worker.

4. **Risk**

Initially, the risks to Connie appeared to be clear. According to the adults who were involved with Connie, it was her father who posed a long-term risk to her because of his problem drug use and because of concerns that he may have exploited her sexually. However, when a joint police and social work investigation found no evidence to support concerns that Connie had been sexually abused, the risks to her became less clear.

> Was Connie at risk from her maternal uncle? Was he grooming or emotionally abusing her?

> Could her maternal family protect her from further trauma?

> Was Connie protecting her father by blaming her maternal uncle?

Finding a way to protect Connie was crucial to her future and ultimately was bound up in the adult relationships she had with her maternal family and her father. Because the 'family' had not been known to the agencies prior to the parental drug overdose, little was known about them. On the surface, her maternal family appeared ordered and supportive. It was only through the investigation that the maternal family members acknowledged that they had been overwhelmed by events, and although they said they were committed to caring for and protecting Connie, they recognised how they had failed her because of their individual and collective relationship with her mother and father. Finding a way forward was essential for Connie's future.

Achieving a positive outcome through child protection

Connie's maternal family had not anticipated that when they sought help for Connie they might find themselves under investigation and involved in a multi-agency child protection conference. Understandably, they felt blamed, and according to research and social work literature (Featherstone *et al.*, 2014), this is not an uncommon feeling of parents and carers. As well as feeling blamed, many parents and carers feel there is a stigma attached to being involved with child protection processes, particularly where legislation drives an approach that is investigative (Parton, 2014). Such an approach can lead to tensions in relationships between social workers and parents that become adversarial. When this happens, it can hamper the assessment process and do little to ensure that the child is protected.

Gathering information from parents, carers and the child becomes fraught with these tensions and ultimately has an impact on the assessment process. It is difficult to make sense of information gathered in such circumstances if those involved feel they need to take up a 'them and us' position. Developing open and honest relationships is essential, and increasingly social workers are faced with having to balance the political needs of the day alongside those of parents, carers and the children. For example, over the years, there has been a concerted effort to avoid the more costly intrusion of child protection processes (Ferguson, 2011) in favour of a welfare approach that considers need over risk and that is underpinned by a philosophy that seeks to protect families from the stigma associated with the intrusion of a child protection investigation (Featherstone *et al.*, 2014).

It is certainly not easy finding a way to bring together the two often opposing positions of delivering child protection and family support services using processes of assessment that in essence are intrusive and can leave all those involved feeling exposed and vulnerable. As a practitioner, I understood the dilemmas and so did some of the parents, carers and children. As far as the many parents, carers and some of the children I worked with were concerned, 'any' form of social work intervention was something to be viewed with suspicion and caution.

It is acknowledged from research and the social work literature that at the heart of good practice in child protection is the relationship between the social worker, the parent, carer and child (Cossar *et al.*, 2014). Developing a relationship that brings about positive changes and outcomes for the child is dependent on the following:

➤ being a good listener

➤ showing empathy and understanding

➤ warmth and honesty

➤ being professional, reliable and respectful

➤ being proactive and willing to take action

Engaging Connie, her maternal family and her father in the child protection process was often challenging and at times exhausting. Not only was I developing my relationships with Connie and her family, I was also trying to make sense of their relationships with each other and the impact of their inter-related histories, which included the impact of parental drug abuse.

Connie was the key and through her perspective I was able to develop a sound professional relationship with her maternal grandparents, her father and her maternal aunt and uncle prior to the child protection conference and throughout the assessment process. My relationship with Connie was based on that described by Mayall (2002) whereby I positioned myself as an adult who is interested in and wants to learn from them. Learning from Connie provided me with information about her experience – before and after her mother's death – that I was able to use in my work with her and the adults. For example, Connie described her life with her parents as being filled with fun, laughter and feeling safe. I was able to test this description out with her maternal grandparents and her maternal aunt. They all agreed to some degree with this description and from this we were able to openly discuss their concerns about her parents' problem drug use and how they had helped to support them both to protect Connie.

Taking a position of an adult who is interested and wanting to learn supported practice that was non-judgemental, sensitive and inclusive. Evidence from research suggests that parents are more likely to be open about their problems and share their concerns about being a parent when practitioners approach them openly, are direct about their role and responsibilities, and keep them informed about social work processes (Cossar et al., 2013).

Tensions between the family and child protection social workers were evident when the child protection conference outcome was to agree to a child protection plan for Connie under the category of emotional abuse. But it was my relationship with Connie and her maternal grandparents that helped to secure a positive outcome for her. Connie went to live with her maternal grandparents as part of the child protection plan and she thrived there. Her father was kept informed of the process and plans and helped the maternal grandparents to seek a section 12 Residence Order under the Children Act 1989. Through solicitors and social workers, arrangements were made for Connie to have contact with her father in prison.

When her father was released from prison, Connie was 15, living with her maternal grandparents and doing well at school. She had remained in education and with the support of her maternal grandparents she had joined a local youth theatre. Connie's relationship with her father continued to be positive and he became an important part of her life.

Learning from Connie

Finding ways to understand the child's environment and space is an important factor when making an assessment of their situation. As a social work practitioner, I remember the many homes I visited where children were observed living in conditions that told a story of neglect, control, poverty, fear, loss, alienation, and despair. Finding a way through to the child in an environment that is colonising their life and effectively obscuring them is critical to protecting them.

There were three important skill sets used in practice to make sense of Connie's lived experience. They were observation, listening and reflection. Using all of these practice interventions supported my learning and increased my knowledge and understanding of her situation. These skills are not specific to the profession of social work. They are all part of human behaviour. It is how they are used and developed by the individual social worker that ensures they become meaningful.

Observing Connie was a key component in my social work practice. I was able to observe her in a variety of different environments, school, different homes, and social work settings and during prison visits. I used two different methods of observation:

1. Narrative/naturalistic observation that was carried out at a specific time and place and focussed on Connie in her *natural* environment. I observed Connie at school using an approach that tends to look in at the child with the aim of mentally recording what is seen without influencing what is happening (O'Loughlin and O'Loughlin, 2014).

2. Scientific/objective observation that was planned and carried out over a period of time. This approach included observing Connie in two different settings: her maternal aunt and uncle's home and her paternal grandparents' home. The purposes of using this approach were to explore and identify a future placement for her.

To support these observations, I used a range of tools to help me in my planning and in recording what I saw. I acknowledge that the pace of practice can mean that many observations of children are ad hoc because the parameters have already been set by the pressures of carrying out the social work task. Carrying out an observation under these circumstances will mean that the social worker will rely on instinct and practice experience. Both are excellent skills to draw upon. However, to support and extend the skills of instinct and practice experience, it is important to plan. Planning will ensure that the focus is on the child. To facilitate planning for a child observation I have provided a framework for carrying out a child observation in Appendix (1). The framework is based on my years of practice experience of carrying out child observations in a variety of different settings and situations and poses reflective questions and offers tips for developing practice in the area of child observation.

Whatever the observation carried out, infants, young children and adolescents will bring to this experience the outcome of their relationships and circumstances. They will be aware of what is going on, and while you are observing them, they will also be observing you and working out whether or not you notice them and are able to make sense of what is troubling and happening to them. How they see you and interpret your relationship with them and others will set the parameters of how they will relate and respond to you. In the words of Gareth (age 12), a boy I worked with as a Youth Justice social worker:

> You can see me and I think you might know me, but you don't know me, not really. All the others (social workers) did not see me. They thought they knew what happened to me, but they didn't really and what they did, they did for themselves not for me. So you won't get in (my head) and I won't let you, not about that.

Listening to Connie and all those adults who had become part of her network required a set of active listening skills that included listening and hearing the immediate (what is being said), what is coming (might be said) and what is under the radar (not being said). The act of listening and hearing tends to be taken for granted within the hearing world. However, it is considered a key communication skill in social work. Trevithick (2000:3) argues that we 'hear how others gather and form their thoughts and feelings, and the meaning they give to particular experiences'.

It took a great deal of hard work and mental activity to accurately present the thoughts and wishes of Connie effectively. Making sense of what she was telling me about her maternal uncle, her father and what she wanted for her future required me to

➢ pay attention to her and concentrate on what she was saying

➢ be able to recall and clarify what was being said

➢ accept and acknowledge silences

➢ be able to respond to pace and timing

➢ be aware of background noises, tone of voice, body language and other clues to help understand and make sense of what she was telling me

➢ be able to evaluate the logic/plausibility of what I had understood

➢ be able to verify what I had understood.

These listening skills were also used to make sense of the adult relationships. They alerted me to the maternal uncle's feelings about Connie's parents and helped me to acknowledge the power of intimate adult relationships in the lives of children.

Making sense of what I was seeing and hearing involved engaging with the practice of reflection. Throughout the work with Connie, her family and other professionals, I had access to supervision and colleagues that supported me to check in and check out my interpretations and evaluations of my communications. Using reflective practice also helped me to focus on how I felt about Connie's current situation, the death of her mother and imprisonment of her father and explore past and present adult relationships. However, I am aware that this description may sound self-congratulatory and somewhat trite in a social work world where the activity of reflection is being squeezed out of practice by time constraints.

How do social workers develop strategies for 'taking back clock-time' (Bryson, 2007:171) from an environment where to practice reflection as a learning activity is now considered to be a somewhat frivolous use of time? Sadly, the practice of reflection appears to have become part of a time-reckoning culture that has separated gaining knowledge from practice in a time-saving exercise that promotes getting the job done at the expense of developing social workers' intellectual knowledge and interpersonal skills. In such an environment taking back 'clock-time' will mean finding ways to promote a culture that recognizes that providing good quality social work requires using time differently. Not as something that can be possessed and turned into a set of activities that lead to cost-effective outcomes, but connected to human relationships and caring responsibilities, such as spending time with a child cannot always be packaged within the constraints of time.

One strategy for taking back 'clock-time' will be the promotion of reflective practice by being explicit about what this mental and often unseen activity is, what it can produce and how it can enhance decision-making for children. During my years in practice, I adopted different strategies that helped me to make explicit the processes involved in my reflective practice. I would highlight words in my recordings, create visual diagrams and developed the practice of talking-out-loud to myself. This talking-out-loud approach usually took place in my car and was a way of helping me to express my feelings. What this talking-out-loud practice did was help me to listen to myself talking and support a process that Peters (2018) suggests can help us to look at things differently. All of these activities helped me to harness the reflective process of looking inwards and outwards to seek clarity and self-awareness.

I learned a great deal from Connie. She alerted me to her maternal uncle's behaviour which helped me to explore his relationship to her parents and what this meant for him and importantly whether these relationships influenced how he responded to Connie. She invested her trust in me to challenge the adult behaviours and throughout demonstrated a level of resilience that helped me to interpret her emotions and those of others. In this context, I believe Connie's resilience was developed and understood within the range of practice frameworks (Daniel *et al.*, 2010) that support practice:

> Where the risks to Connie and the negative chain reaction of risk was reduced

> She was listened to and her emotions taken seriously.

> Opportunities were created that fostered caring relationships within her maternal family and contact with her father.

Placing Connie at the centre of practice provided insight that helped her family and the professionals to piece together bits of information and fill in the gaps. As a result, a fuller picture emerged that supported a clearer understanding of the risks to Connie and her needs. Her account and perspective became the driving forces for developing and reinforcing positive relationships, all of which enabled the adults to find a way to secure a future for her.

Conclusion

Evidence from research suggests that children living with parental problem drug abuse are more likely to suffer significant harm as a result of chaotic life-styles and parents' inability to recognise and meet the needs of their children (Cleaver *et al.*, 2011). One of the major difficulties for social workers is being able to identify and engage with parents who misuse drugs. Because this behaviour is against the law, parents will hide and minimise their problem, and although some will have access to support networks, the impact on children of parental problem drug use can be long-term and significant.

Connie's life was severely disrupted as a result of her parents' drug abuse. It was the cause of her mother's death and the imprisonment of her father, and although her maternal family tried to provide a stable environment for her, the impact of these traumatic events on everyone produced a negative outcome for Connie.

Reducing these negative outcomes was achieved through positive social work relationships with Connie and, through her, with her family. The quality of the relationship with Connie was established very early and it developed because Connie recognised that I might be able to wrest some power away from her uncle. She understood that I, as the social worker, had the power to make decisions about her future. Findings from research (Cossar *et al.*, 2013:109) suggest that a trusting relationship between children and social workers offers *'opportunities to promote self-confidence, feelings of safety and self-efficacy'*. It was a trusting relationship with Connie that helped me to advocate on her behalf and ensure that the adults could see her trauma and recognise the impact of their behaviour on her.

Building relationships with children is emerging as an important skill for social workers working in child protection. Of equal importance is recognising the power that adults hold over narratives and decisions about children. Supporting social work in times of political upheaval when adult themes and needs will overshadow those of children will be the challenge of the future. Undertaking direct work with children requires that organisations invest in social work staff across all levels. This fits with supporting relationship-based practice (Ruch et al., 2010) where the relationship between the social worker/ professional and the child is central to making sense of what is happening.

Understanding Connie's behaviour in the context of trauma was a key factor in developing practice interventions and a good social worker/child relationship. Using a range of communication skills that included observations provided a wealth of information about Connie within her family networks. Watching as she moved away from the family unit of her maternal aunt and uncle was a powerful communication that showed her struggle with what was going on. It highlighted her vulnerability and need for support and protection.

Protecting children involves taking action and child protection processes play an important role in this. There will always be debates that challenge thinking and actions about the rights and needs of parents alongside those of the children. Pursuing the protection of children is all about getting the balance right. Providing checks and balances in the child protection process is important because too often the narrative and needs of the adults tip the balance. When this happens, the position of the child becomes precarious. They are overwhelmed and often left outside of the protective processes designed to protect them (Cossar et al., 2013).

Pursuing the protection of Connie through the formal process of a child protection investigation, conference and plan, particularly where protective concerns were unsubstantiated, was an important and positive step. It sent a message to the adults and Connie that social workers and other professionals were taking the issues seriously. As a positive practice, it also framed future interventions and strengthened Connie's central position.

Taking Connie seriously and examining her life using her perspective led to an outcome that supported her mental well-being, the development of relationships and educational achievements. Working with vulnerable children and their families requires investment of time and engaging in respectful, inclusive and reflexive practice. Such an investment is good for the child, their family and the social worker.

6

Accumulative Risks. Parental Capacity. Darren's Story: I'm the 'Man' of the House But I Am Frightened and Cannot Look After My Mum and Sister

The concept of risk in child protection social work in England has been constructed over time and understood within the sociological constructs of childhood and a child's vulnerability to abuse (Daniel, 2010). In the narrow world of child protection, this relationship has been used to predict the likelihood of abuse and the harm resulting from the abuse (Lonne *et al.*, 2009). For Parton (2014), this concept of risk as a future focus to make predictions based on probabilities was encapsulated in the 1989 Children Act, which provides the legal mandate whereby social workers make those enquiries necessary to determine whether a child is suffering or likely to suffer significant harm. There have been considerable debates and commentary in the social work literature (Ferguson, 2003; Lonne *et al.*, 2009; Daniel, 2010; Parton, 2014) about the ambiguous legal wording and how concepts of 'likely', 'harm' and 'significant' are interpreted by social workers in child protection. But it is now widely accepted that they are all associated with 'risk' and are bound together in the language of prediction and prevention, concepts that entail making an assessment of risk in the social sphere of child protection where the probabilities are unpredictable and complex (Daniel, 2010).

Assessing risk and making a judgement about which child is in need of protection are central to child protection social work (Wilkins, 2013). From making an initial assessment to working with a child and their family under the direction of a child protection plan, the issue of predicting and managing risk is at the centre of social work assessment and practice. Social workers know that the assessment of risk and the needs of the child is an ongoing process that places them under considerable pressure to be accurate with their predictions about the risks to the child and thorough in their plans to manage the risks. However, research has shown that social workers are dealing with limited and poor-quality information that is unlikely to come with identifiable risk factors (Barlow *et al.*, 2012; Wilkins, 2013; Kirkman and Melrose, 2014). This means that social workers often are faced with only part of the puzzle as many of the parts are missing. With little or poor information, social workers enter into a process of investigation that requires them to gather as much information as possible about the child and their family before making an initial judgement about whether the risks to the child are imminent (high) or whether they are manageable.

Formalising how risk and need are assessed is carried out by using the assessment framework (Department of Health, 2000) guidance with specific reference to the three domains of child development, parental capacity and the environment. While research has shown that social workers using this model are good at gathering information (Wilkins, 2013), research has also highlighted that they are not so good at analysing it (Barlow *et al.*, 2012). This issue has been identified in a number of serious case reviews and used by subsequent governments and the media to blame social workers for not understanding or seeing the risks to children they were involved with (Ferguson, 2011).

Undoing risk as a concept and as a practice in child protection social work has been a source of debate between researchers and social work academics for some time. There is an extensive literature base that examines how risk is understood and applied in child protection social work. This base comes from researchers and writers who examine the rise of risk ideology within a political context (Houston and Griffiths, 2000; Webb, 2006; Parton, 2014; Warner, 2015) and those who have explored how risk is understood and applied in practice (Scourfield, 2003; Ferguson, 2003, 2011; Shlonsky and Wagner, 2005; Munro, 2008, 2011; Daniels, 2010; Broadhurst *et al.*, 2010; Barlow *et al.*, 2012; Wilkins, 2013; Houston, 2016). While the extensive debates emanating from this literature base have provided a broad range of findings, the focus has tended to be on two main issues: (a) the use of technical assessments and tools to predict and manage risk and (b) the use of professional wisdom (intuition) to perceive and predict risk. Although the debates have produced a range of information and tools aimed at helping social workers analyse risk, the spectre of making a sound prediction (getting it right) remains an illusion in a profession that is dealing with the unpredictable nature of human responses to human tragedies.

In the midst of the debates, the growth and development of risk-based assessment tools from the Orange Book to the assessment framework have grown, and social workers now use supportive assessment tools such as the Multi-Agency Risk Assessment Conference (MARAC) to identify risk in relation to domestic violence (Featherstone *et al.*, 2014). The rise of 'specialist' assessment tools to use alongside the assessment framework acknowledges that risk in child protection social work houses a range of what are referred to as predictive factors that impact on parenting capacity. These predictive factors based on parental behaviours are identified as

➢ parental mental health

➢ parental problem drug and substance misuse

➢ parental learning disability

➢ domestic violence.

Research has focussed on parental behaviours, but researchers acknowledge that a wide range of factors in the parental background and socioeconomic and family environments affect the risk of child abuse (Department of Education *et al.,* 2016). Research has paid attention to risk factors, what these are and their effect on the child, producing findings that suggest that the strongest risks are from socioeconomic deprivation and factors in the parents' own background. But there is an overall acknowledgement in the research findings that one factor alone cannot predict risk of significant harm and that it is more likely to be an accumulation of these identified factors that will place the child at risk of abuse (Cleaver *et al.,* 2011). For example, parental mental health + problem drug use + poverty + learning disability = risk.

However, although having an understanding and knowledge about identifiable and predictive risk factors is important, there is a lack of detailed discussions about how social workers using the conceptual assessment framework model navigate the domains to make sense of the factors in relation to the different dimensions of parental capacity, the child's development, and family and environmental factors. Cleaver *et al.* (2011) provide a comprehensive analysis of parental behaviour risk factors and the effect of mental health, domestic violence, alcohol and substance abuse, and learning disability on the child, but there is little or no discussion about the accumulation of risk within a dimension. For example, the domain of parental capacity has the following dimensions:

➢ basic care

➢ ensuring safety

➢ emotional warmth

➢ stimulation

➢ guidance and boundaries

➢ stability

(Department of Health, 2000:21)

This chapter seeks to examine how risks can accumulate within these dimensions and whether this accumulation can provide better insight into how risk factors are perceived and understood. The chapter takes the specific domain of parental capacity and examines how risks to a child accumulated within the dimensions when the adult responsible for the child has learning disabilities and when the parenting behaviours of this potentially vulnerable adult had implications for keeping the child safe. The reader will be asked to consider how risk is understood in an ever-changing environment for the child who is fearful of what they are seeing and experiencing. This chapter will use illustrations from a case study. Darren's story will show how the rights of the child and their best interests were overshadowed by practice that promoted the rights of the adult parent in terms of their freedom of choice and actions. Importantly, this chapter will identify how social workers can develop their listening skills when undertaking direct work with children and how social workers can actively engage the child in the process of protection while ensuring that plans for their future are developed with the child in mind.

Darren's story

Darren (age 8) lived with his mother (Annie) and sister, Leanne (age 6). Annie had a learning disability. Darren was considered by health professionals to be small for his age. He had fair short hair that often stuck up and out, giving him the appearance of having just got out of bed. He had brown eyes that stared out at the world with defiance and a knowingness that was beyond his years. He often appeared like a small adult in a child's body that was constantly moving in a way that suggested he was anxious and unsettled. He loved his mother and sister and was very protective of them both. He would sit close to his mother and either gently place his hand over hers or pull at her clothing when he thought she was behaving in a way that brought attention to her. He did this when she was in the company of professionals and social workers. Throughout Annie's childhood, she attended a school for children with special educational needs and disabilities. Her intellectual disabilities translated into having limited cognition and learning. Her numeracy and literacy skills were limited. Annie said she could read a bit but didn't like big words. She struggled to communicate effectively. When she was upset, frustrated or angry, she would use a range of expletives to express herself. She found it difficult to manage relationships. She did not understand the social mores of developing and having an intimate relationship with men. This meant she would accept the attentions of men she hardly knew, allowing them to stay in her home. Annie failed to comprehend the risks her actions posed to Darren and Leanne. After a report was made by the police to Children's Services that a known sex offender was living in the home, a child protection conference was held and both children's names were placed on the child protection register under neglect. Annie and her children were supported by their maternal grandmother (Agnes), who

▶

◀

also had a level of learning disability. Agnes described her learning disability as being 'slow' and explained that she had also attended a 'special school' when she was a child because she was made fun of by other children. The child protection plan included direct work with both children. The focus of the direct work was to establish how safe the children were and to use this work to inform a core assessment that would help to determine Annie's parental capacity.

Parental capacity

The 1989 Children Act makes it clear that the responsibility for providing care and protection to children rests with the parents (May-Chahal and Coleman, 2003). Supported by the *Working Together* (2015:34) policy guidance and the Department of Health Assessment Framework (2000), professionals and social workers providing services to children should ensure that they are 'growing up in circumstances consistent with the provision of safe and effective care'. Most of us would accept the language of 'care', 'protection', 'safe', 'effective' and 'consistent' to describe the expectations and responsibilities of being a parent, and although policy documents acknowledge that there is 'no single, perfect way to bring up children' (HM Government, 2015a, 2015b:29), they go on to state what good parenting involves:

> caring for children's basic needs, keeping them safe and protected, being attentive and showing them warmth and love, encouraging them to express their views and consistently taking them into account, and providing the stimulation needed for development and to help them achieve their potential, within a stable environment where they experience consistent guidance and boundaries.

> (HM Government, 2015a, 2015b:30)

Being a parent is challenging. While I as a parent acknowledge and accept the above description, I don't doubt that if I had become the subject of external scrutiny, I may well have fallen short of such expectations, especially around issues of consistency, allowing an expression of views and taking them into account. There has been a proliferation of literature, media programmes and technology all professing to be *the* guide to being a 'good' parent plus private and state programmes aimed at supporting and educating parents. But it continues to be the case that most parents would acknowledge that they didn't know what they were signing up to.

For those parents with learning disabilities, parenthood continues to be controversial. This is because in Westernised cultures parents with intellectual disabilities continue to be viewed with fear and suspicion and treated to a large dose of paternalism, which over the years has marginalised them within the larger population and led to the perception that this specific group of parents is more likely to pose a risk to their children (Wade *et al.,* 2008). What these risks are remain contentious. While being a parent with a learning disability is now identified within the social work literature as a risk factor, it is understood from research that social work assessments fail to consider the range of different abilities and disabilities held within the term 'learning disability' (Booth *et al.,* 2005).

'Learning disabilities' is a limited term for a wide range of needs. The range of terms used to describe specific learning needs has evolved over the years as a result of disability activism that has challenged the preconceived ideas about adults and children with cognitive difficulties (Orme, 2001). However, these challenges have brought about limited changes in terms of health, education and social care provision. Seven years after the BBC Panorama programme exposed the systematic abuse of young people and adults with learning disabilities at Winterbourne View hospital in Gloucestershire, the outcome of the subsequent police investigation and public inquiry aimed at learning lessons was described by the care minister at the time, Norman Lamb, as a complete failure (*Guardian,* 2018a, 2018b, 2018c). The Equality Act of 2010 clearly prohibits service providers from discriminating on the basis of a person's disability, and section 47(1) of the National Health Service and Community Care Act 1990 places a duty on local authorities to consider the needs of those with a learning disability and, where necessary, to provide health and community-based support. So it would appear that as a society we remain stuck in attitudes or perceptions that consciously or unconsciously marginalise and oppress people with disabilities on the basis of a knowledge framework that sees able-bodied(ness) as the 'normal' template to measure disability against (Oliver and Sapey, 2006).

For Orme (2001), the generalised categorisation of disability is a contributing causal factor in how we tend to see or not see people with a disability. According to Orme (2001), the generalisation of disability fails to acknowledge individuality, identity and the vast differences in skills, abilities and experience of people with physical and learning disabilities. Wong and Donahue (2002) support this argument by suggesting that, as a society, we do not want to see the range of identities embodied by people with learning disabilities and that – when faced with the challenge of recognising them in the context of being a mother, father, lover, son, daughter, aunt, uncle or grandparent – we find the overarching generalised identity of disability contested.

The Department of Health's definition of learning disability encompasses people with a broad range of disabilities. They include the presence of:

➢ significantly reduced ability to understand new or complex information, to learn new skills (impaired intelligence); with

➢ a reduced ability to cope independently (impaired social functioning);

➤ which started before adulthood, with a lasting effect on development.

(HM Government, 2010:279)

Mencap provides a wider description of learning disability:

> A learning disability is caused by the way the brain develops. There are many differ-
> ent types and most develop before a baby is born, during birth or because of a seri-
> ous illness during early childhood. A learning disability can be mild, moderate, severe
> or profound, but all are life-long. Many people with a learning disability, however,
> live independent lives.

(Mencap, www.mencap.org.uk)

Although the definitions and descriptions provide helpful information to aid
understanding, there is an important question to address. Can social workers
confidently carry out an assessment of parental capacity from a position of
knowledge and understanding about parental learning disability? I suspect
that, for many child protection social workers, the area of parental learning
disability presents some challenging issues, specifically those associated with
applying definitions of mild, moderate, severe or profound learning disability
to the practice of assessing and making sense of their effect on parenting
capacity. Equally, they may be struggling with their own internalised attitudes
about disability and parenting. According to Cleaver *et al.* (2011), 'there is
still a widely held belief that adults with learning disabilities should not have
children' (p. 55).

Pause and consider:

The statement by Cleaver *et al.* (2011) and identify the assumptions being made.

In *Children's Needs – Parental Capacity: Child Abuse: Parental Mental Illness,
Learning Disability, Substance Misuse and Domestic Violence*, Cleaver *et al.* (2011)
identified the following issues in relation to parental learning disability and
parental capacity:

➤ 'Traditionally scores on standardised intelligence tests (IQ) have been used
to define learning disability. However, classifications of learning disability
using IQ tests have caused confusion and inconsistencies as a result of people demonstrating a variety of different levels of skills and abilities in the
different elements of the test. In reality an IQ score is not something to
measure parenting capacity' (p. 34).

➤ Research suggests that people with a learning disability are more likely to have 'suffered childhood abuse and as a result will have physical and mental health needs' (p. 35).

➤ 'Parents with learning disabilities have been found to be amongst the most socially and economically disadvantaged' (p. 35).

➤ 'Referrals to child protection teams are less likely to record parental learning disability' (p. 36).

➤ Parental learning disability plus other contributing risk factors, such as domestic violence, mental health, and alcohol and substance misuse, 'are frequently identified as impacting on parental capacity' (p. 36).

➤ 'Whilst there is no association between parental learning disability and child abuse, there is evidence to suggest that children may be neglected by omission' as a result of a lack of knowledge and understanding and support (p. 35).

➤ 'Some mothers with learning disabilities are particularly vulnerable to the financial, practical and emotional support offered by men who are paedophiles and whose primary concern is gaining access to the children' (p. 35).

However, while research has identified the effects of parental learning disability on parental capacity, it would be safe to suggest that it not only remains a contentious area of assessment in child protection social work fraught with the challenges presented by attitudes, knowledge and understanding, the question about whether or not social workers can make a confident assessment of parental capacity that is unbiased and keeps the child in mind becomes more pressing. As Cleaver *et al.* (2011) point out:

> To suggest that all parents who suffer from mental illness, learning disability, problem alcohol/drug use or are subjected to or perpetrate domestic violence present a danger to their children is misleading and dangerous. Indeed, much research indicates that with adequate support, parents who are experiencing a single disorder are often able to be effective and loving parents and present little risk of significant harm to children (p. 63).

What is becoming clear from the research findings on parental learning disability is that social workers carrying out an assessment of risk or need (or both) face having to get the balance right between the rights of the child to be safe and the rights of their parents with learning disabilities to care for their child or children. A first step to carrying out a balanced assessment is to acknowledge the attitudinal barriers and be open to challenging these through reflection and supervision. Although finding out as much as possible about parental learning disability and what this may mean for their child or children is a good start, the next step is to examine how this knowledge and understanding are applied in practice. An example of how this can be carried out is now described and discussed. Drawing upon dimensions of parenting capacity from the assessment framework (Department of Health, 2000), the experience of Darren and his sister, and research findings, the next section aims to expose the barriers and challenges that social workers faced when trying to identify whether or not Darren and his sister were safe.

Undoing risk within the domain of parental capacity

In this discussion, I argue that the focus on predictive factors in relation to parental problems has not served social workers well in terms of helping them to understand risks to children. Developing knowledge and understanding around parental behaviours such as mental health, drug and substance misuse, domestic violence and learning disability provide a tangible 'coat hanger' upon which we hang our judgements and decision-making about risks to a child. But there are less visible, more fluid and less tangible parental activities that in practice present social workers with challenges.

These challenges are often realised in practice that seeks to measure dimensions of parenting capacity that are open to a set of values and beliefs much of which are based on our own lived experiences of being a parent or being parented. This set of values and beliefs will screen what we see and hear. Research has found that they harbour bias and have become fertile ground for growing rigid and fixed thinking about perceptions of parenting – what this looks like and how parenting should and shouldn't be performed (Kirkman and Melrose, 2014; Featherstone *et al.*, 2014). This perception of parenting is based on theories of confirmation bias (Kahneman, 2011) whereby our brain uses a back catalogue of lived and practice experiences to make sense of what we are seeing, but it is also the trigger for setting off an emotional roller coaster driven by fear. How social workers acknowledge these fears and try to understand which ones pose a threat and which ones don't is the underlying issue for social workers as they try to undo risk around notions of parenting capacity where measuring the single concept of providing basic care is fraught with subjectivities. What one social worker judges to be acceptable basic care may be viewed differently by another and both will have different views of about which risks are significant and which are not worth bothering about. As Horwath (2013) argues, there is an overall interconnectedness between the issues of parental problems, parental backgrounds and parental needs that 'make it difficult for practitioners to establish exactly what impact the parenting issues are having on the parenting' (p. 183).

I agree with this argument in part. First, I accept that social workers faced with what Horwath (2013:182) refers to as a 'web of disadvantage' will find it difficult to makes sense of parenting capacity in this context. This is because they will be faced with inconsistencies. For example, in amongst the parental lived and living experiences that take parents' energies and attentions away from their child, there are times when their parenting is perceived by social workers to be good enough and in effect seen to be meeting the child's needs. Many social workers have been faced with parents who struggle to meet the demands of parenting. In amongst the scene of chaotic, dirty and unhygienic homes where the children appear oblivious to their surroundings, they observe parents showing care and attention to their child. Importantly, seeing the child responding to this emotional warmth with a hug or smile presents a picture that the brain finds difficult to comprehend.

In this situation, social workers will see the positives and this will generate feelings of optimism and interventions based on providing support as opposed to protection (Jeffreys et al., 2011). My addition to the argument posited by Horwath (2013) is that the difficulties faced by social workers trying to make sense of parenting capacity are due to the fact that the term 'parenting capacity' is adult-focussed and as a result the frame of reference for determining cause and effect unconsciously and consciously connects adult to adult. This adult connection sways how parenting capacity is interpreted and ultimately marginalises the child as social workers grapple with trying to make sense of what parenting capacity looks like as an adult performance as opposed to what this performance means for the child.

This adult-focussed approach to making sense of parenting capacity has had far-reaching consequences for children. From the death of Maria Colwell to the recent serious case review of the death of Ellie Butler, the view of parental capacity has defined the outcomes for the children. In the case of Ellie Butler, independent social workers reported that they 'were able to see child D (Ellie) and her sibling (child S) and their parents were in a relaxed state 'smiling and happy' which was … attributable to the care being offered to them at that time' (Sutton, Local Safeguarding Children Partnership, 2016). A year later, Ellie Butler, amid a range of concerns expressed by different agencies about the parental care she was receiving, died from head injuries inflicted by her father.

There is no doubt that social workers are trying to make sense of parenting capacity in the midst of a range of parental behaviours and activities that often present complex and inconsistent scenes and behaviours. As I acknowledged earlier in this chapter, parenting requires being able to provide care through behavioural activities that enable the child to grow into adulthood. How this is achieved is also acknowledged as a challenge for all parents, and as this chapter is focussing on parental learning disability, the research suggests that, for this specific parenting group, the challenges are much greater (Cleaver et al., 2011).

Undoing risk within the context of parental learning disability and parenting capacity is now examined in the story of Darren. This discussion aims to examine how risk accumulated within the dimension of parenting capacity with specific reference to the impact on Darren and his sister, Leanne. It is hoped that, through a focus on the child, the issue of risk is viewed with more clarity and that a greater understanding is achieved about how social workers measure parenting within the contested, confusing and challenging area of parental care giving.

Basic care

Darren lived with his mother, Annie, and his sister in what is now referred to as social housing. The house was spacious and there were three bedrooms. The house provided warmth and shelter but was chaotic. There were dirty and clean clothes piled on the sofa, food left on the work surfaces and piled up in the sink, and dirty toilets and bath suites. The children's bedrooms had distinctive furnishings. Darren had Ninja Turtles bedding and his sister Care Bears and in both rooms there was evidence that care and attention had been taken to provide the children with their own individual space. Although the basic care in terms of the provision of warmth and shelter was being provided by Annie, Darren's experience of his mother's basic care was that he often wore dirty clothes, suffered head lice and smelled from not being bathed regularly. His dental health was poor and he had missed optician appointments to ensure that he wore appropriate prescription glasses. Darren was often late for school and frequently complained of being hungry. As a result of his appearance, he was often bullied by other children. His school confirmed that he was often wearing dirty clothes and they shared their concerns about his eyesight and how they felt this was having a detrimental effect on his learning. The school also confirmed that when Darren did get to school they would always provide him with breakfast as part of an early breakfast scheme.

The Department of Health (2000:21) defines basic care as:

> Being able to provide for the child's physical needs, and appropriate medical and dental care. This includes provision of food, drink, warmth, shelter, clean and appropriate clothing and adequate personal hygiene.

Research shows that parents with learning disabilities need encouragement and support to establish and maintain regular routines as they often find it difficult to cope with the unexpected and as a result life easily becomes disorganised (Cleaver *et al.,* 2011). For many parents, caring for children is best described as something akin to undertaking a military operation where the skills and abilities to implement timetables, produce lists of things to do, buy and prepare food, do laundry and so on are learned from our own parents, family networks, friends and reading. Annie's childhood experience was similar to the one her son was now experiencing. She was not able to comprehend what the problems or concerns were when she spoke with social workers. According to Annie, her mum's house was the same as hers. Although her mother visited her regularly and appeared to provide some emotional support and infrequent care for the children, she was not able to influence or provide Annie with the practical support that would enhance her parenting skills and abilities. Agnes had her own learning disability and this generational factor – which research suggests is a feature in parental learning disability whereby children of parents with learning disabilities are more likely to be born with a learning disability or psychological disorder (McGaw and Newman, 2005) – meant that Darren and his sister were dependent for their basic care on two adults with moderate learning disabilities who were struggling to provide this.

While social workers assessed that Annie was not meeting Darren's basic care needs, it was agreed that this area of parental capacity could be resolved through social work, health and education interventions that focussed on providing support to encourage routines that helped to meet Darren and Leanne's needs. Although there is strong research evidence to suggest that family and social support can make a significant difference to a child's experience of parental learning disability (Ghate and Hazel, 2002), how long this should be provided for and by whom remain issues that often produce tensions between professionals (Rogowski, 2013). The issue of resources and who should be providing them, especially when levels of risk are being disputed, is often resolved by budget cuts and workload pressures. This means that social workers are pressured to close cases where the risks have been reduced and parenting capacity is deemed *good enough* or the risks have been resolved through the courts and children are removed and placed in care. Before we move on in this discussion, it is important to examine what is meant by good-enough parenting in relation to basic care.

Pause and consider:

The issue of good-enough basic care in relation to current practice and parental learning disability. For example, is there a benchmark of standards for meeting the basic care dimension of learning disability and parental capacity? When would you consider that basic care needs are not being met and are placing the child at risk? Do you think Darren's basic care needs were being met?

What was becoming clear was that Annie needed ongoing and probably long-term social work support to ensure that she was able to meet her children's basic care needs. Darren's lived experience reflected research findings that show how children of parents with learning disabilities, where basic care is inconsistent and limited, are more vulnerable to societal isolation, health problems, bullying and neglect, which increase their risk of significant harm (Cleaver *et al.*, 2011), but there was some evidence of emotional warmth.

However, the level of risk and the level of significant harm associated with parental learning disability tend to take place in an ever-changing environment where support provided in one area is overshadowed by problems in another. Darren and his sister faced increasing risk and social workers became increasingly concerned about their mother's capacity to ensure that both children were safe and protected.

Ensuring safety

Ensuring that a child is safe and protected from harm requires the parent to be able to see potential dangers and to make sure the child's environment is hazard-free. As the grandmother of a two-year-old, I am constantly being caught out by her physical agility and her ability to work out how to climb from one piece of furniture to another as she explores my home and her parents' home. Although furniture has been re-arranged, kitchen cupboards fitted with child locks, ornaments taken down, and rugs removed and a general attempt has been made to ensure that the home environment is child-safe, she continues to be one step ahead. This means that her parents and I have become hyper-vigilant in our attempts to keep her safe.

However, according to the Department of Health (2000), ensuring a child's safety includes being aware of and understanding the potential dangers of the outside world, particularly 'from contact with unsafe adults' (p. 21). The image conjured up by the term 'unsafe adult' is most likely to be the predatory paedophile who seeks out disadvantaged and vulnerable children (Pritchard, 2004) – an image that has evolved from the stranger-danger fears of the 1950s and 1960s and that permeated a discourse aimed at raising parents' awareness to the dangers of extra-familial abusers. This image of the stranger lurking around housing estates and playgrounds and waiting to abduct a child has been seared into society's consciousness, leading to a belief that harm is not close by but out there in someone else's environment, an environment of disadvantage and vulnerability, and that as long as parents are vigilant they will keep their children safe (Pritchard, 2004). However, this image has been challenged and people have become more aware that paedophiles are living and working in all areas of society – the teacher, social worker, police officer, GP, paediatrician, judge and member of parliament – as a result of Jimmy Saville and other celebrities and high-profile politicians being exposed as unsafe adults.

For many parents, this new knowledge has meant developing different parenting skills that include being knowledgeable about safeguarding policies in schools, youth activities, nurseries, churches, and swimming and football clubs. Whereas many parents will have increased their knowledge about unsafe adults, parents with learning disabilities who have limited literacy will find it difficult to access information or make sense of it in a way that is meaningful to them. As research has shown, this area of ensuring that children are safe from being abused by someone outside of the family poses specific issues for children dependent on parents with learning disabilities (Cleaver *et al.,* 2011).

Both Darren and his sister had been made the subject of a child protection plan because of concerns that their mother was allowing a known sex offender and paedophile into the family home. Annie initially denied all knowledge of the man, saying it was all lies. However, when confronted by information passed to social workers by her mother (Agnes), Annie admitted that he had visited 'sometimes'. She said he was a friend who was nice to her and she did not believe what the police and social workers said about him. It was her inability to comprehend the seriousness of her actions and the danger she was placing her children in that raised alarm bells for social workers and all those in the core group. However, as a result of the sex offender's being re-arrested and placed in custody, many of the core group believed the children were now safe and there was an overall view that, as a result of Agnes's actions, future support could now include helping Annie to understand the dangers that some men pose to her and her children. Although those involved in the core group, including Annie, saw this as a step forward (specifically in regard to the role of Agnes, who appeared to better understand the concerns), it has to be said there was little detail in the planned work to 'educate' Annie about men in general and those who may pose a risk.

The issue of social workers' being able to communicate and discuss with parents their intimate relationships was identified in Chapters 4 and 5. This is an area of practice that Featherstone *et al.* (2014) argues has been neglected, suggesting that social workers should pay attention to the power of intimate relationships and how adults may place these above the needs of their children. Sex and its relationship to the body in terms of identity, status and positive and negative experiences are powerful concepts. Understanding the power of these concepts and their influence on risks to children presents social workers with a challenge that asks them to be open and honest about not only how they feel about the issues but how they would go about talking about them to others, especially to parents and particularly to parents with a learning disability where it is acknowledged that the challenges are increased as a result of attitudinal barriers (McCarthy, 1999).

Pause and consider:

How would you plan direct work with Annie that focusses on intimate relationships and educating her about the dangers of unsafe adults?

The issue of Annie's having an intimate relationship raised a number of issues that centred on her rights as a woman. These issues hung over the core group and many found it difficult to communicate to Annie and each other what they meant by being concerned about Annie's entering into an intimate relationship. This caused tensions and barriers between the professionals as some focussed on Annie's rights to privacy and family life, opposing suggestions of monitoring and surveillance. This situation did not help Annie. She was confused about what everyone was saying about her and her life, and her responses confirmed each side of the argument – her rights as a woman to privacy versus regulation and monitoring. The two issues were never fully resolved between the professionals. However, because Annie complied with a core group recommendation to attend a day group for women whose children were subject to a child protection plan, core group agreed that this approach, though supportive, was also a way of monitoring her capacity to ensure that her children were safe.

When Annie was attending the group (as she did regularly), she appeared to gain support from the other women. She engaged with all the activities, formed friendships and appeared to gain confidence. Core group members commented on the difference in Annie: she was more confident and organised at home, and the school reported that Darren's attendance was better, he did not appear to be hungry and he had been for an eye test. The risks to Darren and his sister appeared to be decreasing. This sense of moving in the right direction to keeping the children safe continued for several core groups to the point that there was an agreement that plans could be made for the child protection plan to be reviewed.

While Annie was attending the women's group, social workers were carrying out direct work with Darren and his sister. The focus of the work was to find out whether they felt safe and to try to understand what this may mean for them. Although the dimensions of parenting capacity set out in the Assessment Framework (DH, 2000) describe what is expected to of parents to ensure the safety of the child:

Ensuring the child is adequately protected from harm or danger. This includes protection from significant harm or danger and from contact with unsafe adults/other children and from self-harm. There should be some recognition of hazards and danger in the home and elsewhere.

(Department of Health, 2000:21)

There is little available in policy or the literature that describes or explains what feeling and being safe mean to a child. As Wrench (2017) points out, we cannot assume that children know what 'safe feels like or looks like' (p. 60). However, I believe that, for children to feel safe, there are important adult behaviours that when carried out provide children with a physical and psychological experience that engenders feelings of safety and trust. The social workers working with Darren and his sister knew that they had to develop a trusting relationship that offered both children the space and opportunity to feel safe so that they could talk about how they felt. Based on research findings and my own direct experience of working with children, developing a trusting relationship with children should include the following:

➢ Be a good listener.

➢ Be honest about what you can and cannot do. Make no promises

➢ Accept the child's language and avoid, as children have said, *'twisting words'* (Cossar *et al.*, 2014:107) to make things sound better or worse. Just tell it how they say it.

➢ Do not put pressure on them to tell you what is happening in their lives.

➢ Be clear about why you are involved with them. As Cossar *et al.* (2014) found out from their research with children involved in child protection services, 'it was clear that children were struggling to make sense of what was going on, and in some cases, their misunderstanding was a cause of distress' (p. 108).

➢ Encourage children to be part of any planning, whether this is about what happens in the future or what they would want to put in place to make them feel and be safe.

➢ Do not put children in the position of having to say what they think about their parents, especially in an open forum or in front of their parents.

The social workers who carried out the direct work with Darren and his sister put the above to good use. It took time and Darren initially was very reluctant to engage with either of the social workers. He did not want to be separated from his sister, and he appeared nervous about activities that involved writing. The social workers tried a range of activities with both children; keeping them together helped to relax Darren. From this direct work, social workers identified that the children enjoyed tearing and pasting papers to make a collage. They both actively engaged in making up a song about staying safe, an activity that Wrench (2017) suggests is helpful with young children when talking about feeling safe and identifying the adults who make them feel safe. However, there is no getting away from the fact that the social workers were trying to find out whether both children were safe and whether they felt safe. During a session where the aim was to engage the children in putting together a protective plan, the following responses helped social workers gauge what their needs were and how they were making sense of their family situation:

SW – Who eats the most?

Leanne – Darren does. He makes lots of bread and butter and eats it all. He can make tea and he makes me cereal and sometimes he brings chips home and we eat them all up.

SW – Who goes to sleep first?

Darren – Leanne. I'm older, so I go to bed much later if mum is not home. Gran lets me stay up and watch telly. If mum is home, I go to bed and watch over Leanne until she is asleep. I watch the door. I watch to make sure no one comes in.

SW – Who wakes up first?

[Silence ...]

Leanne – Darren wakes me up when he shouts and screams. He shouts at the monsters when they come into my room. He shouts and screams when he is in mum's room. He says he fights off the monsters.

Darren – Shsssssssss. Leanne don't tell. Mum said not to tell.

SW – What did mum tell you not to tell?

Leanne – She said not to tell anyone about Uncle Eddie and Uncle James. I don't like Uncle Eddie. He smells and he pulls me onto his lap and wriggles around. Uncle James, he shouts at mum and he gives me sweets and tells me to go and play outside.

Darren – [Jumped up and ran across the room. He picked up a small chair and threw it at the social workers. He was screaming and shouting. He ran outside of the building and refused to come back into the room. He stayed outside and hid behind a car.]

SW – Is it okay if I sit here?

Darren – [Silence... silent crying and holding his head which he said is hurting him. He eventually asked the social worker:] Are you still there?

SW – Yes. I will stay until you feel okay to come into the centre.

Darren – There will be trouble now. I'm in real trouble. Mum said I'm the man of the house. I'm supposed to look after Leanne and my mum but I'm frightened. Eddie and James scare me.

SW – You have done a good job looking after Leanne. She knows that you look after her. Do you think you could come into the centre and tell me about Eddie and James?

Darren – Okay, but I'm hungry. Can I have something to eat first?

From the direct work with both children, it was very clear that Annie was not able to ensure the children's safety or her own. The impact on Darren of not feeling safe was clear to see. He was emotionally distressed and living in fear because he believed he could not protect his sister and mother. Research confirms that children between 8 and 10 years old, particularly boys, feel they have to intervene to protect a parent or sibling from violence and abuse. This means they are more likely to suffer significant harm and are at risk of suffering physically and emotionally through injury and trauma (Cleaver *et al.*, 2011).

A picture was building that confirmed research findings that women with learning disabilities are vulnerable to being singled out by paedophiles who are seeking to gain access to their children (Cleaver and Freeman, 1995). These men offered Annie financial support, companionship, sex and (she believed) some status in her community. The impact on Darren and Leanne was severe. Although social workers felt strongly that the information provided from both children was evidence of significant harm, there was also a desire to ensure that the issue of Annie's parental capacity was fully understood in terms of planning the children's future. Social workers had no doubts that Annie loved her children and could respond to them with cuddles and praise them for doing something well, but she was not able to sustain this and sadly she could not protect them from violent or predatory paedophiles.

Emotional warmth

The Department of Health (2000:21) provides the following definition of parental emotional warmth:

> Ensuring the child's emotional needs are met, and giving the child a sense of being specially valued and a positive sense of their own racial and cultural identity. **This** includes ensuring the child's requirements for secure, stable and affectionate relationship with significant adults, with appropriate sensitivity and responsiveness to the child's needs. **It also includes providing** appropriate physical contact, comfort and cuddling sufficient to demonstrate warm regard, praise and encouragement.

A question that needs to be asked at this point is, how is the definition of emotional warmth understood and translated into practice? There are several examples from serious case reviews that refer to children's behavior being interpreted by professionals as a response to parental emotional warmth. This was evident in the case of Ellie Butler, where independent social workers interpreted her smiles as being a response to her parent's emotional warmth. This interpretation of parental emotional warmth in relation to a child smiling is fraught with issues and is easily clouded by adult feelings and emotions. It now poses the question – how else would a child's smile be interpreted? The issue of children smiling in the presence of a parent or adult carer is one that was examined in the case of Victoria Climbié when professionals explained their responses to

Victoria and her aunt. Professionals said they interpreted and understood the smile of Victoria in the presence of her aunt to indicate a relationship based on strict cultural parenting that demanded respect but was tinged with levels of emotional warmth (Ferguson, 2011).

Pause and consider:

What you think children in difficult situations are telling us when they smile? Do you believe that this may have to do with their knowledge and understanding of their social situation and a script they have come to learn and use? Can you think of a current case in which you are trying to make sense of a child's presentation in the presence of their parent or parents? What are the issues?

Social workers assessing Annie's parenting capacity witnessed Annie hugging Darren and Leanne at home and after direct work with social workers. Both children responded to this demonstration of emotional warmth. Leanne would jump up and down to gain her mother's attention to show her what she had made, whereas Darren would tend to stand back, allowing his sister to get his mother's attention first, before hugging her. Both children always appeared to be pleased to see their mother. Trying to make sense of the children's affection towards their mother in the context of the fears Darren had expressed was unsettling. Social workers found it difficult to make sense of this shared emotional warmth between Annie and her children. However, they went back to what Darren had told them about his experiences and how he felt frightened. They recognised that Darren's experience was shaped by his relationship to his mother and his understanding about what was taking place in the home. He understood that his mother could not protect him or his sister. The emotional relevance of his experience provided him with a framework to understand his feelings of fear and what this meant to him in terms of risk.

Darren fully understood the risks he was facing from the men who came into his home, and he knew that his mother's expression of emotional warmth through hugs and cuddling was not enough to protect him. According to Thompson *et al.* (2003), children develop an understanding about a lived experience through talking with others. That understanding includes gaining some insight into why they feel the way they do – the intentions and motives behind their feelings. Darren had gained his understanding about his lived experience, emotions and feelings from listening to his mother, the men who frequented the house, his sister, his grandmother and now the social workers.

How social workers test out and measure emotional warmth against the Department of Health (2000) definition is best understood when this is brought back to focus on the child. This approach is not about using the child's experience as a way of blaming the adult, although within the context of child protection that is exactly what is being asked of social workers when they assess parenting capacity. I argue that the parent/parenting/child relationships should not be competing narratives but should be understood and viewed as relational. As Burman (2008) suggests, the child's interests should not be understood at the expense of the parents and equally we should not seek to understand parents and parenting at the expense of the child. Somehow, we need to understand how this relationship intersects and has the capacity to provide positive life experiences for both or frustrate them as well (Katz, 2004).

To help this process, I offer the following modest model that aims to bring into sharp focus the needs of the child in a way that asks critical questions about how social workers are assessing emotional warmth in relation to parenting.

Child's needs

Emotional

Sense of value: How would you know that a child has a sense of value? What behaviour would you expect to observe and witness in a child who feels valued?

What parenting style do you think would provide a child with a sense of value? What parenting activities would you expect to be involved in supporting and developing a child's sense of their own value?

Would you expect a child to be confident, curious, ambitious, questioning, aware of others, appropriately cautious of adults, independent, socially skilled, loved and loving?

Would you expect a parent to be affectionate, encouraging, interested, responsive, loving, sensitive and available?

Sense of belonging: How would you assess a child's sense of belonging? What would you consider to be important to a child in developing a sense of belonging? What parenting practices would you consider to be crucial to ensuring a child felt they belonged?

Would you expect to observe a child secure in their relationships with siblings and significant adults and secure in their immediate environment and their outside world (schools, nursery and clubs)?

Would you expect parents to be able to attend health appointments and educational functions; keep family, holiday and spiritual rituals; and provide a level of consistency at food, bed and bath times?

Sense of their own racial and cultural identity: How would you assess a child's sense of racial and cultural identity? What parenting values and beliefs do you think would be present?

What would you expect a child to say about their racial heritage, their language, their traditions, their immediate and extended family, their community and their religion?

What would you expect a parent to say about their racial heritage, their language, their traditions, their immediate and extended family, their community, and their religion?

Physical

Providing appropriate physical contact: What is your understanding of appropriate physical contact? Do you believe that smacking a child is okay? Do you believe the age of the child will influence what is understood as age-appropriate contact? How would you apply your understanding of appropriate physical contact to assessing the needs of a child with a disability?

What would a child's behaviour tell you about how they are experiencing physical contact? High levels of self-awareness, happy/sad, withdrawn/outgoing, anxious/relaxed, misinterpret the intentions of others, hyper-vigilant, lacking in confidence, poor communication skills, aggressive, angry, injuries (hidden and obvious), fearful and fearless.

What parenting behaviour would you expect? Displays of affection towards the child and significant adults? Cuddling, hugs, kisses, being responsive to each other when they are crying, upset, angry, fearful and frightened? Providing secure and stable adult and child relationships?

Language

Praise and encouragement: Think of the language used by adults to praise and encourage children. How have you developed as a consequence of your lived experience? How is language used in different environments? Is the language in the home different from that of, say, teachers at school? How would you demonstrate praise and encouragement to a child you are doing direct work with? Is the language used age-appropriate? Is it accessible – does the child understand?

How would take notice of the child's responses to praise and encouragement? Would you expect them to present as self-assured and resilient; have self-esteem; be ambitious and self-sufficient; want to achieve; have friendships as opposed to being isolated, fearful, withdrawn, hyper-vigilant and aware; lack confidence; and have limited communication and social skills and low self-worth?

What are your ideas about language and its importance in parenting? Would you expect to observe and hear positive and affirming language as opposed to language filled with criticism, rejection and abusive swearing?

How the dimension of emotional warmth is understood in the context of parenting capacity is not simple. Within the model offered, there will be critical questions asked not just of the model but of our own ideas about how we have experienced being parented and indeed our own parenting. If you have had a positive and affirming life experience, this will influence how you understand and interpret actions of emotional warmth. Your experience will have set a benchmark that you will use consciously and unconsciously to gauge the parenting of others. It is often worth reminding ourselves about our own lived experiences in a way that helps us tune in to the child within all of us – the positive and negative experiences we may have had and what impact they have had on our adulthood.

Darren's understanding and experience of emotional warmth were inconsistent and confusing. His mother outwardly expressed her feelings towards her children with hugs and cuddles but not always in the presence of professionals. Her mother, Agnes, confirmed that they both showed the children affection and this was observed in the home. However, Annie was also unpredictable and vulnerable and unable to ensure that Darren was surrounded by appropriate adult relationships. She had confused Darren and Leanne by referring to the adults as uncles when they were not related. This is a common approach in communities. Many of my friends and I grew up referring to adults in the community as aunt or uncle and this was understood as a sign of respect and recognition of their significance to the family. For Darren and Leanne, the term 'uncle' had a very different meaning. Equally, Darren had referred to himself as the 'man of the house', a term Annie had used to affirm that he was growing up. She had believed that this was a positive term that showed she valued him. However, for Darren, it had the opposite effect. He was living in an environment where he witnessed his mother being physically, sexually and verbally abused by his 'uncles'. He interpreted his mother's reference to his being the man of the house as taking on the burden of responsibility for protecting his mother and his sister. He worried about his mother and his sister. He was torn between his love for his mother and his experience that left him feeling powerless and disconnected from his mother and as a result he felt unprotected and at risk.

Recognising how Darren felt provided social workers with an understanding about how emotional warmth was being played out in the relationship between him and his mother. They began to understand that the displays of affection, though real, were not enough to meet all of Darren or his sister's needs. As a consequence, social workers were beginning to understand the impact of Annie's parenting behaviour on the children and how these were accumulating in a range of unmet needs that were having an impact on all aspects of his health and well-being. Understanding this accumulation of adverse outcomes in relation to unmet need provided social workers with a clearer view of Darren. They began to understand his behaviour in relation to his fears and anxieties. Now they needed to make sense of his unmet needs in order to make a considered decision about his future and that of his sister.

Stimulation

We will all have a view about what is meant by providing stimulation that supports and promotes the child as they grow and develop. Apart from the specific textbooks that social workers may refer to, a growing technical world is offering new ways to engage parents in stimulating their children. It has to be acknowledged that stimulating children is set within theories aimed at ensuring children develop into *good citizens* with the appropriate and accepted social skills and abilities to become independent, self-sufficient and able to give something back to society through employment and taxes. While this is a goal that many parents set out to achieve, it is one that requires the finances, tenacity, patience, creativity, time, knowledge and skills to get even close to achieving, especially when it feels like the goalposts keep being moved.

Research findings suggest that children living with parental learning disability where there are parenting issues will experience emotional and behavioural problems, cognitive and language delays because of their parents' inconsistent and sometimes erratic behaviour, and lack of stimulation (Horwath, 2013). It is the lack of stimulation – defined by the Department of Health (2000:21) as 'Promoting the child's learning and intellectual development through encouragement and cognitive stimulation and promoting social opportunities' – that social workers will refer to when measuring the effects of parenting issues on the child. However, how social workers measure 'cognitive stimulation' and 'promoting social opportunities' is unclear and open to interpretation by the individual social worker. According to Tarlton *et al.* (2006), interpretation has been shown in research findings to house negative and stereotypical attitudes towards parents with learning disabilities and influence assessments and judgements. A consequence of this negative and stereotypical approach is that the parenting bar is set very high for parents with a learning disability.

Understanding what parental stimulation is needs unpicking in a way that helps us to critically reflect on how this is being assessed as a dimension of parental capacity. We cannot assume that there is a clear benchmark understood and used by all social workers. Equally, we cannot assume that an understanding is used appropriately and effectively to make sense of the child's lived experience. Children's experiences of parental stimulation will vary and depend on age and their parents' understanding and their skills and abilities to provide this stimulation. Where there is a range of parental problems, it is therefore not surprising that providing a child with stimulation will be limited, and for many children, by the time they reach school age, they have unmet needs that mean they have a starting point very different from that of many of their peers (Horwath, 2013).

Darren (age 8) already had a range of unmet needs by the time he began school. Before we look at these in more detail, it is worth exploring your own understanding of stimulation as a dimension of parental capacity.

Pause and consider:

How do you interpret the dimension of stimulation? What is your parenting benchmark for providing a child with stimulation? What would you expect a parent to do to ensure that their child was being cognitively stimulated? What is your understanding of promoting social opportunities?

For school-aged children, attending school promotes their learning and social and intellectual development. School is a place where children learn about each other, learn about themselves and learn about parenting. We all know from personal experience that school can be a challenging and difficult environment. We all have memories about the good times and the not-so-good times. From the pressures of fitting in with everyone else to suffering the anxieties of coping with tests and exams, attendance and non-attendance at school can provide a wealth of information to help professionals and social workers understand what is going on for the child at home (Portela and Pells, 2014). For those children living with parental problems, school can be a place of sanctuary and peace as well as a place of hostility and aggression (Cleaver and Nicholson, 2007). Where children are dependent on their parents for support and encouragement to attend school and are living with parental learning disability, the problems they face are wide-ranging and the impact on their lives can be profound.

Darren was not attending school regularly. Because he was not being encouraged or supported by Annie to make the most of education, the impact on his life was wide-ranging and the outcomes for him were as follows:

➢ Who counts? – Being late and often not attending school caused Darren to become singled out and isolated. He was singled out because being late meant that he missed out on early-morning activities associated with classroom assemblies. He became isolated because other children avoided him, did not notice him and did not include him in their games and activities. He became undone by this experience. His sense of self-worth and value were both devalued. In the day-to-day life of school, he simply did not count.

➢ What counts? – Darren was hungry, poorly dressed and dirty. His appearance singled him out and made him an easy target for bullying. He responded to the bullying by being verbally and physically aggressive or running out of the classroom. His behaviour showed his distress and his body was telling him 'fight or flight'. He also understood that what counts is fitting in and he knew he was not subject to the same type of parenting other children were subject to.

➢ Why it counts? – The relationship between not counting and what counts had an impact on his engagement and learning. He had a range of unmet development and educational needs. He struggled to keep up with the other children – physically, intellectually and emotionally. He felt outside of their experience and found it difficult to make sense of what teachers were asking him to do. His poor eyesight meant that he was further disadvantaged. It counted because Darren's starting point was different and was difficult for him to understand or accept.

➢ Where it counts? – Darren was tied to the school community. It was a big issue in his life. While it was fraught with fears and anxieties, it paradoxically offered him a level of protection from the adult males in his home. However, the school community was a small experience of the social processes he was experiencing at home and in the community. Whether he was at school or at home, he was vulnerable. In places that should count towards keeping a child safe, Darren was not safe and importantly he did not feel safe.

Understanding the role of parental stimulation in the lives of children cannot be underlined enough and its role as facilitator in relation to the other dimensions to enable the child to thrive physically, emotionally and intellectually is important. However, how the benchmark of parental stimulation is set is worth clarifying and thinking about. Darren's cognitive development had been impaired and this became evident when he started school. His reading skills were assessed as being that of a five-year-old and he found it difficult to tell the difference between a 'C' and a 'G'. When Darren tried to do addition and subtraction, especially when he was faced with higher numbers, he would become frustrated and angry. When he was working with the social workers, they noticed that he found it difficult to hold and control a pencil or crayon, suggesting that there may be some developmental delay. Although Darren appeared to understand what he was trying to achieve and the goals he needed to reach, he just didn't have the thinking development to get there. This would cause him to become angry and upset. He would test out boundaries by being aggressive and threatening or refusing to complete tasks and this would result in his being taken out of the classroom.

According to Cleaver and Nicholson (2007), delays in a child's cognitive development may be caused by genetics or by inadequate parental stimulation and poor school attendance. But with support this need not be the case for many children of learning disabled parents. Because Annie had not been able to prepare him for the experience of attending school, he was not ready for or able to cope with the transition into a social world that placed him under huge pressure. As a result of Darren's limited cognitive development, the many social opportunities that present themselves through school – taking day trips or being invited to a birthday party or over to a friend's home – were often denied to him because he failed to attend or was bullied and isolated. For Darren, the lack of parental stimulation plus the genetic factors and the additional impact of experiencing fear were beginning to accumulate, providing evidence of a child suffering significant harm.

Guidance and boundaries

All children need guidance and boundaries. Building a moral values fence around a child to provide them with a set of rules, regulations and expectations is a key task of parenting. This moral values fence is extended as the child grows and develops and is something that can and will be challenged and negotiated.

The term 'moral value' is used by the Department of Health (2000:21) in its definition of the guidance and boundaries dimension of parenting capacity:

> The key parental tasks are demonstrating and modelling appropriate behaviour and control of emotions and interactions with others, and giving guidance which involves setting boundaries, so that the child is able to develop an internal model of **moral values** and conscience and social behaviour appropriate for the society within which they will grow up in. The aim is to enable the child to grow into an autonomous adult, holding their own values, and be able to demonstrate appropriate behaviour with others rather than having to be dependent on rules outside themselves. This includes not over-protecting children from exploratory and learning experiences.

We have a passion for boundaries, whether these are internal or external. According to Gullestad (1997), the focus on boundaries is the outcome of modern-day capitalism, in which the state, religions and the popular media all have some influence over debates about how we parent our children. Alongside the external influence of state, religion and the popular media, there is the role of immediate and extended family, which will be hugely influential in creating family scripts containing models of moral values, conscience and behaviours that will have an impact on parenting styles that affect the lived experience of the child.

During the 1990s, government and media debates on parenting produced the term 'toxic families' to describe parenting that was understood to be out of control, lack moral values and fail to provide appropriate guidance or set boundaries in line with the societal standards of the day (Warner, 2015). The use of emotive language grew and politicians began referring to children from problematic and problem families as 'feral' while promising the voting public that legislative and policy changes were in place to bring such families in line with the rest of society (Drakeford and Jordan, 2010).

The use of 'toxic' and 'feral' to refer to particular families and their children increased when the media reported the findings from a controversial serious case review into the physical and sexual assault on two boys by two young brothers of primary school age living in foster care. The attack left one of the boys with life-threatening injuries, and the findings from the serious case review reported that, before being placed with foster carers, the two boys lived with their parents and were known to all the agencies. The reporting described the parenting as follows:

> The children were raised in appalling circumstances of violence, drugs and neglect. They accessed violent and pornographic films and were left to run wild in the community, foraging in bins for food and carrying out acts of violence.

> (*Guardian*, 2010)

It will always be the extreme outcomes of violent parental behaviours and neglect that hit the media headlines, prompting knee-jerk responses from politicians that lead to debates about broken families and how to fix them. Social workers across the country will be accountable for children living in similar environments where problematic parenting is causing, and is likely to cause, significant harm to the children. But there will also be those children and families where the parental guidance and boundaries are fluid, inconsistent and less than stringent and where the children appear to demonstrate appropriate behaviour, cognitive development and a level of autonomy. However, how parents carry out the key parental task of providing guidance and setting boundaries is a contested site where the overtones of moral values and frameworks will influence how this is understood and assessed by social workers.

Horwath (2013) makes the point that making a judgement about the quality of parenting is filled with bias and is formed by a scale of different standards that vary depending on the socioeconomic status of the parents. She refers to the reporting on the 2007 abduction of Madeleine McCann (age 3) from her parents' holiday apartment. Madeleine was left alone in the apartment along with her twin siblings while her parents had dinner downstairs with a group of friends. She was abducted and to this day what happened to her remains unknown. Although her abduction caused a media furore and both parents were subjected to public outcry and anger about the quality of their parenting, such attacks were tempered and rationalised by a discourse that focussed on their middle-class credentials and standing in the community.

Pause and consider:

The term 'model of moral values' and how you would interpret what you think would be contained in such a model. Think about your own model of moral values and how this may influence how you judge the quality of parenting.

Social workers working with Darren and his sister, Leanne, judged Annie's parenting to be lacking in guidance and boundaries. Based on the direct work with the children, they determined that both children were suffering forms of neglect that placed them at risk of significant harm. They based their concerns on listening to both children and trying to make sense of what they had been told. As discussed in Chapter 2, the art of listening to children requires that adults tune in to the child, using a range of sonar-like skills that ensure that everything the child is saying and not saying is gathered together in a data set that can be examined through reflection.

How social workers carry out the process of making sense of what a child is telling them is unclear. I am not convinced that, as a profession, we have come up with a clear way of analysing the information we gather from direct work with children or their parents. I suspect this is at the core of concerns raised from serious case review findings that social workers struggle to analyse information (Brandon *et al.*, 2012). The social workers working with Darren and his family used a range of processes to reach their conclusions about the lack of parental guidance and boundaries in the home. They brought together the facts available, the outcomes of the direct work with the children and the concerns expressed by professionals about Annie's parental learning disabilities. I do know that the process of analysis they leaned heavily upon was their professional wisdom, an unseen process of thinking that brings together knowledge, practice and personal experience to make a judgment about the risks to the children. I also know that they would have found it difficult to explain the processes involved in their professional wisdom decision making. For this reason in order to provide readers with something they can take away and use in practice, I have used the words of Darren and draw upon the work of Hardwick and Worsley (2011), who advocate using thematic analysis to analyse research findings, to set out a visible analytical method with clear guidelines to use to test out basically how you have listened to children.

In short, thematic analysis is a tool to support a process of thinking and questioning and developing ideas. It is underpinned by theoretical frameworks from psychology and the social sciences and adopted by social work researchers. It has become the most used qualitative method of analysis in social work research and, according to Hardwick and Worsley (2011), the most important. To break it down, it is a staged process that takes place after you have collected information from listening and recording what the child or parent has said. The staged process includes the following:

1. reading through recordings

2. identifying important features and patterns

3. identifying themes and relationships

4. making sense of the themes and relationships

To show how thematic analysis can be used in practice, I have used the words of Darren and Leanne to take us through the staged process. However, as with all methods, models and tools, how they are used is dependent on the individual social worker's skills, knowledge and capacity to reflect. Adopting a thematic analysis approach to recordings means the social worker has to be involved, immersed and active in the process. They will be constantly looking and thinking about what the words, connections and ideas mean to them, outcomes for the child and their families and practice. So as a word of caution, this is not an easy approach or process. There will be times when you get caught up in a circular process whereby you go through all four stages several times. However, although it may take time, it is a way of ensuring and reinforcing the importance of the child's words and their meaning. More importantly, a thematic analysis approach will provide social workers with a tool that helps release the voice of the child by using a method that supports them to find out what it is they want to know and make clear decisions.

In the following activity, the themes from the dimension of guidance and boundaries have been used in relation to both children.

Emotions:	Interactions with others:
Fear, scared, anxious, sad, distressed, angry, unsure, hyper-alert, worried, out of control, afraid and confused	Inappropriate adult expectations of children, leading to neglect Modelling poor adult behaviour – secretive, exploitative, violent, abusive and risky
Moral values:	**Boundaries:**
Not considering the needs of the children. Placing the children at risk of abuse from dangerous men. Not supporting education. Not providing the children with the skills and discipline to shape their behaviours	No set meal times, bed times or bath times. No boundaries around what the children can watch on television. An inability to respond assertively and set boundaries around adult behaviours towards the children

As we use thematic analysis and identify headings (themes), a picture begins to emerge out of the words of the children that their home environment is a place of disharmony and risk. According to Brandon *et al.* (2012), the coexistence of family disharmony, violence and neglect places children at higher risk of suffering significant harm. Both Darren and Leanne were living in an environment where the parental guidance was inappropriate and ineffective and the boundaries were inconsistent, fluid and risky. The lack of guidance and boundaries on both children was having a traumatic effect on Darren and Leanne. According to Wrench (2017), social workers should not underestimate the impact of trauma on children and particularly how this is manifested in the child's body as it responds to constantly experiencing feelings of fight or flight. She goes on to explain that children will have a sense of feeling undervalued and overlooked by adults that increases the likelihood of developmental behaviours that are over-reactive and aggressive. It is important that we understand the impact of poor and inappropriate parental guidance and the outcomes for children when boundaries are not set. Equally, it is important that connections are made between the different dimensions and how in each case outcomes in one area can trigger events and outcomes in another. For example, there was evidence in the case of Darren and Leanne that connections between the lack of parental guidance, poor parental supersivion and boundary-setting were having an impact on their development, their safety, their health and well-being. As a result, these connections and their outcomes had an effect on how both children experienced being cared for by their mother and grandmother. For Darren and Leanne their parental and care experience was bound up in feelings of insecurity, fear and instability.

Stability

Lack of stability in the lives of children can have a long-standing impact on their adult lives. In the process of completing this book, I read a commentary piece in the *Guardian* (2018a, 2018b, 2018c) by Iain Maitland about his childhood. He described how, as an only child, he experienced instability as a result of his parents' relationship and marriage breaking down. What caught my attention was his description of a family scene when he was 6.

> It was 1968 and we sat in the car outside my grandparents' house in West Norwood, London. My father and his mistress in the front, my mother and I in the back. My father turned to me … and said forcefully, "if your nan or grandpa ask, Alison is your teacher and she is staying with us for a while" … he had told me earlier in the year that she was our housekeeper. I knew she wasn't my teacher. I looked to my mother for explanation but she turned away from me, as if this was all perfectly normal, ignoring what was going on around her (p. 61).

Maitland (2018) goes on to describe an unsettled childhood as he was passed between parents when they eventually divorced and how he felt starved of love and affection and the impact this had on his physical and emotional well-being. I have used this description because it is not a social work case study where stability and the lack of it in the lives of children tend to create extreme images of chaos, aggression and unstable relationships. Though not as extreme as those cases that social workers come into contact with, it underlines the importance of a stable adult/family environment to enable a child to develop cognitively, physically and emotionally.

The Department of Health (2000:21) provides the following guidance on the dimension of stability within the domain of parenting capacity.

> Providing a sufficiently stable family environment to enable a child to develop and maintain a secure attachment to the primary care giver(s) in order to ensure optimal development. **This** includes ensuring secure attachments are not disrupted, providing consistency of emotional warmth over time and responding in a similar manner to the same behaviour. Parental responses change and develop according to the child's developmental progress. In addition, ensuring children keep contact with important family members and significant others.

In the lives of Darren and his sister, social workers were aware that Annie was struggling to provide both children with a stable family environment. Although with support some progress was made in terms of school attendance, there was concern about the appropriateness of the adult relationships and the danger they posed to the children and Annie. Most importantly, there was the issue of attachment and its relationship to Annie and her children, specifically how Darren was interpreting the drives and intentions of his mother when she told him that he was the 'man of the family' and how he appeared to be struggling to understand this in the context of the situation he was facing. What Darren was facing was the presence of predatory males and what he was beginning to understand was that his mother could not protect him or his sister. In theories of attachment, it is the strength of the emotions involved in the development of the parent–child relationship that, if cracked or broken, affects the emotional and psychological development of the child (Bowlby, 1988). In terms of Bowlby's influential theorising on attachment, Darren was experiencing anger, grief and depression because the lack of protection by his mother broke their attachment. The consequences were Darren's violent and aggressive outbursts.

Having concerns about the role of attachment in the lives of children and their parents and carers is worth some reflection on how this is understood and used in practice to make sense of the relationships between children with particular reference to stability. This is because, according to Bowlby (1988), 'healthy, happy and self-reliant adolescents and young adults are the products of stable homes in which both parents give a great deal of time and attention to their children' (p. 1). The work of Bowlby (1988) has been roundly criticised by feminists for its focus on the child in relation to *its mother* and the assumption of heterosexual relationships between a *husband and wife* all rooted in a belief that parenting is biologically pre-programmed and organised through a gendered order (Duchinsky *et al.*, 2015). But it remains a powerful template upon which social work policy and child protection practice are defined (Featherstone *et al.*, 2014). Although central concepts of attachment theory continue to guide child protection policies and practice and serious case reviews have called for social workers to 'understand the child within the context of attachment and the parent-child relationship' (Brandon *et al.*, 2012:52), how it is applied by social workers has become contested. Researchers and academics argue that attachment theory is applied too narrowly and punitively to the parenting capacity of single mothers (Krane *et al.*, 2010) or misapplied when trying to make sense of a child's behaviour and development (Shemmings and Shemmings, 2014). Given these arguments, it is worth taking some time to consider attachment theories in the context of parental learning disability and parenting capacity.

Pause and consider:

How do you use attachment theory to guide your understanding of the child's lived experience within the context of the parent–child relationship? Do you use observations, assessments, or educational or psychological reports about a child's developmental behaviours to make sense of stability and parenting capacity?

The effect of parenting that lacked stability on Darren and Leanne was presenting social workers with clear concerns for their safety and the long-term effects of both children becoming increasingly aware that the environment they were living in was not safe. Outcomes for Darren, short and long term, did not look positive. His self-worth and sense of identity were being seriously affected by his understanding of his role in the family and not being able to protect his sister and mother. Darren was also displaying and demonstrating anxiety and aggression as a response to living in an environment that was not providing him or his sister with stability of:

➢ Ensuring that his health needs can be met. Research findings suggest that children of parents with learning disabilities may suffer health problems because of a lack of hygiene and a lack of understanding about the importance of attending medical appointments and being able to carry out instructions (Cleaver and Nicholson, 2007). *The school reported that Darren's poor hygiene, which included head lice, and his poor eyesight were having an impact on his health.*

➢ Ensuring that his educational needs can be met. Research findings suggest that a child's cognitive development may be impaired or limited when parents with learning disabilities do not encourage school attendance, support school work and encourage learning in general (Cleaver *et al.,* 2011). Research also identified that children living in unsettled home environments are unable to concentrate because what is happening at home takes over their thinking (Abrahams, 1994). *The school reported that Darren's poor attendance, lateness and his unsettled behaviour were having a detrimental impact on his learning.*

➢ Ensuring that his cognitive and emotional development needs can be met. Research findings suggest that children exposed to violent relationships will suffer from anxiety and will either withdraw and become quiet or act out and become aggressive verbally and physically. According to research, there is an acceptance that boys are more likely to act out their distress by becoming anti-social and that girls are more likely to internalise their worries and become withdrawn and anxious (Velleman and Orford, 2001). Also, where the child is frightened by their parents' behaviour and there is no alternative safe adult around to help out or protect them, the impact on the child's feelings of self-worth and value are seriously impaired (Stanley *et al.*, 2010). *Social workers observed his aggressive and distressed behaviour and heard from Darren about his fears about the adult behaviour.*

➤ Ensuring a sense of a positive identity. Research findings suggest that if children are not provided with positive responses about who they are or their skills and abilities are not celebrated or they are left to fend for themselves, they are not able to develop a strong sense of self and identity (Cleaver and Nicholson, 2007).According to Aldridge and Becker (2003) where children feel they cannot protect themselves from parental violence or be able to protect a parent from violence they feel guilt, despair and develop a poor sense of identity (Aldridge and Becker, 2003). *Darren's sense of self was bound up in the identity of being the man of the house, and when he could not protect his sister or mother or enact this role, his sense of self-worth and value were clearly affected.*

➤ Ensuring that children experience positive and supportive relationships. Research findings show that where there are inconsistent parental behaviours, unsettled environments, and lack of guidance and boundaries, children feel anxious and have poor attachment experiences characterised by fear and uncertainty and that unplanned separations may lead children to assume roles beyond their years and to have feelings of helplessness and loss (Cleaver *et al.*, 2011). *Darren was assuming the role of protector and provider. His relationship with his mother and grandmother were affected by the feelings of fear, uncertainty, and unplanned separations.*

Emerging research evidence suggests that children living with parental learning disability face a range of challenges that are linked less to the intellectual limitations of their parents and more to the wider sociological ecology of poverty, isolation, stigmatization, vulnerability, unemployment, family histories, health problems and lack of support (Horwath, 2013). This ecology of need and pressures creates the conditions wherein the separate dimensions of parental capacity absorb and transform each other into accumulative risks of significant harm to the child. In the words of Gergen (2001), the 'the text becomes a skipping stone, flung along a pond, and as it skips and sinks it makes circles that ripple to the shores' (p. 605).

Where did all the ripples go?

What I would want to underline from this discussion is that there will be a number of Annies and Darrens being provided with supportive social work interventions across the UK and all will be different. We cannot make generalisations about learning disability parenting or assume that their children are more at risk than other children. Each parenting experience will be different and will be affected by the range of ecological, biological and societal demands and issues that cause different levels of stress. All of these stressors and issues will be experienced by all parents. Some will have the support and guidance from a network of family and friends, agencies and communities that can make all the difference to the child's living experience. However, if these networks of support are not available or break down or are simply not enough to protect the children, then social workers are often faced with intervening in challenging circumstances whereby they need to balance the needs and rights of the parent with the needs and rights of the children.

The social workers working with Darren and his sister continued to provide a range of interventions aimed at addressing the parenting issues that were impacting on the children. This included the following:

➤ Family support services aimed at helping Annie develop her parenting skills (that included her continued attendance at the parents' group) and introducing a range of visual aids to help her organise around the children's daily lives. Family support workers worked alongside Annie in her home to ensure that these were useful and meaningful.

➤ Direct work with Annie and her mother that focussed on providing a protective environment for her children and included work with Annie on developing an intimate relationship. Police and social workers worked together to remove Eddie and James from the children's home.

➤ Direct work with both children that focussed on feeling safe.

➤ Several agencies worked together to provide a network of universal and community-based services with the aim of ensuring that the children were safe at home.

It was acknowledged at core group meetings that support for Annie and her children needed to be long term and regular with the focus on helping her to develop and maintain good-enough parenting skills. It was agreed that this social work intervention should take place under a formal child protection plan because the children had already suffered significant harm and core group members believed the risks to the children remained a cause for concern. At this stage of the social work intervention a decision was made not to seek a legal framework, such as care or emergency proceedings via the courts to protect the children by seeking to remove them from their family and home. Instead a decision was made that the children's welfare and protection could be met by ongoing support provided using the registration of the children on a child protection plan. This decision was reached based on the 'no order' principle of Children Act 1989 – Section 1 (4) 'the court should not make an order unless to do so is considered better for the child than making no order' (White *et al.*, 1990).

The social work intervention and support continued for some time, and reports to the core group suggested that progress was being made. However, those working with Darren continued to be concerned about his behaviour. The school reported that although his attendance was better and his basic care was appropriate, his behaviour had become more aggressive and volatile. Social workers carrying out the direct work with Darren and his sister found that he had withdrawn completely from them, refusing to engage with activities and being verbally sexually aggressive towards them. This all came to a crisis one day when Darren ran away from school and, when found by staff and a family support worker, was so verbally and physically aggressive – his teacher described him as 'a bundle of spitting and hitting rage' – that they could not get near him to find out what was causing him so much distress.

Finding out what was happening for Darren was not achieved by talking to him or his sister or grandmother. While social workers speculated about his behaviour and the impact of the trauma of trying to protect his mother and sister from Eddie and James, Annie told another social worker during the parenting group what she thought was causing Darren to be so distressed. It transpired that while Annie appeared to understand and accept that James and Eddie posed a risk to the children, they continued to visit the family home late in the evenings, when they believed neither the police nor social workers would 'find out' and according to Darren 'he didn't like this'. More concerning was that Annie told the social worker that James and Eddie had introduced her to another male who lived on the same estate and who (she said) was nice to her and Leanne. According to Annie, he was just a friend and she did not 'do it with him' since he was 'not like that'. Through further investigation, concerns were confirmed that Annie was visiting a registered and known sex offender and taking Leanne with her.

The social work intervention changed and both children were taken 'into care' under the auspices of a section 31 Interim Care Order under the Children Act 1989 and placed with foster carers. Annie was supported through the process by advocates, social workers and a solicitor. Both children remained together in care, moving to a long-term fostering placement. They saw their mother regularly at the foster carer's, an arrangement that was reached after Darren told his foster carer that he did not feel safe with his mother at the children's centre. Darren was helped to attend school, and after receiving a Statement of Educational Needs, he developed and progressed. He attended a range of social events, and although he continued to present as anxious and challenging, he was helped to find different ways of expressing his feelings. Leanne also developed and responded well to living in foster care. Neither of the children returned to live with their mother. They both remained with their foster carers, who later became their adoptive parents.

Conclusion

What is evident from this exploration of risk and how this accumulates within the domain and dimensions of parental capacity as they are applied to parental learning disability is that we need to have a clearer understanding of each area and how they feed into one another to create either a positive childhood experience or an environment filled with fear, uncertainty and harm. While the Department of Health (2000) guidance provides a baseline of what is expected of parents, how these are understood, measured and applied in social work practice is vulnerable to misrepresentation, debate and bias, particularly for parents with a learning disability (Cleaver et al., 2011). I hope that as the discussion has evolved, it has provoked considerable reflection and challenged the reader to consider how they perceive and assess risks to children where parental learning disability is a factor. I also hope that the discussion and examination have prompted thinking about how parenting capacity is being assessed across the identified and predicted factors that currently dominate the risk factor milieu.

Without a doubt, assessing parenting capacity within the context of risk in child protection social work is a challenge. It is also a site of contested knowledge and understanding about parenting styles, parenting rights and parenting problems and how these impact on the child. This focus reinforces how social workers look at parenting. During this process of trying to make sense of parents with problems and why the parents are experiencing these problems, the needs of the child and the impact on them can take a back seat in a journey that has only one destination: a crossroads of decision-making about risk.

Understanding risk within the context of child protection social work is a swamp of messiness, uncertainty and riskiness where social workers try to navigate their way around problem parenting and how this impacts on the child. In this environment, social workers can find themselves lost and disorientated as they try to ensure that they are making the right decision – for the child and their parents and families. In response to their situation, social workers (the adults) focus on the problems of other adults (parents) at the expense of seeing the child and the impact on their lives. When social workers are faced with parental learning disability, this particular area of parenting challenges their skills and abilities to navigate risk and harm to the child. It is an area where social workers' knowledge and understanding about parenting capacity become tested, specifically as they try to make sense of how this impacts on the children. In the words of Sjoberg (2004:7), 'everyone is seeking to manage risk and they are guessing, because if they knew for certain, they would not be dealing with risk'.

What is also evident from the examination of parenting capacity in the context of parental learning disability is the impact on the child when the risks stack and gain momentum, producing an environment in which they are not only disadvantaged but also vulnerable to the risks posed by dangerous adults. In the case of Darren and his sister, their home situation was influenced by the tensions of different agency attitudes towards parental learning disability. Finding the most effective social work interventions to support Annie to address the cause and effect of the problem parenting, social workers failed to grasp the profound impact on Darren of his taking on responsibilities that were not appropriate, the effect on his education, his relationships and social opportunities and being exposed to violence and sexual abuse. It could be argued that the consequences for not grasping the issues meant that Darren and his sister were left too long in an unsafe home. This is one of the many challenges faced by social workers as they intervene in the complex lives of children like Darren and Leanne, and getting the balance between parental rights and needs and the needs and protection of the child is precarious. As Horwath (2013:203) points out, social workers need to ensure that they are not caught up in 'working at a pace that focusses primarily on the parents'. Ofsted (2012:13:35), reporting on child protection practices in Doncaster, opined that 'in too many assessments there was a lack of focus on the individual children and young people in favour of the adults in the household'.

How social workers achieve a balance when faced with complex family situations is an outstanding question with few meaningful answers. There is the political response that highlights the rise in referrals to Children's Services and specifically child protection teams as a result of growing poverty and greater deprivation where it is difficult to recruit skilled and experienced social workers (Hood *et al.*, 2016). There is the argument that the system of child protection and assessing risk is procedurally driven, leaving social workers to manage the formal and informal processes for predicting and managing risk (Broadhurst *et al.*, 2010). Finally, there are the debates about where social work is going in terms of their value base and keeping to the principles of social justice (Gray and Webb, 2013). While all the above debates provide important insight into the political, policy and ethical terrain in which child protection is operating and provide valuable discussions about the direction of social work as a profession, they all have a tendency to focus on adult needs and outcomes. As a consequence the impact and outcomes on and for children remain out of focus.

To help refocus on the child, I offer the following practice points:

➤ Ensure that you know the child in the context of their environment – their home and their community. Ask yourself how much you know about the locality and the estates where the child lives and what resources are available to them. For example, social workers working with Darren knew the estate and the community well. They had developed good relationships with neighbours and the community centre and knew how far he had to go to get chips. They also found out that the local chip shop frequently gave Darren sausage and chips to take home and did not ask for payment. They also found out that the neighbours were concerned for both children because they saw them playing outside in 'all weathers', unsupervised and being around older children who were actively involved in anti-social behaviour.

➤ Ensure that the child's experience is understood and acted upon. This should include understanding the impact on the child of taking on or being given responsibilities that are inappropriate, whether this is as a young carer to parents and siblings or as a protector. Some children will try to avoid telling social workers what their responsibilities are and how they have come about since they do not want sound disloyal to their parents. In the case of Darren, it was his sister, Leanne, who provided the information that told a story about what was happening in the home. Annie denied that she had told Darren he was the 'man of the house'. She also denied that both children were left to sort out their own breakfasts. However, when confronted with the issue of the free food from the chip shop, she acknowledged that Darren frequently brought home chips but she saw this as an achievement – getting something for free – which she found amusing.

➤ Ensure that the child's experience and how you have interpreted this are recorded. Use the words of the child as the focus for analysis. The words Darren used to describe how frightened and scared he had become as a result of not being able to protect his sister and mother were used by social workers to support their decision that he was suffering significant harm and was likely to continue to suffer.

➤ Ensure that you understand the needs of the child by having a sound knowledge of child development. Use this knowledge to understand the impact of problem parenting or parenting issues on the child in relation to their age, ethnicity, culture, health, education, cognitive and emotional needs. Darren was 8 and the social workers had a wealth of information from education, health and historical case notes to work with. They used this information, drawing up brief child-focussed chronologies that told them about his culture, family background, health and education and past behaviours.

➢ Ensure you engage and develop a relationship with the child that is based on trust and respect. Being clear about the social work role and responsibilities with children sets the ground rules. Some children will have a greater understanding than others why social workers are involved with them and their families. They may be suspicious, frightened and relieved. They may also have a range of expectations associated with the social work role, and how social workers help them become less suspicious or frightened depends on their relationship with the social worker. Both social workers working with Darren developed a good relationship with him and his sister which came over time and was influenced by the fact that they recognised the importance of the children's relationship with each other. This relationship was used to good effect when one of the social workers worked closely with other social workers to place him with foster carers and support contact with his mother, Annie.

Outcomes for children depend on the skills, knowledge and practice of the social worker in understanding their experiences of being parented and the impact on the child's health and well-being when things go wrong. There are multiple challenges for social workers to recognise the cause and effect of parenting capacity on children and none more challenging than those faced when parents have a learning disability. However, the child will be, in many senses, the compass. The words and actions of Darren and Leanne provided social workers with a way to navigate the complexity of their family situation. It did take time and they advanced across a tightrope that meant they could not rush at the situation but knew they had to stay focussed if they were to get to the side that met Darren and Leanne's needs.

7

Women and Neglect. Christopher's Story: My Mum Doesn't Want Me

Millet (1977) highlights the insidious meaning that lies behind the words used by influential Freudian theorists to argue and describe what it takes to be feminine.

The glorification of femininity, the family, female submission and above all motherhood. (Millet, 1977:208)

This archetypal myth of femininity wrapped in notions of motherhood has influenced how society has perceived mothers since time immemorial and more importantly has been used to construct ideas about mothering through a powerful discourse about its relation to the functions of the family. What defines being a good mother continues to influence government policies and shape professional social work practice through perceptions of mothers and mothering.

Women as mothers continue to be judged by whether they live up to the iconic saintly expectations of mothering myths that construct mothers as being committed to the care and protection of their children 'come what may' (Featherstone et al., 2014). Or they are judged by their transgressions (sins) of being childless, selfishly pursuing a career or a relationship that subsequently results in their failing to nurture and protect their child. The worst kind of mothering transgression is to openly say you are not coping or do not want your child or children.

This chapter explores the neglect of children with a specific focus on the over-representation of women as mothers in cases of neglect. I explore the construction of mothering in British society and its impact on social work policy and practice by posing questions about how we understand a mothering identity in relation to the neglect of children. In the work of feminist theorists, the term 'mothering' refers to the experiences associated with the role, responsibilities and practice of being a mother (O'Reilly, 2004).

Using the story of Christopher, I will examine how neglect was understood within a powerful discourse of mothering and describe how this shaped social workers' responses. An important feature of Christopher's story will be an explanation about how his wishes and feelings were gathered and presented to a family group conference (FGC). This explanation will highlight the tensions and dilemmas of bringing a child's voice to an adult protective process.

Christopher's story

Christopher (age 6) lived with his mother, Penny, and his sister, Lauren (age 4). They are white British and though not practicing any religion Penny was baptised into the Church of England. Penny originated from London and moved to Cross Towns with her partner after Christopher was born. Shortly after the birth of Lauren, Penny and her partner separated and she moved to live in social housing on a well-established estate with access to a range of public services.

Both children attended their local primary and nursery school based on the same site. The children attended regularly and were well presented in terms of their clothes and personal hygiene. Christopher was described by teachers as a 'bit of a challenge' to teach because he struggled to concentrate on set tasks and became silly and was easily distracted by others. His reading was below average and he could withdraw into a mood, refusing to talk or take part in classroom activities, which meant that he was isolated and had few friends. His sister presented as the opposite. She was lively and well liked at school by peers and teaching staff. Although her reading was below that of her age, she was considered to be a little girl who tries hard and is 'lovely to teach'.

Both children were white British and were described by education and health staff as attractive and pretty children who looked like they had 'stepped out of a glossy magazine'. However, their mother suffered from depression and health professionals became concerned when she told them she was struggling to provide basic care for the children. A referral to child protection was triggered when both children's school attendance and appearance changed significantly over a short period of time and Lauren told teaching staff that she and Christopher were looking after themselves because mum had 'gone away'.

As a result of a child protection investigation under section 47 of Children Act 1989, it was revealed that Penny had left the children in the care of her brother while she went away to stay with a friend. Her brother said that he had agreed to care for the children for only a few days and when Penny had not come back after a week he had gone back to work, asking a neighbour to 'look in on them'. What this meant for both children was that they were often waking up to an empty house and having to fend for themselves until their uncle or the neighbour arrived. As a result of the investigation, it was agreed that a family group conference (FGC) would be held to look at the issues of need and risk with a specific focus on identifying how to help Penny to care for her children.

Before the FGC, social work interventions included working closely with Penny, her brother, the children and professionals from health and education. During the social work intervention with Penny, she told social workers that she did not want her children. She said she could not provide them with the love and care they needed. She said that she had too many needs of her own and that her children were not safe with her. It was this information that was presented at the FGC and that led to social work interventions that included placing both children with short-term foster carers while social workers pursued a legal framework that released them for adoption.

Neglect – A mother's voice?

Research tells us that neglect is the most common form of child abuse, and findings from serious case reviews highlight that neglect is a feature in 60 per cent of child deaths (Brandon *et al.,* 2013). Research also suggests that neglect is a *crime* of mothers, and the social work literature about neglect of children confirms that mothers tend to be the focus of social work assessments (Horwath, 2013). However, although mothers appear to be the focus of social work attentions in cases of neglect, Farmer and Owen (1998) point out that when women as mothers do ask for help from Children's Services, they are signposted to alternative services such as their GP or told to seek help from their families or their needs and those of their children are minimised. Of equal concern are research findings that suggest that referrals of neglect may not be considered to be child protection. Indeed, the risks to the child or children are not considered to be high or imminent and in many cases referrals of neglect tend to be sifted out of the child protection system (Davies and Ward, 2012), a practice approach that Brandon *et al.* (2013) argue is set within a professional mind-set of 'this is only neglect' (p. 10).

Although research has provided a significant contribution to our understanding and knowledge about neglect of children and how in some cases it can lead to fatal outcomes, the social work literature also acknowledges that definitions of neglect are contested (Howarth, 2013). As a result, professionals will have different views about what constitutes neglect and in practice this has led to tensions and disagreements about whether a child is at risk or in need. The operational definition of neglect for England is:

> The persistent failure to meet the child's basic physical and/or psychological needs, likely to result in the serious impairment of the child's health and development. Neglect may occur during pregnancy as a result of maternal substance abuse. Once a child is born, neglect may involve a parent or carer failing to:
>
> ➤ provide adequate food, clothing and shelter (including exclusion from home or abandonment)
>
> ➤ protect a child from physical and emotional harm or danger
>
> ➤ ensure adequate supervision (including the use of inadequate caregivers).
>
> It may also include neglect of, or unresponsiveness to, a child's basic emotional needs.
>
> (HM Government, 2010:38)

An important aspect of neglect is that it is considered an act of omission. It is the failure to perform parental duties that provide physical and emotional support and attention and the failure to act and take actions to protect the child.

Tanner and Turney (2003:26) posit that neglect can be understood as the 'sustained and chronic breakdown in the relationship of care'. Understanding the specifics involved in a breakdown of care has been helpfully set out by both HM Government (2010) and research findings (Davies and Ward, 2012; Brandon et al., 2013).

Malnutrition   Defined as the life-threatening loss of weight or failure to gain weight or serious consequences of neglecting to nourish the child. Findings from serious case reviews identified that many children who died or nearly died of malnutrition were not in the child protection system, and issues of isolation, non-school attendance, parental aggression towards professionals and withdrawal from family members and the community were important factors that can 'signal life-threatening harm for a child' (Brandon et al., 2013:8).

Medical neglect   Described as the neglect of parents to follow or seek medical advice. This is particularly relevant where the child has complex health needs. Consideration also needs to be given to those children whose basic health needs are not met as a result of failures to keep immunisations up to date or be registered with a GP. Health professionals tended to be overly optimistic about parents' neglecting to keep appointments, giving them the benefit of the doubt and in some cases 'shielding them from children's social care' (Brandon et al., 2013:9). Missed appointments should be followed up and should not be, as in the case of Hamzah Khan, the reason GP services were withdrawn (Warner, 2015). Children can easily disappear from view, placing them at risk of significant harm.

Nutritional neglect   This is a much-debated and contested area and one which has received media and government attention. There has been an array of celebrity chefs promoting healthy foods in school and government drives to improve the health of the nation with the publication of the Eatwell Guide (Public Health England, 2016), aimed at protecting and improving the nation's health. Although the definition of nutritional neglect is challenging to most health professionals, the domain of parenting capacity from the assessment framework (Department of Health, 2000) outlines that a failure to provide appropriate diet is a type of neglect. Inadequate nutrition linked to poor diet has been associated with poor behaviour, lack of concentration, malnutrition, poor bone development, low academic achievement, malnutrition and obesity, which all have implications for children's long-term health and development (Sabin et al., 2007).

Emotional neglect   Failure to meet the child's emotional needs, including developing their sense of a positive self through the development of a safe and good child–parent relationship. As Brandon et al. (2013:11) assert, parents can 'wittingly and unwittingly be a source of danger rather than comfort to their child'. Examples of a parental emotional neglect are where a parent is not able to make a cognitive connection to the child. Simply, the parent or carer is unable to see the child as a child in terms of their emotional maturity and/or their physical skills and abilities. Expectations of children become unrealistic resulting in children being overly criticized, denigrated or teased for not being able to meet the adult's exacting standards (Howarth, 2013).

Educational neglect Failure to provide learning or support intellectual development can have a significant impact on the child. According to the Department of Education (2016:14) final report *Pathways to harm, pathways to protection: a triennial analysis of serious case reviews 2011 to 2014*, school 'can promote good overall development and provide a buffer against adversities for the child both within and beyond the home'. Although serious case review findings highlight that neglect featured highly amongst infants and pre-school children, non-school attendance for pre-school and older children leads to isolation and the invisibility of the child (Brandon *et al.,* 2013) and, where neglect is already occurring, can increase the risk of harm to the child (Department of Education, 2016:14).

Physical neglect The failure to provide stimulation, appropriate clothing and basic hygiene. Physical development depends on providing children not only a good diet but also a range of opportunities to develop their skills to run, jump, climb and skip. The child who is strapped in a buggy or a high chair for long periods of time or locked in a room or the infant left in a cot will demonstrate apathetic behaviours, will be withdrawn and show levels of anxiety when they try to explore the world around them (Horwath, 2013). Those children who have been physically neglected are susceptible to bullying, rejection and social isolation. Learning from serious case reviews highlights that those children who have suffered rejection through chronic physical neglect suffer from long-term mental ill health and find it hard to trust others or ask for help (Brandon *et al.,* 2013).

Lack of supervision and guidance The failure to provide a safe and child-friendly environment with good adult supervision can lead to life-threatening accidents and place the child at risk of significant harm as a result of drowning, poisoning, falls and fires (Davies and Ward, 2012; Brandon *et al.,* 2013). There is growing evidence that children who are technically left to fend for themselves with little or no adult supervision and guidance become anti-social and aggressive and are more likely to become involved in risk-taking behaviours that lead to social isolation or violent out-of-control behaviours (Howe, 2005). These behaviours were evident in the case of the two young brothers (ages 11 and 12) who, after years of neglect that included a lack of parental supervision and guidance, carried out a violent crime of physical and sexual assault against two other children and who the sentencing judge said showed a 'chilling detachment and lack of remorse' (*Guardian*, 2010).

Findings and outcomes from research and serious case reviews are salient reminders that there should be no mind-set that suggests that neglect is somehow a less harmful type of abuse. The fact that neglect can be harmful and fatal needs to be better understood, and a mind-set that seeks to minimise this needs to be critically examined. There are feminist concerns that the mind-set of 'it is just neglect' has been perpetuated by the language of mothering which has influenced an interpretation based on an understanding that a mother's participation 'in the daily care of children is obligatory' (Risley-Curtiss and Heffernan, 2003). As a consequence, other feminist theorists and I believe that the phrase 'it is just neglect' is being interpreted as 'it is poor mothering' (Warner, 2015).

It is this interpretation and understanding that feminist theorists and I believe have led professionals to see neglect as a different type of abuse closely associated with femininity, mothers and mothering. Although there appears to be an acceptance that neglect is a fluid and diverse concept, this knowledge is not afforded to concepts of mothering (Milner, 2001; Featherstone *et al.*, 2014; Warner, 2015). In contrast, the social work literature and research findings highlight that parental changes in neglect cases focus on mothers and their mothering capacity (Cree, 2015).

In this discussion, I pose the question, is neglect the voice of mothers? Are women as mothers trying to express their fears, anxieties and frustrations about the burden of responsibility and accountability for their children in their neglectful behaviours? Certainly, Christopher's mother, Penny, was expressing her fears and anxieties about being a mother to two children whom she did not believe she could care for and protect.

After the birth of Christopher, she had asked for help, saying that she could not cope because he was a 'colicky' baby and she needed some respite from him. Penny was not offered the support she wanted, but arrangements were made via the health visitor for Penny to attend a mums-and-baby massage group. When Lauren was born, Penny was diagnosed with post-natal depression and again sought help from Children's Services by requesting some respite care. At the time, Penny was offered a range of community support services – mother-and-baby groups, a post-natal depression group and a Home Start visiting scheme to help mothers who were isolated.

Although Penny initially agreed to accept the support offered, she later declined any help because she said she had found a part-time temping job. There was no follow-up to these requests from Penny. Social workers closed the case, and health reduced their involvement because both children were accessing education. When later social workers, health and police became involved with the family, Penny's response to agencies' empathy and anger at her neglect of Christopher and Lauren was to 'dig in' by refusing any help or any interventions aimed at helping her to change her parenting or, as she put it, 'her mind'. What Penny knew that the professionals appeared to be ignoring was that she was living in fear of how far she would go – how far she had to descend in her neglect of the children before anyone would listen to her and take her seriously. For Penny, her neglect of her children was a cry for help.

Becoming and being a mother are set within a vision of the all-giving, ever-present and self-sacrificing mother (Bassin *et al.,* 1994). Equally, motherhood is presented and deemed to represent the pinnacle of womanhood and femininity. We only have to take the time to examine how motherhood is depicted in the media and the growing trend that associates being a good mother with physical attributes of being thin and attractive alongside being successful in the home, work and choice of male partner with whom to produce attractive children. The language used is normative and seeks to promote heterosexuality, class and whiteness in a world where the alternative – schoolgirl mums who choose to get pregnant so they can get a flat; drunken, drug-addled, hardened, pinch-nosed women who produce multiple children to multiple partners from different racial and ethnic backgrounds; 'lard-gutted slappers who will drop their knickers in the blink of an eye'; mothers who choose to stay with violent men; and single black mothers whose children become violent gang members – is feared and vilified and seen as the 'scourge of contemporary Britain' (Tyler, 2008:18). Whereas one narrative is evocative and symbolic of the respectable, responsible and resplendent mother, the other generates feelings of disgust, anger and anxiety over female sexuality, fertility and reproduction (Tyler, 2008).

The narrative of disgust and anger has been used effectively in the media to characterise a mothering identity requiring moral regulation through state interventions designed to constrain, contain and change (Warner, 2015). This narrative has been used to motivate social work policies and practice and sustain a 'binary discourse of good and evil' (Warner, 2015:93) about mothering that has been translated into assessment practices that not only look at risk and the needs of the child but also seek to change parental behaviours by using state interventions in ways that are understood as punitive, finger-wagging and threatening (Horwath, 2013).

Mothers who are primarily at the sharp end of these practice approaches find themselves bound up in a situation whereby their identity as a woman and as a mother is dispossessed by the state. How they go about reclaiming an identity that helps them to function, even if they know this may not be accepted socially or may place them at risk, is fraught with tension, self-blame and loss. How do women as mothers perform within a legislative and socially constructed child protection framework that they did not choose to enter? When they do choose to enter this framework, they find that their survival depends upon their performing to a set of mothering norms that seek to improve and fix them in order for recognition of good mothering to be conferred.

How should women like Penny and the many others who have faced the condemnation of the media and courts have asked for help from the state and their institutions that recognise only a certain set of mothering norms? To get the help they believe they need, what would these mothers say to social workers? Do we understand what these women as mothers are asking for? When Penny says she feels she can no longer care for her children or protect them, do we dismiss this as a woman being over-dramatic? In the situations below, what would social workers' responses be to the mothers asking for help?

Pause and consider:

What would the social work response be to each mother's request in the following vignettes? As you consider both requests, reflect on the political and policy implications of mothers asking for help.

'My head is so mixed up as a result of what my dad did to me. Social workers did nothing when I told them. The drugs help and the shoplifting means I can provide for them. I want them to have what I didn't and I need help. It is not really neglect – and I know what real neglect is. I am trying to be the best mother I can and you are trying to take my kids off me'.

'I need you to take my kids into care. Not forever but for a short time so that I can get my life sorted out. I have got involved with a man who is 'pimping me' out to friends and other men and I have to leave them alone most nights to avoid being beaten up by him. I try to do the best I can during the day and I have a few friends who will take them during the day. But I left them too long with a friend and now they won't help unless I pay them half of what I earn'.

I suspect there will be two responses to the above cases. First, there will be a response that harbours feelings bound up in exclamations about motherhood and mothering. For example, a question that seeps into our subconscious is, how did these women get into this situation in the first place? Second, this question will be quickly followed by thinking that is bound up in institutional policies and practice related to budget-led resources.

It is unlikely that mothers asking for help will be as candid as the women in the above cases. Many women know how they will be judged should they be so open about the help they need. They know that asking for help as a mother is a very mixed-up declaration. Equally, many mothers who struggle to parent are themselves at a loss to understand why they are not able to be the instinctive mother they are told is their natural position.

There is a connection between mothering and being lost. In familiar metaphoric terms, when it is a question of mothering, we get lost in the passions and tend to run wild with visceral emotions, which take us to the deepest and most remote of places. There the dual identities of woman and mother become entwined in a dual relationship so intense that the dimension of parenting is lost or forgotten. Meanwhile, the women have to fight for their own survival because of the violence of others, mental illness, childhood fears and experiences of poverty and social deprivation. Being a mother fighting for survival under the overbearing weight of a dominant discourse that blames *them* for their situation – whether this is being poor, living with violence or having mental illness – means that achieving the idealised concept of mothering becomes impossible (DiQuinzio, 1999).

However, the impossibility of a mother's situation is rarely recognised, and when they do neglect their child, this is rarely understood as a cry for help; rather, it is viewed and perceived within a moral framework designed to punish and oppress them. Warner (2015) observed that, in the reporting on the death of Hamzah Khan, 'the domestic violence in the case was constructed as something that should not arouse compassion for Hutton *(mother)* but as something she was using to deflect attention from her accountability as a mother who failed her child by neglecting him' (p. 61).

Being compassionate and empathetic for mothers who neglect their children is fraught with psychological challenges because our thinking about motherhood and mothering is shaped by ideologies that cast mothers as the child's primary protector and provider of care. According to Warner (2015), these ideologies are difficult to resist and have influenced social work practice in areas of neglect where the focus tends to be on 'fixing' the mothers as opposed to seeing the needs of the child and making a decision about removing them.

What does this focussing on the mothers mean for the child or children? In many high-profile child deaths, the issue of failing to see or understand the needs of the child is a constant (Brandon *et al.*, 2013) and is a reminder that, while social workers and other professionals set their sights and practice on changing mothering behaviours, paradoxically the needs and risks to the child are neglected.

How can social workers resist a dominant discourse about mothering to refocus their attention on the impact on the child? How can they do this in such a way that considers the needs of the child and mother equally? When a child tells social workers that his mother 'doesn't want him' (as Christopher did), how do we consider his needs without becoming caught up in the turmoil of emotions that lead us down a pathway of interventions we feel bound to follow because the alternative goes against all that we understand about constructions of mothering?

In the case of Christopher, the practice approach was to hold an FGC. The practice of the FGC is now discussed with an explanation of the approach and its impact on decision-making in relation to Christopher and his sister, Lauren.

Family group conferencing: A message to mothers

Family group conferencing is a method to aid social work decision-making and was introduced to child care social work practice in England in the early 1990s. It is a decision-making method that originates from New Zealand, where it was introduced to meet the needs of the indigenous Maori population at a time when state interventions were felt to be failing to meet the needs of Maori children and their families (Provan, 2012). The introduction of the FGC to social work practice in New Zealand was an acknowledgement of the power and role of the family, communities and community leaders to discuss and make decisions about the problems affecting their families and their children. The intent of the FGC for New Zealand was to 'return the decision-making power back to family networks from the state systems that had usurped them' (Merkel-Holguin and Marcynyszyn, 2015:725).

When the FGC was introduced to child care social work practice in the UK, it was initially used as a response for dealing with family breakdown. It is now widely used across the UK in cases of abuse, neglect and youth offending (Merkel-Holguin and Marcynyszyn, 2015). Although the model of the FGC as a decision-making process has been translated into social work practice across the UK with some success (Burford, 2017), there are critical questions emerging about how it has been used with families in the UK. Many of the questions focus on the translation of a method from New Zealand, where the FGC was rooted in community-centred approaches, to the UK, where families and communities are becoming increasingly fragmented and isolated as a result of high unemployment and poverty and, more importantly, where the *traditional* role of social services to work in communities has been diminished (Pranis, 2017).

While the debates about the use of the FGC as an intervention for promoting change through collective responsibility and accountability continue and more questions are asked, a question I pose through the experience of Penny as a mother attending an FGC is, does family group conferencing send a message – not by name but in subliminal thinking that comes out as a message – to mothers that their mothering is being questioned? Of course, in reality, this is the case. By using the word 'family' and promoting a family focus, we are creating the words and language to shape thinking and notions of how a certain type of family unit should look and behave and, in particular, what type of mother and mothering we would expect to see. This frame of thinking, other feminists and I have argued, has been used to full effect in the decision-making process of the FGC (Provan, 2012).

In the case of Christopher and his sister, the FGC was used as a social work intervention for responding to the concerns about neglect. Although the FGC is considered a formal multi-agency decision-making process and can be used effectively as part of protective processes where children are considered to be at risk (Pennell and Burford, 2017), it does not carry the weight of decision-making associated with a child protection conference. While the outcomes from an FGC can lead to legal social work interventions, the ethos and practice approach are about prevention and support.

The FGC was introduced in Cross Towns in the early 1990s to address a range of parental problems that were considered a community-based response to growing unemployment, alcohol and drug use, and adult mental health issues after the town's largest employer closed down. Like some new towns in the UK, Cross Towns had been built around a large industry, and the town was influenced by the range of different Celtic cultures of the people from Scotland and Northern Ireland who moved to the town for work. This migration brought with it a strong cultural connection that centralised motherhood through religion, philosophy and social status.

For many Scottish and Northern Irish families, motherhood was symbolic of status, continuity and progress (Walter, 2000). The archetypal white middle-class family divided into two oppositional spheres of caring and providing was not overtly that of Scottish or Northern Irish culture. Mothering was something that all women of the immediate and extended family took responsibility for. The emotional care and protection of the children were interdependent, complementary and interwoven and overseen by the grandmother, who was very much the head of the home and who promoted the image and social identity of the strong mother (Walter, 2000). The financial provision to the family was not always the exclusive responsibility of men, and for these Scottish and Northern Irish women, their influential role and status in their homes and the community were highly valued.

Although there were variations among the many Scottish and Northern Irish heritage families, the role of the mother and mothering was hugely influential in the community. This relationship between motherhood and mothering and issues of family and home were complex. For these migrant women, the notion of family and home had a specific resonance as they were 'simultaneously linked to a homeland of origin and to settled homes of destination' (Walter, 2000:51). The cultural identity of these women was central to how they managed and negotiated living in a different place and space, and they used their family positioning of motherhood and mothering when actively engaging with the community and state-led agencies.

Adapting the FGC to respond to the needs of the Cross Towns community drew upon the cultural identities of these women, reducing the number of children being made the subject of child protection plans and care proceedings. The community response to the FGC as a method for bringing together families, the wider community and professionals to provide creative, pragmatic and protective solutions to family problems was considered successful. However, although the use of the FGC appeared to meet the needs of this specific community, few questions were asked about the impact of imposing a cultural mothering identity on the mothers who were central to the process. It took the experience of Penny to bring into stark focus issues of a lived social experience that simply did not mirror that of the 'other' group.

Penny was white British and her own cultural background was in contrast to that of the more influential Scottish and Northern Irish culture and she was essentially outside of the dominant culture. The dominance of the culture was often underlined by many of the professionals who themselves were from the same ethnic and cultural backgrounds and through the use of FGC co-produced a mothering ideology that promoted the notion of being a strong woman and mother. My own Northern Irish heritage was steeped in a cultural mothering ideology that promoted mothering practices of self-sufficiency, being fiercely independent from 'outside' help and doing what was necessary in terms of managing domestic and paid work to ensure my motherhood entitlement and social standing.

I understood the women of Cross Towns and comfortably slipped into a relationship of inclusiveness and knowingness that essentially provided a cultural template for belonging. For Penny this cultural and ethnic template influenced the FGC process, and under the full glare of a strong mothering ideology of standards and expectations, her mothering was judged as not belonging. Her own social identity and culture were submerged into a generalised and homogenised cultural notion of motherhood and mothering.

Penny attended the FGC with her brother and maternal aunt. A range of professionals attended the FGC, head teacher (woman), class teacher (woman), social worker (woman), child care manager (man), health visitor (woman) and police child liaison officer (man) who knew the children, had been in contact with Penny and had come to know the family situation as a result of being involved in the section 47 investigation. All of the professionals attending the FGC were experienced and well used to this method of decision-making. They were used to families and specifically the women of the community working closely with professionals to resolve the issues. However, on this occasion, Penny's starting point was that she did not want her children and the only help she would accept was both children being taken into care.

The group found it difficult to find a response to what they perceived as a challenge to the dominant 'home' culture and its and mothering. Attempts to engage Penny in any plans aimed at keeping her and the children together were either dismissed or resisted. Everyone present believed they were trying to find a way that promoted the best outcome for the children. Professionals and the family made a range of offers of services and support aimed at helping Penny meet what they believed was her mothering commitment to her children.

The group of professionals found it difficult to find a language to help them understand that Penny's needs may be separate from those entangled with meeting the needs of her children. All those present became caught between a discourse that promoted the centrality of motherhood in the lives of women and children and an alternative that not only challenged the dominant ideology but questioned the notion that mothers must be mothers.

This failure to consider that Penny may have separate needs and what these may be or look like without her children meant that the support and interventions proposed were all understood through ideas and notions of being a child whose mother was rejecting them. It was difficult to shift the focus away from mothering that fosters nurturing, love and commitment because all those present were looking at the situation through a 'prism of their own gendered ... *childhood* ... identities' (Hollway and Featherstone, 1997:4). It took time to shift the focus. Through the skills of the FGC chair, the support of the social worker and the words of Christopher and Lauren, decisions were made that the children would be taken into care using section 20 of the 1989 Children Act:

> Every local authority shall provide accommodation for any child in need within their area who appears to them to require accommodation as a result of
>
> (c) *The person who has been caring for him being prevented (whether or not permanently, and for whatever reason) from providing him with suitable accommodation or care.*

It was also agreed that, during the period of care, the local authority social workers would engage Penny in the adoption process, which would include providing her with information and access to counsellors to ensure that she fully understood the decision she was making. This decision was accepted and agreed to by Penny, who said that for the first time in a long time she could 'breathe', and although she remained frightened for herself, she no longer felt frightened for her children since, in her words, 'she was now being a good mother'.

The impact on the group, particularly Christopher and Lauren's head teacher and class teacher, can only be described as shattering. Neither of them agreed with the decision, which they felt was too final and extreme. They both said that they believed neither of the children had suffered any real significant harm, and although Penny had been neglectful, they felt that the factors contributing to her neglect of the children could be overcome with counselling and practical support to help with the children.

According to Horwath (2013:1), this professional response to parental neglect is not unusual and is in keeping with findings from research that suggests that professionals focus their attention on resolving the presenting parental problems rather than look more closely at the impact on the child. It has been surmised by research findings that professionals respond differently to parental neglect because they fail to understand the 'root cause' of this specific type of abuse (Horwath, 2013:1).

However, there is something in the language of neglect and its close association with aspects of mothering that might offer an explanation. To be a mother is to be committed to meeting the demands and needs of your child. To neglect these commitments and demands is to transgress a mother's maternal and feminine instincts. It is this close association that other feminists and I believe is worthy of examination (Warner, 2015). If we are to fully understand neglect, we need to begin a conversation at the practice level about how we respond to and understand mothering. If we fail to have an open discussion about the inter-relatedness of neglect and mothering, we will continue to lose sight of the child because of a narrative that focusses on condemnation as opposed to understanding. The power of this narrative was evident in the case of Hamzah Khan; in the summing up, Judge Roger Thomas, QC, said he was sentencing Hamzah's mother, Amanda Hutton, for 'the terrible failures to fulfil the most basic responsibilities that you, as a mother, should have fulfilled' (*The Times*, 2008:31).

Engaging the neglected child in protective decision-making

We are all able to conjure up a mental image of a neglected child. Images are readily available from the media and practice. However, it is more difficult to capture the impact of neglect on a child. Whereas bodily injuries from physical abuse are often visible or can be detected on the bones through old injuries, a child's fear, isolation, secrecy, poor hygiene, hunger, worry and general feelings of uncertainty are not easily seen or readily connected to the formal lived experiences of abuse (Phillips, 2014).

Evidence from research (Davies and Ward, 2012) suggests that neglect and emotional abuse often overlap because parents who ignore or who are unable to provide basic care are indicating that they either do not understand or do not care. This overlapping produces a set of complex emotions that together have a significant impact on the child and how they relate to the outside world. For example, children living in neglectful environments are less likely to tell anyone what is happening and, even when they feel frightened and confused, are more likely to want to protect their parents (Davies and Ward, 2012). This places children living in neglectful family environments under further pressure to remain silent. However, when they do signal to professionals that they need help, this may be followed by a reluctance to readily engage with social workers.

For example, in their research, Cossar *et al.* (2013) identified a number of factors that hinder children from being able to talk about their experiences to social workers.

➢ They feel that they deserve what is happening to them.

➢ They find it difficult to acknowledge that the parent they love is being abusive.

➢ They struggle to understand their parents' unpredictable behaviour when the relationship is sometimes good.

➢ They feel confused about the often fluid boundaries in their relationship and don't understand when they are expected to be more grown up than they are.

(Cossar *et al.*, 2013:iv)

How do social workers engage and intervene in the lives of the neglected child? The *Working Together* guidance provides a set of principles for working with children who come into contact with social workers:

➢ developing a direct relationship with the child

➢ obtaining information from the child about his or her situation and needs

➢ eliciting the child's wishes and feelings – about their situation now as well as plans for the future

➢ providing the child with honest and accurate information about the current situation, as seen by professionals, and future possible actions and interventions

➢ involving the child in key decision-making

➢ providing appropriate information to the child about his or her to protection and assistance

➢ inviting children to make recommendations about the services and assistance they need and/or are available to them.

(HM Government, 2015a, 2015b:1.18)

How these principles are employed in practice remains a challenge. Particularly challenging are those principles that focus on ensuring the participation of the child in decision-making processes through direct work that seeks to find out what they are feeling, what they want now and what they want for the future. This is because including the child's voice in decision-making in the field of child protection is a relatively new concept (Cossar *et al.*, 2014). Practical guidance such as ideas about how this is done and how to present a child's wishes and feelings to formal meetings is limited in the social work literature (Kennan *et al.*, 2018). Existing social work literature tends to focus on ensuring the participation of the child rather than offer ideas about how to do this. As a result, eliciting and presenting a child's wishes and feelings to formal meetings continue to be a mixed bag and to depend on the relationship and skills of the individual social worker (Kennan *et al.,* 2018).

Social workers working with Christopher and Lauren carried out direct work with both children that included observing them at home and at school and in a children's centre. This direct work also included engaging both children in a range of creative activities designed to find out what was going on for them. The activities included drawings and artwork. Evidence from research suggests that engaging neglected children in drawing is a useful way of helping them express how they feel and a way of gaining some understanding about what they are experiencing (Davies and Ward, 2012). However, although drawings can be useful, we need to take care when interpreting them. According to Cossar *et al.* (2014), social workers are all too ready to adopt adult interpretations of a child's wishes and feelings in their presentations to an adult audience.

Christopher and Lauren did engage with the direct work. Over a period of time, they expressed how they felt about their situation through drawings and talking. They did this very differently. Lauren readily responded to the activities and questions of the social workers. She told social workers that Christopher cried all the time, but she didn't since she wanted to go live with someone else, not her uncle, 'so that mummy could get better'. She also told social workers what she wanted

- a new mummy and daddy
- a pink bedroom
- not to feel sad or frightened.

Christopher was more reserved in his response. However, he told social workers that 'his mummy doesn't want him and he is scared of going to live with someone else because, he knew he would never see her again'. However, he also said that he wanted

- mummy to be happy
- not to be left alone
- to be fed
- to feel safe.

From Lauren's pragmatic and practical response to the situation whereby she showed that she wanted to have some control over what the future might hold to Christopher's sense of loss and finality, both children were saying, albeit in different ways, that they were unhappy in their current daily lives. What this information told the social workers was that if the current problems were not attended to, both children were facing rather bleak futures, a situation both children already knew.

Social workers decided to present Christopher and Lauren's wishes and feelings using their artwork with no interpretations. This decision was taken when Lauren told the social workers that she wanted her 'thinking and feeling clouds' to be shown to the people. Christopher was not as eager for his work to be presented but he did agree that the social worker could tell people how he felt. Although the social workers believed that they were able to present the wishes and feelings of both children authentically, they were fully aware of the potential tensions that this information may bring to the decision-making process of the FGC.

These tensions are best described by the adults who attended the FGC concerning Christopher and Lauren. Some found it difficult to put aside their adult reasoning and interpretations and were particularly concerned about Lauren's pragmatic perspective and whether this should be used to inform decisions about her future. Others said Christopher's statement was a heartfelt plea for his mother to change her mind which subsequently led to her feeling pressurised by those present to accept support to keep both children at home.

Presenting the wishes and feelings of Christopher and Lauren did support the decision-making of the FGC. The children were placed together with foster parents under section 20 of Children Act 1989 and although this was an outcome that neither child really wanted, they did settle and remained in care until they were adopted. During this period, social workers did hope that with support both children could be returned to Penny's care. However, Penny remained resolute that she did not want to parent her children.

When the adoption process was completed, Penny disappeared from her children's lives. She had said she did not want any contact with her children. Both children remained with their adoptive parents, and although Christopher had some difficult teenage years, they both had successful adoptions. Christopher gained an apprenticeship as an electrician and with the support of his 'father' worked locally. Lauren went off to university, moving away from home to become a graphic designer.

Conclusion

The construction of mothering continues to be a flawed ideological vision. This devotion to a fixed vision of maternal perfection has had a disastrous effect on how mothers and mothering are constructed in social work. This construction is binary and is presented as a simple either/or of 'good/bad' that is translated into 'deserving/undeserving' of services. The damage that this thinking does to service provision and practice is made visible in the discourse that surrounds neglect and how this form of abuse has become located within understandings of femininity and all that is maternal.

When women show any ambivalence to the role of mother and their performance falls short of societal expectations and they neglect and abuse their children, they face a storm of anger, resentment and censure. These emotions swirl around mothers and the professionals who become involved, gaining momentum and creating a whirlwind that sucks up mothers and professionals into a contest of preserving the archetypal fiction of mothering and leaves the children in its wake.

In the case of Penny and her children, policy and practice were influenced by an underlying assumption of the primacy of the role of the mother as the primary caregiver and protector. To that end, the FGC was set up to respond to a problem of neglect that was understood as a problem of mothering. The focus on Penny and her mothering failed to acknowledge that the significant changes in Penny's behaviour – leaving the children alone – were indicators that the children were in a harmful environment. Even when Penny forcefully rejected the role of mother, professionals continued to remain focussed on how to solve what they believed was a breakdown of mothering.

How to ensure that the child is seen in cases of neglect is a challenge to social workers and other professionals. Notwithstanding the gender stereotyping associated with concepts of care and nurturing, neglect as a form of abuse continues to be the most durable and poorly defined category in child abuse (Brandon et al., 2013). It is also vulnerable to individual subjectivities about what constitutes an unhealthy environment, a poor relationship and inappropriate supervision. While research and serious case reviews highlight that neglect can be life-threatening, the child's experiences of this form of abuse in the short and long term are rarely examined. This has led to current research conclusions recommending that, to make better sense of what might be going on for the child, social workers should ask the question, *'what does this child mean to the parent and what does the parent mean to the child?'* (Brandon et al., 2013:12).

For Christopher and Lauren, what their mother's parenting meant to them was captured in their responses of fear, anger, worry and uncertainty. They were two young children who did not know what direction their mother's parenting would take next and what this would mean for them. The harmful effects of Penny's physical and emotional absence of care meant they were unsafe. The children recognised that they were unsafe and unwanted. What the children meant to Penny was responsibility, accountability and impossibility. She found the role of mother too difficult and the expectations overwhelming and for her the only way she believed she could be a good mother was to place her children with someone else who could provide a safe, nurturing and protective environment.

The FGC was a practice method chosen to respond to Christopher and Lauren's family situation. Although this approach has found a level of success and popularity across the UK as a way of dealing with a range of family situations (from abuse to relationship breakdowns and understanding youth offending), it has also been acknowledged as a mothering-centric approach that places the burden of 'cleaning-up the mess and making the world a safer place' firmly with mothers (Rose, 2018:22). However, it is important to point out that the FGC that took place in Cross Towns was not representative of many others that I have chaired and attended.

What made the FGC of Cross Towns a different experience were the terms of reference. Penny wanted her children to be cared for by others. She did not want to be Christopher and Lauren's mother, because she felt strongly that this was a role she could not fulfil, and although she wanted help, she did not want it on the terms being offered. Her frank and open statement that she did not want to be a mother and care for her children created a 'disempowering context' that left all those involved feeling lost and unsure about how to approach a situation that called for them to practice and think differently (Morley, 2014:169).

Listening to Penny was difficult for all of the professionals, and because she drew attention to the 'fraudulence of the things she was being asked to do', this generated feelings of anger and incredulity (Rose, 2018:22). This level of emotion drew the focus away from what was happening to the children. The issue of how and why she had neglected the children slipped out of professional mind-sets as they struggled to understand the complex mother–child relationship and Penny's request to be discharged of her motherhood.

Presenting the children's wishes and feelings to the FGC in this context exposed these tensions and dilemmas. Christopher's recognition that his mother did not want him was a powerful lesson in a child's ability to cut through adult psychological explanations of parental behaviours and see the situation for what it was. Lauren's practical solution was a demonstration of a child understanding the urgency of their daily lives.

While the overall effects of neglect are not fully understood by the adults, the children who experience rejection, abandonment, poor or no basic care or protection show us through their behaviour and sometimes by telling us that they are frightened and scared in our adult world. When the adults take notice of the children, we find that they can also provide us with long- and short-term solutions to the problems they are facing.

The critical learning points that emerged from working with Christopher and Lauren were the following:

➤ being alert to neglect as abuse

➤ making sense of their experience

- ➤ how minimising the effects of neglect can lead to poor and dangerous outcomes for children

- ➤ be critically aware of mothering and how it is understood and interpreted in relation to the child, social work policy and practice

- ➤ taking notice of the child

- ➤ engage with them but do not be over-reliant on the child to be the one to speak out about what is happening to them.

For Christopher and Lauren, it was a crisis that alerted agencies to their experience of neglect. Because Lauren spoke out about being left at home alone, professionals were able to intervene. Her readiness to speak out and willingness to engage with social workers suggest that she knew that keeping silent would not protect her or her brother. Although Christopher was less responsive, he was given the opportunity to say how he felt. Both children provided social workers with information that was used to make plans for their future. Although it was a future that neither child expected or wanted, nor was it an outcome that some professionals agreed with at the time, it was what Penny believed was the best for her children.

Undoing the woven texture of mothering that has taken centuries to create will be a challenge. The challenge calls us to look closely at how we see and understand the child in relation to a mothering narrative that has consciously led us to become unconscious of the dimension of neglect.

8

Known to All the Agencies. Kevin, Jenny, Darren and Sarah's Story: Mum and Derek Said Social Workers Would Take Us Away to a Scary Place

Time and again, serious case reviews of child deaths in the UK highlight how a breakdown in multi-agency communication can and has become a factor in children being left in unsafe families (Department for Education, 2016). Reviews have identified a range of factors that create communication barriers between professionals and their agencies. Although structural and procedural changes have been made to support the sharing of information about vulnerable children, communication between professionals working to safeguard children continues to be fragmented, complex and difficult (Department for Education, 2016).

While some of the problems associated with effective multi-agency communication can be situated in the structural and procedural changes experienced by all the agencies responsible for safeguarding children, there is the important issue of inter-personal relationships and professional identities and the barriers created when there is a difference of opinion about risk and need. Where there is one child considered to be at risk, these tensions can erupt and boil over as each professional takes a particular view on how to protect or meet the needs of the child. When there is more than one child living with parents with complex needs, the tensions and views are multiplied and the potential for ineffective communication is increased.

This chapter examines how the interests of a group of siblings who were known to a range of agencies, which had expressed a number of concerns about the children's safety, were eclipsed by professional and personal identities and led to ineffective communication between the agencies. To explore a range of professional communication problems, the story of four children – Kevin, Jenny, Darren and Sarah – will be used to provide a real-world experience that highlights how the range of concerns about the children (individually and as a group) escalated, causing professional confusion, anger and frustration that led to professional paralysis about how to intervene effectively, leaving the children at risk of further harm.

There will be a discussion about how the children found the child protection process frightening and confusing, and there will be opportunities to stop and consider how social workers can work effectively in situations where the child fears the consequences of talking to social workers. The tensions between the social work tasks involved in this case study and building effective relationships with the children will be addressed with the opportunity to identify best practice when working with a sibling group in the child protection process.

The children's story: The Culvert family

Kevin (10), Jenny (8), Darren (7) and Sarah (4) lived with their mother, Debbie, and her husband, Derek, in a council house in an old market town. The oldest children attended the same school while Sarah remained at home. Debbie and Derek had been married for two years and he was the father of Sarah. Neither Debbie nor Derek was in full-time employment. They claimed benefits and did casual work with a local fair that travelled around the county. Debbie had traveller heritage and working with the fair was a family tradition. When Debbie and Derek worked with the fair, the maternal grandparents cared for the children. Derek was known to the police and had a criminal record for burglary of commercial properties (shops and factories) and assault on an adult. He had served several custodial sentences. Debbie had a record of shoplifting as a teenager. Both Derek and Debbie had disrupted education and this meant they had limited literacy and numeracy skills.

The family were well known to a range of universal and statutory services. The school had a range of concerns about the children, such as a lack of basic care, poor school attendance, appearing hungry, looking dirty and dishevelled, and wearing inappropriate clothing. All of the children had attended the local accident and emergency hospital during their childhoods to seek treatment for what appeared to be a range of accidental injuries: Kevin – cuts to his head from falling out of a tree; Sarah – cleaning fluid sprayed into her eyes by Darren; Darren – two occasions of a dislocated thumb and small fractures of bones in the hand from falling from a tyre swing and being on bumper cars at the fair; Sarah – cuts to her head from falling from a chair she was climbing on, drinking cleaning fluid from an unlocked cupboard, an ankle sprain caused by jumping out of living room window and a broken wrist after falling from a slide at the local park.

The children were made the subject of a child protection plan after repeated referrals from school about the children's welfare and a police report of domestic violence and finding the children home alone when they called. Debbie and Derek said they had called maternal grandparents to come to the house to care for the children before 'running away from the police', who they claimed were now harassing them. They disputed the report of domestic violence and failed to acknowledge professional concerns about leaving their children alone without adult supervision; they said the maternal grandparents had been 'round the corner' and the children would not have been alone for long.

▶

◄

As social workers tried to implement the child protection plan, concerns from school and police increased and professionals demanded that Children's Services take action to remove the children. A professionals meeting was held to discuss all the concerns, and legal services attended. It was accepted that parenting capacity was limited and the children had likely suffered significant harm, but because both parents agreed to work with social workers (accepting that unannounced home visits would be made, Sarah would attend a nursery and social workers would undertake direct work with the children), those present agreed (reluctantly) to the child protection plan's continuing.

Social workers carried out unannounced home visits during the day and evening, and two visits were made at weekends. Each time social workers called at the home, they found all the rooms to be clean, tidy and organised. They also reported that there was food in the home, and during one visit, the children were eating pizzas while watching an appropriate children's film. Nothing appeared to be amiss and the picture of the home appeared to be contrary to the concerns being expressed by school and police. Both parents appeared compliant and willing to work with social workers. However, Sarah failed to attend nursery and social workers never got to carry out the direct work; the parents offered a number of excuses – children being ill, not wanting to see social workers, Sarah refusing to go to nursery.

Before social workers could organise a professionals meeting, Sarah was admitted to hospital with a broken arm that parents said had happened when she was at the fair. When Sarah arrived at the hospital, she was wearing a fancy dress costume of a cat and her face was painted. When nursing staff removed the costume and face paint, they found a number of old and new bruises on her face and body. Sarah refused to say how she had broken her arm or how she got the bruises. Both parents were arrested.

The background of this case will resonate with many social workers across the UK. It has all the issues of professional fears, anxieties and concern that a child or children are 'at risk'. In the above case study, some professional fears were related to concerns about parental care and supervision, whereas other emotions appeared to be related to professional anxieties about the families' cultural travelling heritage. What the case of Kevin, Jenny, Darren and Sarah shares with other social work cases is the fear of the unknown, of missing something vital, all overlaid by conflicting values and evidence that individually and together begin to attach themselves to the situation, where they multiply and generate more fears. As Lupton (1999:641) posits, 'emotions create risks and risks create emotions'.

In terms of the arguments and debates in this chapter, the coming together or clash of risk and emotions becomes a driving force that influences and shapes professional relationships, responses and practice. As a result, barriers between professionals are created. As they face each other across tables and rooms, the volume of emotion and risk increases, producing a 'white noise' of blame and threats that paralyse thinking and practice.

Known to all the agencies

Since the death of Peter Connelly, known as Baby P, the phrase 'known to all the agencies' has become synonymous with media reporting of professional failings. Baby P had been known to social workers, paediatricians, police officers and health professionals before he died. When his death was investigated and reported, according to Shoosmith (2016:11), *'those professionals who knew Peter and his family shared that sense of shock and disbelief'.*

This sense of shock and disbelief was used by the media to generate a public and government outcry about professional involvement with the family. This culminated in questions of why those professionals who were in such proximity to Peter and his family networks were unable to see the obvious.

Since the serious case review (Haringey, Local Safeguarding Children Board, 2009), there has been an outpouring of analysis about the many factors believed to have contributed to Peter's becoming lost in a failed child protection system (Munro, 2011; Jones, 2014; Shoosmith, 2016). While the more tangible factors became the building blocks for change, the more nebulous issues such as practitioner relationships, cultures and values and how these do or don't *work* within the context of assessing risk remain unclear.

What many social workers know is that child protection and issues of risk cannot be solved by one agency alone. Although the Children Act 2004 and *Working Together* (2018) guidance both underline the importance of developing and maintaining good professional relationships that work together to ensure that information about children who may be at risk is shared openly and quickly, social workers and professionals know that in practice this poses a number of challenges.

The challenges are found in developing trusting and effective relationships against a backdrop of politics, ideology, values and money that can be divided into different headings of professional perspectives and cultures (Turney *et al.*, 2011). The differences cause tensions and conflict, and when another professional feels strongly about a specific group in the population and finds it difficult to hold an empathic position about those children's social circumstances, this is where the conflict begins. Over the years, I have worked with a range of professionals who have had very different world views about the children and families we were working with. During this period, I was presented with a range of statements that often left me wondering whether we could ever find common ground:

➢ 'Why can't you prevent these families having children?'

➢ 'I don't want you to tell the family that I have referred them. I want to remain anonymous'.

➢ 'The adults are too dangerous and I will not attend a multi-agency meeting if they are present'.

- 'The mother has two male partners. The children's father appears to visit regularly and she has another male partner in the house. What are you going to do about it? This can't be good for the children to see such inappropriate behaviour'.

- 'They are such a nice family living in such a nice area of the town. I don't believe the father meant to hit his daughter or cause the injuries. She can be challenging – you know and I do not agree that social workers have to trample all over such a nice couple'.

- 'He would never sexually abuse children. He is a Christian and an important member of our church and school'.

These often-challenging value-laden judgements can distort thinking and develop barriers to inter-professional working. What often accompany these value-laden judgements are issues of racism, sexism and ageism interspersed with conflicts about class and status. The above statements that professionals made to me about cases I was involved with caused me to feel angry and defensive. The struggles I experienced are all very real in the arena of child protection. Although I was able to challenge many of the statements by being clear about roles and responsibilities, findings from serious case reviews have acknowledged that, where statements about children and their families go unchallenged, issues of risk become lost in what Ferguson (2011:182) refers to as 'destructive dynamics' that lead to a stand-off between professionals.

I was able to find ways of working with most of the professionals who made the above statements. I did this by acknowledging that what they were saying was coming from a place of anger, fear and loss. For example, the education professional who made the statement about preventing certain families from having children told me, as we had a chat over a coffee, why she found working with a mother and her children too painful. She told me she was angry with the unfairness of life. What she saw was a mother abusing drugs, whose fertility was not impaired and who appeared to be having children she could not look after. Meanwhile, my colleague's own daughter, who lived a 'good life', could not have children. Finding a way to have an informal chat with colleagues from different agencies has opened up a number of conversations about the challenges of working in child protection. As Ferguson (2011:183) reminds us, 'professionals bring all their human frailties as well as their strengths to the practice of *child protection*. They not only communicate through the head but the heart'.

Over the years, along with legislation and guidance implemented to bring about better inter-professional and multi-agency communication, training and different systems and structures have been introduced. Most notable of these has been the establishment of multi-agency teams to respond to child protection referrals and the introduction of the common assessment framework (CAF). The CAF introduced the idea of building a team around the child by using statutorily governed and integrated working approaches to ensure there was a joined-up approach to assessing children where a range of needs had been identified. However, although these initiatives have had some success in bringing about good inter-professional and multi-agency working (Turney *et al.*, 2011), the emotional context in which child protection takes place continues to be fertile ground for professional differences and barriers to grow.

Before we move on to discuss how the professional differences and barriers developed in the case of the Culvert family, it is worth taking time to consider the post-qualifying standard: knowledge and skills statement for child and family practitioners – 10 (Organisational Context) – *'Maintain personal and professional credibility through effective working relationships with peers, managers and leaders both within the profession, throughout multi-agency partnerships and public bodies, including the family courts'. Act in ways that protect the reputation of the employer organisation and the social work profession while privileging the best interests of children* (Department for Education, 2018:7).

> **Pause and consider:**
>
> What barriers have you experienced and how have these impacted on your ability and your agency's ability to privilege the best interests of the child?

Creating barriers to multi-agency and inter-professional working

Privileging the child in good multi-agency and inter-professional working is not just about developing inter-personal relationships. In my practice experience, when we (social workers and professional colleagues) got this right, it was because the emotional context was acknowledged and we understood the effect of these individual and collective emotions on our relationships and practice. It was not just about doing the mechanical processes of passing on information; it was about understanding how we were touching and being touched by the experience and processes (Woods *et al.*, 2010).

For example, a number of themes emerge from biennial analysis of serious case reviews that highlight how internal and external processes handled by professionals turn into barriers that subsequently influence how tasks are performed and how the focus of these performances effectively renders the child invisible. In the case of the Culvert family, there were three areas where barriers and tensions between professionals were allowed to develop, causing tensions, conflict and often open hostilities.

Silo practice This is the failure of professionals to look at aspects of the children's needs outside of their own specific brief (Gilbert *et al.*, 2011). Silo practice developed in the case of the Culvert family when a number of referrals were made by the school expressing concerns about the level of basic parental care of the children and the parents' apparent lack of awareness or willingness to work with the school to address issues of poor attendance, lateness, hygiene and children being hungry. When these referrals were received by Children's Services, duty social workers responded by using section 17 of Children Act 1989, identifying the children as in need rather than at risk.

Several home visits to parents were made and social workers chaired a meeting with parents at the school to discuss the concerns for Kevin, Jenny and Darren. As a result of the parents' apparent cooperation and agreement to work with the school, the case was closed. This outcome was strongly contested by the school as they believed the children were at risk of further harm. There was a difference of opinion between the school and social workers about thresholds of risk. While social workers believed that there were low-level needs within the family, they did not agree that the children were at risk of significant harm; therefore, having met the parents and gotten an agreement from them to work with the school on issues around their children's education, they argued that they had discharged their duties under section 17 (b) *'so far as is consistent with that duty, to promote the upbringing of children by their families'.* Effectively, Children's Services believed that they had met their legislative and organisational brief. This action set the tone and pace of ongoing multi-agency working. When further referrals were made to Children's Services, the tensions between professionals grew; the school believed that their concerns about the children were not being taken seriously, and social workers believed that there was a hidden agenda bound up in the family's traveller heritage.

However, in the early days, when the school was making referrals to Children's Services about their concerns for the Culvert children, a range of political agendas were being played out, locking the school and social workers into silo practice. These were connected to thresholds set in place as a gate-keeping process to services for children and were influenced by a range of factors:

➤ staffing shortages

➤ pressures to ration demand for services

➤ time constraints

➤ limited resources – specifically foster placements

For those professionals involved – specifically the school and social workers – the impact of silo practice meant that the children's individual needs were not being looked at since a more comprehensive assessment of their situation was not pursued. If a core assessment had been initiated much earlier in the process, social workers would have had access to information from police and health that had the potential to support an analysis that focussed on risk. Of course, the ifs and buts that litter this example of silo practice will resonate with social workers and professionals working with children and their families where the issue of timing is all too familiar. Although research tells us that intervening earlier in the lives of children where concerns about their welfare have been highlighted has the potential to stop further harm to children (Munro, 2011), it is not always that straightforward. In the case of the Culvert children, a delay in decision-making led to entrenched views about interventions and responsibilities that were heavily influenced by parents' behaviour, lifestyle and cultural heritage.

Parental defensive behaviours This means working with parents who present a range of defences against social work interventions. These parental defences include a range of behaviours such as being hostile, abusive, resistant, dishonest and aggressive that the social work literature has referred to as *parental disguised compliance* and *highly resistant* (Gilbert *et al.*, 2011; Clapton *et al.*, 2013). Whatever term is used, social workers will at some point in their career have to make sense of parental defensive behaviours and what these may mean for the child and practice.

Debbie and Derek presented a range of parental defensive behaviours:

➤ They were abusive and hostile to school staff, which they were suspicious of because of referrals to Children's Services.

➤ They agreed to cooperate with social workers and the school at meetings and then failed to keep to this agreement.

➤ They agreed to home visits by social workers but were not in when social workers called.

➤ They claimed that the school was treating them differently because they were from a travelling family.

➤ They accepted social work involvement because they believed that social workers could advocate on their behalf.

➤ They demanded to see managers to express their concerns about the school and different social workers.

➤ They denied that their intimate relationship was violent.

➤ They lied about the children's injuries, basic care and supervision.

Evidence suggests that parental defensive behaviours come from a fear of losing their children, a feeling of powerlessness, a suspicion of social work interventions, and being exposed as a parent who is abusing their child or who is trying to parent against unassailable odds of poverty, violence and adult needs (Clapton *et al.,* 2013). Developing an open and honest relationship with parents in this context can prove taxing. Even when social workers try to understand what it must be like for parents in this position, there will always be those parents who keep moving the goalposts in an attempt to stay ahead of state interventions.

This was the case with Debbie and Derek. As social work interventions became more crisis-led, social workers became caught up in what can only be described as a form of emotional and psychological 'tunnelling' (Woods *et al.,* 2010:13). That is, the social workers' field of vision and thinking narrowed as their operating environment became a game of 'cat and mouse'. Social workers became caught up in a dysfunctional game driven by the parents' need to hide what was really going on in the home. This 'game' was being played against a backdrop of pressure and high demands that required them to pay attention to and keep track of a wealth of information from parents, school, health and police.

Social workers and other professionals found it increasingly difficult to gain a foothold on what the truth was. In this situation, social workers were using trust as a determinant to establish a working relationship with the parents. Once any notion of trust between social workers and parents disintegrated, what was left were less-than-healthy feelings of anger about how their mandated authority had been effectively 'torn up' by both Debbie and Derek.

Social workers found themselves managing a set of challenging emotions and contradictory imperatives:

➢ fear about the uncertainty of the situation

➢ anger that their professional credibility had been challenged

➢ pressure from other professionals to take action and remove the children

➢ management demands to provide evidence of significant harm based on resources

Being angry with Debbie and Derek for their parental defensive behaviour, not liking them very much as a result and responding to the anger of other professionals are not grounds for seeking a legal framework to remove children from their parents – at this time. Although the social work literature has highlighted how the 'coarsening of social work attitudes' towards parents and families in child protection may be leading us in this direction (Clapton *et al.,* 2013; Warner, 2015), how to resist and find a different way of responding to parental defensive behaviours remains a contested area of practice.

The 'rule of optimism' When professionals apply the rule of optimism, they make efforts not to be judgemental or make negative judgements about parents' parenting, lifestyle and backgrounds (Gilbert *et al.,* 2011). The Culvert family had traveller heritage. Both Debbie and Derek were from traveller families. Whereas Debbie's mother and father had given up the travelling life to settle, Derek's family continued to travel across the country, returning to towns with the seasonal fair.

Research suggests that a 'child's ethnic affiliation evokes little significant approach by social workers, confirming a largely universal approach' (Williams and Soyden, 2005:901). However, in the case of the Culvert family, it was significant and underpinned how parental behaviours were interpreted and understood. For example, both Debbie and Derek expressed their distrust of formal education and said they found it difficult to engage with teachers they believed were 'looking down on them'. Social workers accepted this and many of their early responses and actions were based on an image of a travelling heritage family trying to 'fit in'. This interpretation of the parental behaviours became all-pervasive, and instead of looking at the relationships within the family (Derek and Debbie's and their relationships with their children), social workers focussed on providing concrete solutions to the problems.

This approach was infused with an 'air of optimism' that parents were trying to do their best for the children against what they believed were judgemental views of travelling families. This became the accepted view of social workers and it clouded how they analysed information from the school and police. As Munro (2008) points out, once 'optimism' sets in, social workers find it difficult to review their position. When social workers in the Culvert case faced increasing levels of concern from professionals, culminating in cries of 'remove these children', there was a readiness to accept the parents' explanations about issues of neglect and claims that the children's injuries were due to accidents in the home, at playgrounds and in school.

According to risk perception researchers, the 'rule of optimism' strongly influences how we seek out and make sense of information and during this process we tend to look for evidence to support what we want to believe (Slovic, 2002). This was evident in the case of the Culvert family. Although elements of need were acknowledged and social workers suspected that the children may be at risk of abuse, their desire to think the best of Derek and Debbie clouded their critical thinking. As a result of this misplaced optimism, social workers were unable to maintain their critical curiosity. As a result, they were unable to find a way through the complex human relationships that were effectively masking the risks to the children.

The combination of the three elements of silo practice, parental defensive behaviour and rule of optimism contributed to social workers' not fully seeing the risks to the children. The children slipped into the margins, and although the children were indeed known to all the agencies, no one really knew that they were frightened

> of Derek, who physically and emotionally abused them
> of social workers, whom they believed were 'monsters' who would take them away and 'bury them'
> of teachers, who didn't really like them and were frightened of Derek
> of their mum, who did what Derek told her to.

Without this information, social workers were unable to reveal the deeper story – a story of multiple complex adult parent and professional relationships that were creating the conditions that led to children being overlooked.

Social worker, social worker – Look at me. Can you see me?

The social work literature and government policy guidance constantly refer to keeping the child in view and ensuring that their voices are heard in child protection social work (Munro, 2011; Cossar *et al.*, 2013). Indeed, the central theme of this book is how social workers see or don't see the child in child protection practice. Although research tells us that good social work practice with children is dependent on developing sound and effective relationships (Cleaver *et al.*, 2011), how social workers do this with children who have suffered trauma and who may be fearful of social workers, as the Culvert children were, remains more difficult to achieve than is so often suggested (Cossar *et al.*, 2013).

Social workers did not fully know or understand what Kevin, Darren, Sarah and Jenny had been exposed to. Although earlier in this chapter a range of factors were identified that explain why and how the children were overlooked, this explanation does not take into account the fact that all of the children were seen and spoken to by social workers, teachers and police officers over a period of time. For example, social workers, teachers and police reported that they saw the children

> playing a board game with Derek and Debbie
> relaxing and watching TV with Derek and Debbie
> enjoying a pizza at home with Derek and Debbie
> playing happily with other children in the school playground

➤ hugging their mum and Derek at the school gates

➤ at home in their bedrooms, which were clean and tidy.

Social workers who saw the children also recorded that they had spoken to Kevin and Darren, who told them that they liked having bunk beds because they sometimes jumped off the top bunk. Social workers also recorded that Kevin appeared very grown up in his presentation and that he told them he 'wasn't afraid of monsters' and that he could look after his brother and sisters.

Social workers did see the children. They were looking at them but they were seeing them and interpreting what they saw and heard in relation to the parents' and their own views about the family. Simply put, the social workers wanted to 'see' the children safe and happy as opposed to being at risk of significant harm. Could they have interpreted what they saw differently? What could they have looked for? According to Thomas and Holland (2010), too often children are only partially represented in social work assessments and social workers tend to describe children in terms of assumptions made about developmental norms. For example, social workers interpreted Kevin's ten-year-old behaviour of appearing polite, walking straight-backed and being able to engage with them as a child wanting to impress them by his adultness. At the time, they did not see the fear that was holding his body straight in an attempt to ensure that he did not open the door to social work scrutiny and ultimately cause Derek to be violent to him, his mother or one of his siblings. His presenting behaviour and how this was seen and interpreted by social worker resonate with the many concerns found in the Victoria Climbié report, in which social worker Lisa Arthurworrey concluded that Victoria's behaviour of 'standing to attention' before her abusers, Kuoao and Manning, was cultural because she understood *'this type of relationship was one that can be seen in many Afro-Caribbean families, because respect and obedience are very important features of Afro-Caribbean family scripts'* (Lord Laming, 2003:345).

Making any assumptions about a child's observed behaviour, whether this is in relation to child development or their parents, brings with it the potential for lost decisions that could place the child in danger. In the case of Victoria Climbié, the assumption made by Lisa Arthurworrey was one of many that escalated. In the case of the Culvert children, making an assumption that Kevin's behaviour was somehow related to his age and a sign of good-enough parenting meant that the social workers lost sight of Kevin and his siblings and the dangers they faced.

There will always be a time in a social worker's professional life that a specific child/children and their family cause them to 'hold their breath' as they consider the 'what-ifs'. This may be after a specific event when the child's situation and the risks they face become visible or as a result of hearing about the death of a child in the media or within your own locality or after reading findings from serious case reviews that remind you of a child and their family and prompt you to think 'this could have been my case'. To support your thinking and reflection, consider the following:

Pause and consider:

how you keep the child in view during professional practice and avoid what Munro (1996) refers to as making assumptions and decisions based on limited knowledge (in the case of Victoria Climbié), inadequate investigation (in the case of the Culvert children) and woolly thinking.

The title of this discussion was influenced by my own granddaughter, who at nearly three years of age frequently says 'granny, granny, look at me' as she demands my attention to watch her demonstrate a newfound skill. She doesn't stop until I do and my enthusiastic response is always critically examined by her as she directs me in a re-enactment of her 'performance', whether this is singing, dancing or expertly balancing on her scooter. She takes no prisoners should I fail to do exactly as she has done. What strikes me about this description is, in all the years I have worked with children as a social worker, how unlikely it was for this group of children to act the way my granddaughter did to gain adult attention. Many children did not overtly ask me to look at them but behaved in ways that demanded my and other adults' attention (such as Connie in Chapter 5). More often, they did everything they could to avert the adult gaze because drawing attention was filled with fear and anxious anticipation about what such adult attention may turn into.

Kevin and his siblings did everything they could to avert the adult gaze in the 'performances' they gave when social workers were around and when they attended school. Even when their physical appearance singled them out, Kevin, Jenny and Darren appeared able to 'manage' their internal fears and anxieties in such a way that they did not spill over into behaviours that would draw further attention to them. Seeing past this performance or presentation and seeing it for what it was – a mode of survival – was not considered by social workers. Although the school held strong views about the children being at risk of living with their parents, they were unable to articulate what this risk was because the children were not verbalising that they were victims of abuse. On the contrary, the children told teachers that they 'loved their mum' and demonstrated this whenever the school set them tasks to make special occasion cards and drawings.

So how do social workers develop a social work gaze that means they are more than an audience to a child's performance? What skills are needed to ensure that the child, while central to the processes involved in child protection, becomes more than one-dimensional? How do we challenge ourselves to take government guidance (Department for Education, 2017) and research findings (Cossar *et al.,* 2013) that ask social workers to ensure the child remains central to social work interventions?

Developing a social work gaze that focusses on the child's behaviour and their mind requires that the adult go on a journey where they examine

➤ the child's sense of self

➤ how they navigate their social and physical world

➤ the vital skills they have developed to cope with their adult world

➤ how they come to understand their experiences

➤ how the narratives they use may set them apart from their siblings and other children.

This journey will mean developing knowledge of children and increasing those skills that support you to work directly and indirectly with children. However, developing a social work gaze is not unlike developing a filmic approach, whereby you direct your view, focussing and refocussing, looking at different angles that ensure you capture the best view of the child and, once this is committed to memory, analyse the scenes by asking critical questions of the images you have in your mind.

If the social workers had been able to adopt such a social work gaze in regard to the Culvert children, they may have been able to keep each child in view and see how hard Kevin was working to keep control of his emotions and behaviours and how when Jenny or Darren were tempted to draw attention to their situation he would distract them with a word or look that said 'careful and be quiet'. They would also have seen that Darren looked to Kevin for assurance and that, when they were at home and observed together, Darren would either stand or sit as close to Kevin as he could while Jenny said as little as possible and tried hard to make herself into what she later referred to as a 'little mouse' that 'no one could find'. Social workers may also have seen through the performance of Sarah, who as the little blonde girl performed by taking a social worker's hand, stroking their arm, looking at them intently and unblinkingly and smiling all the time or making faces that made everyone laugh. During these individual and collective performances by the children, social workers may also have seen how Jenny and Darren avoided looking at Debbie and Derek or how Kevin would surreptitiously sneak a look at Derek to measure his response and how Sarah's performance was somewhat mechanical and rehearsed.

When Derek and Debbie were arrested, the children were taken into care and placed with foster carers, an event that was traumatic for the children and social workers. Although current statistics confirm that the number of children being removed from their families and being made the subject of legal frameworks has increased over the last nine years (Department for Education, 2017), it is never a decision taken lightly by social workers. While pressures on social workers to protect children have grown over the last two decades, carrying out such a specific social work intervention is an emotional roller coaster that leaves all those involved feeling drained and exhausted.

Removing the children from Debbie and Derek was what the children had come to fear and so the event of being placed with adults they didn't know was a frightening experience. Their fear was reflected in behaviour that was distinct in its intensity and actions, and each child demonstrated their anxieties in very different ways:

➢ Kevin physically lashed out at social workers and ran away.

➢ Darren was verbally abusive and also tried to run away.

➢ Jenny cried silently.

➢ Sarah smiled and clung tightly to social workers.

What became clear to social workers and foster carers was that it was going to take considerable time to unravel what had been their physical and emotional world. The trauma experienced by all the children had impaired their communication skills. Before anyone could engage the children in any realistic plans for the future, there needed to be a period in which the children had to be supported to develop some confidence in those adults around them. They needed to feel safe and secure before they could trust anyone to tell them what had happened to them and be able to communicate their wishes and feelings.

How do you get children to trust you? What works?

Although there is no off-the-shelf aid for ensuring that the child is central to practice, there are some important areas of best practice that are worth considering. However, before we look at some of these, it is worth reminding ourselves that much of what social workers do is often developed over years by working with children and learning from this experience, from having the professional experience of working alongside others, from drawing upon their own lived experience and from reading.

Many social workers will use these developed skills on a 'what works' basis. I worked with a number of social workers who had a small library of toys, games and reading that they referred to and adapted to use with different children. However, although building a personal library of ideas and activities takes time, it is also helpful to have a pre-designed guide that you can dip into and that allows creative thinking – a bit like a colouring book that allows you to focus on the task at hand but also helps you to colour outside the set lines. In developing such a guide, you need to direct your attention to what is around in terms of literature and research.

I offer the following thoughts and ideas to help social workers develop their skills for gaining the trust of children who have been abused, victimised and traumatised by the adults in their lives. I also direct you to some further reading that will help you consider how you will engage in a process of 'making what works – work'.

Gaining a child's trust: We are all dependent on others for our survival, and when that has been undone, this leaves us feeling vulnerable to feelings of anger, failure and fear that all have an impact on our emotional and physical well-being and capacity to trust (Brotherton and Cronin, 2013). For children, this will be accompanied by feelings of confusion and will contain elements in which they blame themselves for the adults' behaviour.

Finding a way of engaging with children who are experiencing all of these feelings will take time and skill to wait and avoid asking questions about what happened. It will feel natural to want to investigate and ask the child questions that may help shape their future. Indeed, there will be pressures on social workers to do this. However, for many children, the timescale will be different. They will have suffered trauma and may be presenting as mentally fragile and they will be worrying about the prospect of a future and what this might mean for them.

For example, Kevin refused to engage with social workers and foster carers to talk about what happened and who did what to whom. Reluctantly, social workers gave up on this approach and, with the foster carers, focussed on helping him to adjust to living in his new and different surroundings. After he had been in foster care for a year, social workers began undertaking direct work with Kevin by using a combination of activities that explored feeling safe (see Wrench, 2017, for ideas). It was during this work that Kevin revealed how Derek had abused them physically (punched, 'belted' and kicked them all) and emotionally (locked them outside of the house at night and made them sleep in the garden after telling them tales about men and social workers who would kill and bury them) and encouraged Debbie to neglect the children as a way of punishing and controlling them. I like the observations of Gilligan (2006:331) in his work on peace and trauma in Northern Ireland. He makes reference to 'traumatic time' and how for *children* this can move forwards and backwards, 'forward from their present anxiety to a pessimistic vision of the future, or backward from a realistic assessment of a bleak future to anxiety in the present'. Kevin's **traumatic time** is described in the following:

1. present anxiety – fear that Derek would find him and come and take him away from foster carers

2. pessimistic vision – social workers were to be feared and he did not know whether his fears of social workers burying him would be realised

3. realistic assessment – his future was uncertain and bleak as he did not know what this held or whether he would be placed with his brothers and sisters

4. anxiety in the present – he was anxious about whom to trust in his present situation

(Taken from Gilligan (2006) and adapted into a numbered list).

Gaining the trust of any child or young person takes time. Gaining the trust of those children who have suffered abuse in all its forms will take longer and understanding this should be central to social work practice interventions. In this situation, social workers need to acknowledge that they cannot engage with children using terms heavily influenced by organizational systems based on outcomes. The terms of engagement will be different. The child's terms of engagement will be shaped and led by their feelings and they will not understand the world of the social worker. Because the children do not understand what is happening to them they will behave in ways that test out social workers and their organizational time frames and structures by being uncooperative, withdrawn, aggressive and disruptive.

Remaining engaged with children who act out all of these feelings can lead social workers to lose confidence and credibility. It can also cause frustrations and these will be manifested in your physical approach. Like a balloon with the air let out, a look of deflation and frustration will be a tell-tale sign picked up by the child, who will feel that you simply do not want to be with them. So I offer the following suggestions that might help you to reflect and reposition an approach that will support gaining the child's trust:

➢ Be clear about why you are trying to gain the trust of the child. This may sound obvious as it will be a means to an end. But to what end? If you are planning for their future, then take some time to think about what this is and what it may mean for this particular child. For example, planning for a future is not an overt process for many children. But children who become part of the child protection process and care system are frequently involved in planning for their future. As Madge (2006:138) found out from research with children, they did not want to 'have to take undue responsibility too early'. Ask yourself, is this approach justification for the institutional processes? If so, it will structure the terrain on which gaining the trust of the child is conducted, and many children may not understand or grasp what future planning means – a fresh start? Be clear that you understand what this may look like for the child and what this may involve.

➤ Avoid placing pressure on the child to engage in either providing you with more details about their experiences or engaging in any therapeutic-based counselling. In your haste to 'help' them through a trauma, you may miss that all they want is consistency of care, shelter and food and time to assess the adults who are providing it.

➤ Promote the identity and strengths of the child. Seeing the child as a victim can be self-limiting and undermine the building of trust. What I mean by this is that the child may not see themselves as a victim in the sense that adults (social workers) understand the term and its relationship to vulnerability. For example, Kevin believed that he had been brave. He had on occasions stood up to Derek in a bid to protect his siblings even when this meant placing himself in danger of physical assaults. Acknowledge what children do to survive.

➤ Take an interest in the child as an individual and as part of a network of siblings and family. Help the child to help you understand who they are and where they are in understanding what has happened to them. While there are a range of activities to do this, I have always found it helpful to ask children to develop their own visual eco-map. Keep it simple and use a range of tools – felt-tip pens and paper. Eco-maps have been used extensively in social work and a range of therapeutic settings with adults and families as a way of understanding family networks and relationships (Rempel *et al.*, 2007). Through the process of tearing, sticking and drawing, the child will set out a visual map that you can use to check out with them relationships, concerns and fears. See appendices for Kevin's eco-map.

➤ Be brave in your ambitions for working directly with children. Develop your skills and knowledge and put together your own 'tool kit' as this is a way of showing children that they are important.

➤ Be active in supervision by ensuring that you get the opportunity to reflect on what you are doing, why you are doing it and your thoughts and views about it.

➤ Seek out other social workers and develop a network of people you can talk to about the work you are doing. Create connections and networks so that you can talk about what you are doing in a way that supports learning and a growth in knowledge.

➤ Working with children is tiring. You will easily engage with and warm to some children; with others, you will breathe a sigh of relief when a session is cancelled. I remember these times very well and it is worth reflecting and talking to others about how you felt. You will not be the only social worker who has felt like this.

Research reminds us that 'it takes a lot to build trust', and children involved with social workers want them to be reliable, competent, available and knowledgeable (Cossar *et al.*, 2013:7). Children will also appreciate a social worker who acknowledges that they do not have all the answers and will know whom to ask to help them. The straightforward answer to 'what works' is that we don't really know. It remains a work in progress. We do know that there are a number of ingredients needed to ensure that children get the best service possible from Children's Services because many of them have told social workers and researchers (Cossar *et al.*, 2013) what they need, want and expect:

> ➢ a critical gaze that takes the child into full view
> ➢ developing and sustaining open adult inter-personal and professional relationships to support the child
> ➢ having knowledge and being knowledgeable
> ➢ taking responsibility for one's own learning
> ➢ valuing the child
> ➢ being consistent and clear about roles and responsibilities
> ➢ being available and committing to the relationship – even if it is short-term

What I know from my work with children is that even when all the ingredients are used and the right measurements adhered to, it is not possible to 'get' a child to trust you. I always reminded myself (or was reminded by others) that to expect children who have been abused to invest in adults again in a way that means they will tell us what their wishes and feelings are or tell us chapter and verse about their abuse is a huge 'ask'. Acknowledging that this is the case is a more honest and healthy basis for developing a trusting relationship with children.

Conclusion

I always believed that with the Culvert children, we social workers 'got lucky' and were able to intervene in the lives of Kevin, Jenny, Darren and Sarah before they suffered further abuse or one of them was tragically killed. Once the children were removed from Debbie and Derek and over a very long period, the older children did tell social workers and foster carers about the range of abuse they had all been subjected to by Derek and their mother. Kevin, Jenny and Darren told different social workers that Derek had 'thrown Sarah down stairs' and 'that's how she hurt her arm'. Although Sarah remained silent on the matter, further health investigations revealed a range of healed injuries to her back, legs and face that were considered to be non-accidental.

All of the children had been subjected to physical and emotional abuse and neglect throughout their very short lives. When this could no longer be covered up because parental behaviours became more erratic and the levels of neglect seeped out into the school arena, sadly the professionals – teachers, social workers, police officers and health professionals – failed to see the impact on the children. Although the school was the first to make the link between the children's presentation and parental neglect, professional barriers were erected very quickly, making it difficult to develop a professional gaze that took in the children and the risks they faced.

This case will certainly resonate with social workers working in child protection. I have no doubts the issues associated with developing and sustaining inter-personal and inter-professional relationships will all have been experienced. I also suspect that, in today's climate, developing professional relationships will be made more difficult by structural and systems changes that appear to be creating more distance between social workers and other professionals involved in protecting children. However, if child care social workers are to position themselves as the 'standout' profession for protecting children in these difficult times, then how we pay attention to children will be crucial. Paying attention to the child calls for social workers to

- ➤ see the child as a child
- ➤ see the child in relation to their family relationships
- ➤ see the child in relation to child protection systems
- ➤ see the child in relation to the social worker

9

Repositioning(s) – The Child and Social Work at the Centre of Social Work Practice

Evidence tells us that children quickly become lost in the protective processes of child protection (Brandon *et al.*, 2012). Even where the existing UK child protection systems are considered to be working well (Department for Education, 2016), children remain vulnerable to adult behaviours and needs. Whether these needs are related to the political and ideological wants of governments and society or the problem behaviours of their parents, children will feel the impact. They will wait, unseen and unprotected, while the adults play out their needs and wants through behaviours and policies that relegate children to the margins of a system designed to protect them.

While children wait, the evidence suggests, social workers – individually and collectively – are also becoming lost in a cycle of budget-led structural reorganisations in response to government attention steeped in political ideologies that promote the family as the place for keeping children safe and social work as the profession for ensuring that this is achieved. Social workers now face two options: (1) take up the state position that places on their shoulders the 'heaviest burden of responsibility' (Department for Education, 2016:4) in ensuring that parents and families do their job or (2) keep their head down. In the first case, social workers hope not to be singled out from the crowd; in the second case, they hope to somehow survive the crash.

This politically led environment appears to have locked the children out and tied social workers to a practice that many argue has less to do with protecting children and more to do with meeting the needs of the state (Jordan and Drakeford, 2012; Parton, 2014). Meanwhile, social workers are becoming increasingly aware that this situation is taking them in a direction they do not agree with. They appear powerless to challenge it. As a group of social workers told me in the process of writing this book:

> It is a new environment. It's competitive. Who can do the most work, respond to the most referrals. Not thinking is an asset. That's the point don't think just do. Create distance between ourselves and service users – be rational and less emotional. It is about survival of the fittest. It is easy to forget all the social work training about values and self-awareness. How you cope is not to be different.

How social workers reposition their practice in this environment will be a challenge. The challenge will be personal and political. Social workers will have to begin by re-engaging with the values they signed up to. They must recognise the political landscape that has created the working environment that is effectively undermining the virtues of the profession and creating a gap between them and those they are mandated to protect. To help this repositioning, they need to take notice of research and the children's testimonies in this book which tell them that children involved with protective services need social workers.

This book has been concerned with bringing the child into focus in child protection social work. Its aim has been to promote the role of the social worker and practice to achieve this. Because it is an area of practice that I have worked in for many years, I believe that social workers are up to the challenges involved in repositioning practice. However, it will not be easy and social workers will have to find the strength and resilience shown by the children in this book if they are to see the child by seeing themselves more clearly.

To help social workers reposition practice, I have introduced a feminist-informed model (FIM) as a tool to aid child-focussed practice. Drawing upon feminist literatures from social work, philosophy and psychology, my own practice and the testimonies of the children who became involved in child protection, I have brought together practice and theory to support arguments about why we need to reposition social work in child protection. In this conclusion, I will highlight the key factors for repositioning practice and include a framework for action.

Key factors to aid repositioning

Through the use of the FIM and the testimonies of the children, three key factors emerge from this book and I believe they are at the heart of repositioning social work practice:

> the politics of the day

> the child in an adult-led world

> relationships

Child protection is political. The politics of child protection are fundamentally set around ideals about the family and a set of parenting norms. These ideals and norms permeate social work policy and practice and influence service provision and practice. Although these politics and ideals are not new to child protection social work, they have taken on a very different tone over the last thirty years. The tone is one of blame, overlaid with moral and state certainty about what parenting is, who can do it, how it should be done and what will happen to those who fail (Shirani *et al.,* 2012). Those who are deemed to be failing in their parenting role and responsibilities face a type of social work weighed down by the burden of state responsibility.

The outcomes of this type of social work are witnessed in practice now conditioned by processes and time. As social workers respond to the day-to-day demands of this politically led environment, they have not had the time to stop and recognise how processes and time have become the standard bearer of front-line child protection social work. As social workers rush to meet the demands of the job, they do not see how this approach is being used to shape and control them and their practice. More importantly, they fail to recognise how the processes and time have created 'different clocks and timetables' (Campbell, 2013:19), where social workers and children are effectively working across different time zones. The consequences for children are that social workers fail to see the uniqueness of the child in the context of child protection processes.

Thinking politically is an important step in repositioning practice. The objectives of thinking politically are twofold: (1) to engage with the political ideals that shape their working environments and (2) to understand how these are expressed through words that influence practice. For many social workers, the idea of thinking politically will be the biggest challenge – not because this may be interpreted as taking some form of political action, but because it means looking closely at how we are translating the political and policy language of parenting into practice and whether or not we are using an internal script that supports a discourse of inequality and oppression.

In Chapter 7, the outcome of a mothering narrative was laid bare when Christopher understood what it meant to be neglected and rejected by his mother, Penny. For the adults working with Christopher, it was a challenge made more uncomfortable when Penny rejected services that she believed tied her to a mothering script she did not want. If the social workers working with Christopher had continued to promote social work interventions that placed pressure on Penny to conform, it would have meant that he and his sister continued to be at risk of significant harm as a result of adult thinking influenced by a mothering ideal.

All the testimonies in this book identify how the adult-led world of child protection makes it difficult for children to be seen, heard, understood and in many cases protected. The children do not ask that the adult-led world of child protection be turned on its head in the process of repositioning. What they do ask is that the social workers who become involved in their lives recognise how important they are to making sense of what is happening to them and to make the best decisions they can to keep them safe. This point was made in Chapter 5 by Connie, who became caught up in adult narratives used to explain her position in an adult world that was consumed by grief, loss and guilt. However, if repositioning can cause the adult-led world of child protection to be turned on its head in favour of seeing the child more clearly, then this has to be an ambition for the future. As Bryson (2007:100) argues, *'any plans for the future should attempt to think beyond what currently exists'*.

Moving beyond what currently exists will be achieved through social workers who develop and understand the importance of relationships. Understanding that relationships can extend beyond individual people to relations between groups, structures, environments, policies, politics, beliefs and emotions will support a new way of seeing the child. The children's testimonies in this book have illuminated why we need to focus on the relational, specifically the relationship between children and adults who become involved in the child protection system. What these testimonies show us is how adult-led relationships create the conditions that lead to children being lost, unseen, unheard and unprotected.

Being concerned about the wider meaning of relationships and where these relationships are taking child protection practice can and should be used to reposition practice. Being concerned about the relational offers an alternative way of making sense of the child's world in child protection. It also has the potential to generate a different conversation about the child, a conversation that ensures that children stay central to thinking and practice.

Drawing on my own practice experience and emerging themes from the book, I offer a practical *aide-mémoire* that is intended to be provocative and challenging.

An aid for seeing the child

Pay Attention	Focus on	Constructing Change
• To who the child is	• Identifying the child's communication skills and your own	• Read up on research that tells us what children want and think about child protection services
• To what you bring to the life of this child	• Increasing your knowledge of child development	• Reclaim the child in child protection by examining your practice in relation to what research is telling us
• To the multiplicity of relationships	• Finding your skills in listening that help you tune into the child and their world	• Read up on feminist social work and what this means to you, your practice and the profession
• To the adultness of child protection policy and practice and where this can take you	• Being open, honest and effective without being reactionary and responding in a way that creates barriers to working with the child	• Engage with a Feminist Informed Model for practice
• To the child's behaviour and what this may tell you. Do not rely on the child to tell you in adult language what is happening to them	• Reflection as a tool for supporting and developing your thinking and resistance	• Find out what your colleagues think about the child in child protection practice
• To the balance of need and risk and how this can easily tip over to a point where the child is at risk of harm		• Become an activist to reposition the child in child protection social work, if you are not one already
• To complexity and how this is created		

I hope that the above aid for seeing the child brings about a sea change in practice through child-centred actions. The aim of the aid is to ensure that the child remains in-focus at all times by asking those adults responsible for protecting them to take time to reflect and question their own and others practice.

Hopes and aspirations

The hopes and aspirations of this book are to generate a conversation about the child in social work practice and to ask social workers to examine more closely those relationships that have a profound impact on the child. More importantly, I ask social workers to take a look at who they are and their practice through the eyes of the child and to understand that doing so will take time – a precious commodity that in social work has become, in the words of Duffy (1993), 'mean time'. Time is 'mean' to child protection social workers. It creates pressures, workloads and stresses for the adults and as a consequence the child and their lived experiences, relationships, thoughts and views become excluded from the social work clock.

I hope the testimonies of the children, who, though all white, are from different socioeconomic backgrounds and live in a cultural environment shaped by unemployment and the politics of the day, have offered some insight into practice that has aimed to keep the child in mind. Whoever the child is, Simon, Katy, Connie, Darren, Christopher, Kevin, Jenny, Darren or Sarah, I hope they have been able to speak to the reader and, through their stories, draw attention to what it is to be a child involved in the adult processes of child protection social work.

Reflections

Like many writers before me, I have painted myself and my practice into the chapters of this book. By doing so, I have been involved in a reflective process that has taken me on a journey back in time when social work and the politics that shaped it were different and social workers were to some degree free to be more politically attuned and active in challenging injustice and inequalities. I am not suggesting (although it would be easy to do so) that, in the late 1970s and early 1980s, the social work project was set in halcyon days when social workers were more radical, steeped in community action and filled with feminist thinking and ideas. No, I am considering whether the challenges faced by social workers today are so different from those faced by my colleagues and me and whether, as a result of media and political attention, we have become accepting of a projected image of social work and social workers that suggests contemporary social work is vastly different because of a more technocratic and technical landscape.

When I am not slipping into this glossy daydreaming of how social work was in 'my day', I remind myself of the children and young people my colleagues and I worked with and the importance of relationships and the challenges we faced. I do question whether the practice of the day would have been different with new knowledge, access to technology and a more authoritarian policy base. If we left children for too long in families where there were insurmountable difficulties and problems, was it because we believed that supporting families in their communities would bring about changes? For example, in the ongoing professional arguments that swirled around Kevin and his siblings, did we forget the child because professional status was more important or because our actions were budget-led and the knowledge that finding and getting a management agreement to take four children into care was a root cause in the decision-making. I have asked myself many more questions, and I hope that in reading the testimonies of the children in this book, students and social workers are asking questions too – whether about my practice or their own.

I am passionately concerned about child protection social work and the direction it is taking and what this will mean for the children and social workers caught up in the politics of the day. However, at present, for the first time in a long time, social work is not receiving government or media attention. This is because politicians and the media attentions are elsewhere with the challenges of Brexit, the Middle East, Windrush and the NHS. During this period, children known to social workers have died and their deaths have not received the attention of their high-profile predecessors Victoria Climbié and Peter Connelly.

Is this the time, when the 'state' is distracted, that social work finds a way to regroup and reposition as a profession? There is no doubt that social workers are gathering together to find their voice, and there is evidence of political challenge in the marches by social workers taking a stand against austerity. This political challenge by social workers is reminiscent of those taken in the past to make their voices heard about new systems, protocols and financial restrictions. I am proposing for the profession that we do more of this challenging and that doing this begins with the individual finding their own starting point. This will not be easy and there will be challenges along the way as ideas and thinking formulate and develop.

To begin this thinking and positioning, I have filled this book with testimonies of children, practice, debates and theoretical perspectives to open up conversations and begin the challenge for social workers to find their place. This place is a profession that, despite being blamed for all that is wrong with our society, remains the profession that the state relies on to protect children. I propose that we use this place and own it by encouraging a practice that ensures that the child is seen in child protection practice.

References

Abrahams, C. (1994) *The Hidden Victims: Children and Domestic Violence,* London: NCH Action for Children

Advisory Council on the Misuse of Drugs (2011) *Hidden Harm – Responding to the needs of children of problem drug users,* GOV.UK

Agerholm, H. (2018) Hundreds of children suffering PTSD after fire, NHS figures reveal, *Guardian,* Saturday, 28th February, 2018.

Aldridge, J., and Beckers, S. (2003) *Children caring for parents with mental illness: Perspectives of young carers, parents and professionals,* Bristol: The Policy Press

Allen, J. (1991) The Teachers and The Children, Award-winning entries from the 1990 WH Smith Young Writers Competition (eds) *Young Words,* Basingstoke: MacMillan Children's Books

Altheide, D., L. (2002) *Creating Fear: News and the Construction of Crisis,* New York: Aldine De Gruyter

Ames, n. (2014) Social Work Recording: A New Look at an Old Issue, *Journal of Social Work Education,* Vol 35(2) pp 227–237

Baird, B (2009) Child Politics, Feminist Analysis, *Australian Feminist Studies,* 23(57) 291–305.

Barlow, J., Fisher, J. D., Jones, D. (2012) *Systematic Review of models for analysing significant harm,* Research Report DFE – RR199, Oxford University: DfE

Bassin, D., Honey, M., & Kaplan, M. (1994) *Representations of Motherhood,* New Haven, CT: Yale University Press

Baumgartner, J., Burnett, L., Di Carlo, C., F., Buchanan, T. (2012) An Inquiry of Children's Social Support Networks Using Eco-Maps, *Child Youth Care Forum,* Vol 41, pp. 357–369

BASW, Northern Ireland (2018), *Insult and Injury: Exploring the impacts of intimidation, threats, and violence against social workers,* Belfast: BASW

Baumann, D., J., Dalgliesh, L., Fluke, J., Homer, K. (2011) The Decision-Making Ecology. *American Humane Association,* Washington DC

Bentovim, A., Cox, A., Bingley-Miller, L. and Pizzey, S. (2009) *Safeguarding Children Living with Trauma and Family Violence.* London: Jessica Kingsley

Bernard, C., and Harris, P. (2016) *Safeguarding Black Children: Good Practice in Child Protection,* London: Jessica Kingsley

Bibby, P. (2017) *Personal Safety Guide for Social Workers,* London: Routledge

Blom-Cooper, L. (1985) *A child in trust: The report of the panel of inquiry into the circumstances surrounding the death of Jasmine Beckford,* London: London Borough of Brent

Bockneck, E. L., Sanderson, J. and Britner, P. A. (2009) 'Ambiguous loss and posttraumatic stress in school-age children of prisoners', *Journal of Child and Family Studies,* Vol. 18 (3), pp. 323–333

Booth, T., Booth, W., and McConnell, W. (2005) The prevalence and outcomes of care proceedings involving parents with learning difficulties in family courts, *Journal of Applied Research in Intellectual Disabilities,* 18 (1) pp. 7–18

Bowlby, J. (1988) *A secure base: Parent-child attachment and healthy human development,* New York: Basic Books

Brandon (2008*) Analysing child deaths and serious injury through abuse and neglect: what can we learn?* A biennial analysis of serious case reviews (England 2003–2005), London: Department of Schools and Families

Brandon, M., Sidebotham, P., Bailey, S., Belderson, P., Hawley, K., Ellis, C., Meson, M. (2012) *New Learning from Serious Case Reviews: A two year report 2009–2011,* University of East Anglia and the University of Warwick: DfE

Broadhurst, K., Hall, C., Wastell, D., White, S., and Pithouse, A. (2010) Risk, Instrumentalism and the Humane Project in Social Work: Identifying the informal Logics of Risk Management in Children's Statutory Services, *British Journal of Social Work,* 40, 1046–1064

Brandon, M., Bailey, S., Balderson, P., and Larsson, B. (2013) *Neglect and Serious Case Reviews, A report,* University of East Anglia/NSPCC

Brockneck, E., L., Sanderson, J., and Britner, P., A. (2009) Ambiguous Loss and Post Traumatic Stress in School-Age Children of Prisoners, *Journal of Child and Family Studies,* 18 (3) 323–333

Bronfenbrenner, U. (1979) *The Ecology of Human Development: Experiments by Nature and Design,* London: Harvard University Press

Brotherton, G., and Cronin, M. (2013) *Working with Vulnerable Children, Young People and Families,* London: Routledge

Bruno, L. (2007) *Reassembling the Social: An Introduction to Actor-Network-Theory,* Oxford: Oxford University Press

Bryson, V. (2007) *Gender and the Politics of Time: Feminist theory and contemporary debates,* Bristol: The Policy Press

Bull, R., Corran, E. (2002) Interviewing Child Witnesses: Past and Future, *International Journal of Police Science and Management,* Vol. 4(4), pp. 315–322

Burford, G. (2017) *Family Group Conferencing: New Directions in Community-Centred Child and Family Practice,* London: Routledge

Burgess, A., and Clarke, A. (1984) *Child Pornography and Sex Rings,* New York: Lexington Books

Burman, E. (2008) *Deconstructing Development Psychology,* 2nd edition, London: Routledge

Burman, E., Stacey, J. (2010) 'The child and childhood in feminist theory', *Feminist Theory,* Vol. 11(3), pp. 227–240

Campbell, B. (2013) *End of Equality,* London: Seagull

Carroll, r. (2012) *Rereading Heterosexuality: Feminism, Queer Theory and Contemporary Fiction,* Edinburgh, Edinburg University Press.

Cixous, H. (1998) *Stigmata,* London: Routledge

Cixous, H. (2008) (eds) *White Ink: Interviews on sex, text and politics,* Stocksfield: Acumen

Clapton, G., Cree, V. and Smith, M. (2013) 'Moral Panics, Claims-Making and Child Protection in the UK', *British Journal of Social Work,* Vol. 43(4), pp. 803–812

Cleaver, H., & Freeman, P. (1995) *Parental Perspectives in Cases of Suspected Child Abuse,* London: HMSO

Cleaver, H., and Nicholson, D. (2007) *Parental Learning Disabilities and Children's Needs: Family Experience and Effective Practice,* London: Jessica Kingsley

Cleaver, H., & Walker, S., with Meadows, L. (2004) *Assessing Children's Needs and circumstances: the impact of the Assessment Framework,* London: Jessica Kingsley Publishers

Cleaver, H., Unell, I., Aldgate, J. (2011), 2nd ed., *Children's Needs – Parenting Capacity, Child abuse: Parental mental illness, learning disability, substance misuse and domestic violence,* London: TSO

Cree., V. (2015) *Gender and Family: Moral Panics in Theory and Practice,* Bristol: Policy Press

Cree, V., E. (2013) New Practices of Empowerment, in Gray, M., & Webb, S., A. (2013) *The New Politics of Social Work,* Basingstoke: Palgrave MacMillan

Crittenden, P. (1999) Child Neglect: Causes and Contributors, in Howard, D. (1999) *Neglected Children,* London: Sage

CSN Policy Briefing, Daniel Pelka Serious Case Review, Coventry LSCB (2013), London: Local Government Information Unit/Children's Services Network

Cossar, J., Brandon, M., and Jordan, P. (2014) 'You've got to trust her and she's got to trust you': children's views on participation in the child protection system, *Child and Family Social Work,* 21, 103–112

Cossar, J., Brandon, M., Bailey, S., Belderson, P., Biggart, L., and Sharpe, D. (2013) 'It takes a lot to build trust', Recognition and Telling: Developing earlier routes to help for children and young people, London: Office of the Children's Commissioner.

Daniel, B. (2010) Concepts of Adversity, Risk, Vulnerability and Resilience: A Discussion in the Context of the 'Child Protection System', *Social Policy and Society,* 9.2, 231–241

Daniel, B., Wassell, S., and Gilligan, R. (2010) *Child Development for Child Care and Protection Workers,* London: Jessica Kingsley

Davies, C., and Ward, H. (2012) *Safeguarding Children Across Services: Messages from Research,* London: Jessica Kingsley

Davies, G. M., Westcott, H. L. (1999) *Interviewing Child Witnesses under the Memorandum of Good Practice: A research review,* Police and Reducing Crime Unit Research, Development and Statistics Directorate, Police Research Series Paper 115, London.

Department for Communities and Local Government (2006) *Tackling Violence at Work: Good Practice Guidance Document for Fire and Rescue Services,* London: Department for Communities and Local Government

Department for Education (2018) *Post-qualifying standard: knowledge and skills statement for child and family practitioners,* London: DfE

Department for Education (2016), *Pathways to harm, pathways to protection: a triennial analysis of serious case reviews 2011 to 2014, Final Report,* London: DfE

Department for Education (2017) *Scaling and Deepening the Reclaiming Social Work Model,* Evaluation Report, London: DfE

Department of Health (2000) *Framework for the Assessment of Children in Need and their Families,* London: SO

Department of Health (2002) *Learning from Past Experience: A Review of Serious Case Reviews,* London: SO

DHSS (1985) *Review of Child Care Law: Report to Ministers of an Interdepartmental Working Party,* London: HMSO

DiQuinzio, P. (1999) *The Impossibility of Motherhood : Feminism, Individualism, and the Problem of Mothering,* London: Routledge

Dominelli, L. (2002) *feminist social work theory and practice,* Basingstoke: Palgrave MacMillan

Duchinsky, R., Greco, M., Solomon, J. (2015) The Politics of Attachment: Lines of Flight with Bowlby, Deleuze and Guattari, *Theory, Culture and Society,* 32 (7), pp. 173–195

Duffy, C., A. (1993) Mean Time, London: Anvil Press Poetry

Dunmore, H. (1994) *Recovering a Body,* Newcastle-upon-Tyne: Bloodaxe Books.

Estes, C, P. (2010) *Seeing in the Dark: Myths and Stories to Reclaim the Buried, Knowing Woman,* Sounds True: Boulder USA

Farmer, E., and Owen, M. (1998) 'Gender and the Child Protection Process', *British Journal of Social Work,* 28, pp. 545–564.

Fawcett, B., Featherstone, B., Fook, J, Rossiter, A. (2000) *Practice and Research in Social Work: Postmodern feminist perspectives.* London: Routledge

Featherstone, B. (2006) Why gender matters in child welfare and protection, *Critical Social Policy,* 26 pp 294–314

Featherstone, B., White, S., Morris, K. (2014) *Re-Imagining Child Protection: Towards humane social work with families,* Bristol: Policy Press

Ferguson, H. (2017) How Children Become Invisible in Child Protection Work: Findings from Research into Day-to-day Social Work Practice, *The British Journal of Social Work,* Vol. 47 (4), pp. 1007–1023

Ferguson, H. (2011) *Child Protection Practice,* Basingstoke: Palgrave Macmillan

Ferguson, H. (2003) *Protecting Children in Time,* London: Palgrave Macmillan

Finkelhor, D. (1984) *Child Sexual Abuse,* Ashgate: Aldershot

Fonagy, P., and Target, M. (2007) The Rooting of the Mind in the Body: New Links between attachment theory and psychoanalytic thought, *Journal of the American Psychoanalytical Association,* Vol 55 (2), 15–25

Fook, J. (2002) Theorising from Practice: Towards and Inclusive Approach to Social Work Research, *Qualitative Social Work,* Vol 1(1) 79–95

Forrester, D., and Harwin, J. (2011) *Parents who Misuse Drugs and Alcohol: Effective Interventions in Social Work and Child Protection,* Chichester: Wiley and Son

Gallagher, B. (1994) Grappling with Smoke: Investigating and managing organised child sexual abuse: A good practice guide, *Policy Practice Research Series,* London: NSPCC

Garrett, P., M. (2013) Mapping the Theoretical and Political Terrain of Social Work, in Gray, M., & Webb, S., (2013) (eds) *The New Politics of Social Work,* Palgrave MacMillan

Gergen, M. (2001) *Feminist Reconstructions in Psychology: Narrative, Gender and Performance,* London: Sage

Ghate, D., and Hazel, N. (2002) *Parenting in Poor Environments: Stress, Support and Coping,* London: Jessica Kingsley

Gilbert, N., Parton, N., & Skivenes, (Eds) (2011) *Child Protection Systems: International Trends and Orientations,* Oxford: Oxford University Press

Gilligan, C. (2006) Traumatised by Peace? A Critique of five assumptions in the theory and practice of conflict-related trauma policy in Northern Ireland, *Policy and Politics,* Vol. 34 (2), pp. 325–340

Gilligan, R. (2000) Adversity, resilience and young people: The protective value of positive school and spare time experiences, *Children and Society,* Vol. 14(1), pp. 37–47

Gray, M, and Webb, S, A. (2013) (eds) *The New Politics of Social Work,* London: Palgrave Macmillan

Guardian (2018a) Barry Bennell branded 'sheer evil' as he is sentenced to 30 years, 19 February.

Guardian (2018b) Seven years on from Winterbourne View, why has nothing changed, 30 May.

Guardian (2018c) Mum and Dad had never been happy. Then he moved his mistress in, 16 June

Guardian (2010) Edlington Brothers Jailed for torture of two boys, 22 January

Gullestadt, M. (1997) *Family and Kinship in Europe,* London: Bloomsbury

Hardwick, L., and Worsley, A. (2011) *Doing Social Work Research,* London: Sage

Hargreaves, R. (2007) *Mr Jelly,* London: Penguin Books

Haringey Local Safeguarding Children Board (2009) *First Serious case review overview report relating to Peter Connelly,* London: DfE

Haug, F. (1987) *Female Sexualization,* Surrey: *Verso*

Hendricks, J, H., Black, D., Kaplan, T. (1993) *When Father Kills Mother: Guiding Children Through Trauma and Grief,* London: Routledge

Hildyard, K., L. and Wolfe, D., A. (2007) Cognitive processes associated with child neglect, *Child Abuse and Neglect,* 31(8), pp. 895–907

Holloway, W., and Featherstone, B. (1997) *Mothering and Ambivalence,* London: Routledge

HM Government (2015a) *Knowledge and Skills Statement for child and family*

HM Government (2010) *Working Together to Safeguard Children: A Guide to Inter-Agency Working to Safeguard and Promote the Welfare of Children,* London: DfCSF

HM Government (2015b) *Working Together to Safeguard Children: A Guide to Inter-Agency Working to Safeguard and Promote the Welfare of Children,* London: DfE.

HM Government (2018) *Working Together to Safeguard Children: A Guide to inter-agency working to safeguard and promote the welfare of children,* HMSO: London

Home Office in Conjunction with Department of Health. (1992) *Memorandum of Good Practice on Video Recorded Interviews with Child Witnesses for Criminal Proceedings,* London: HMSO

Hood, R., Goldacre, A., Grant, R., Jones, R. (2016) Exploring Demand and Provision in English Child Protection Services, *British Journal of Social Work,* Vol 46 (4) pp. 923–941

Hooper, C. A., & Warwick, I. (2006) Gender and the politics of service provision for adults with a history of childhood sexual abuse, *Critical Social Policy,* Vol. 26, pp 467–479

Horwath, J. (2016) The Toxic-Duo The Neglected Practitioner and Parent Who Fails To Meet the Needs of Their Child, *British Journal of Social Work,* Vol. 46 pp 1102–1116

Horwath, J. (2013) *Child Neglect: Planning and Intervention,* Basingstoke: Palgrave Macmillan

Houston, S., and Griffiths, H. (2000) Reflections on Risk in Child Protection: is it time for a shift in paradigms, *Child and Family Social Work,* 5, pp 1–10

Houston, S. (2016) Beyond Individualism: Social Work and Social Identity, *British Journal of Social Work,* Vol. 46 pp 532–548

Howe, D. (2005) *Child Abuse and Neglect: Attachment, Development and Intervention,* Basinstoke: Palgrave MacMillan

Iwaniec, D., Larkin, E., Higgins, S. (2006) Research Review: Risk and resilience in cases of emotional abuse, *Child and Family Social Work,* Vol. 11 (1), pp. 73–82

Jones, R. (2014) *The Story of Baby P: Setting the records straight,* Bristol: Policy Press

Jordan, B., and Drakeford, M. (2012) *Social Work and Social Policy under Austerity,* Basingstoke: Palgrave Macmillan

Jay, A. (2014) *Independent Inquiry into Child Sexual Exploitation in Rotherham 1997– 2013,* Rotherham Metropolitan Borough Council

Jeffreys, H., Rogers, N., and Hirte, C. (2011) *Keeping the Child in Mind, Child Protection, Practice and Parental Mental Health,* Adelaid: Government of South Wales, Department for Families and Communities

Jordan, B. (2010) *Why the Third Way Failed: Economics, morality and the origins of the 'Big Society',* Bristol: The Policy Press

Kahneman, D. (2011) *Thinking, Fast and Slow,* UK: Penguin Random House

Katz, C. (2004) *Growing up Global: Economic Restructuring and Children's Everyday Lives,* Minneapolis: University of Minnesota Press

Kelly, L., and Karsna, K. (2017) *Measuring the scale and changing nature of child sexual abuse and child sexual exploitation,* Scoping Report, Centre of Expertise on Child Sexual Abuse, London Metropolitan University.

Kennan, D., Brady, B., and Forkan, C. (2018) Supporting Children's Participation in Decision Making : A Systematic Literature Review Exploring the Effectiveness of Participatory Process, *The British Journal of Social Work,* 48 (7), pp. 1985–2002

Kenward, H. (2002) Chapter 8 Integrated Review, Ainlee Labonte, Newham Area Child Protection Committee, London.

Kirkman, E., and Melrose, K. (2014) *Clinical Judgement and Decision-Making in Children's Social Work: An analysis of the 'front-door' system:* Report by the Behavioural Insights Team, DFE-RR337. London: DfE

Krane, J., Davies, L., Carlton, R., and Mulcahy M. (2010) The Clock Starts Now: Feminism, Mothering and Attachment Theory in Child Protection Practice, in Featherstone, B., Hooper, C. Scourfield, J., and Taylor J. *Gender and Child Welfare in Society,* Oxford: Wiley-Blackwell

Laird, S., E. (2013) *Child Protection: Managing conflict, hostility and aggression,* Bristol: Policy Press

Lamb, M. E., Hershkowitz, I., Orback, Y., Esplin, P. (2011) *Tell Me What Happened: Structures Investigative Interviews of Child Victims and Witnesses,* John Wiley & Sons: Chichester.

Laming, H. (2003) *The Victoria Climbie inquiry: Report of an inquiry by Lord* Laming, London: HMSO

Latalova, K., and Prasko, J. (2010) 'Aggression in borderline personality disorder', *Psychiatric Quarterly,* vol 81, pp 889–99.

Littlechild, B. (2005) The Nature and Effects of Violence against Child Protection Social Workers: Providing Effective Support, *The British Journal of Social Work*, Vol 35 (3), pp. 387–401

Littlechild, B. (2008) Child Protection Social Work: Risk of Fears and Fears of Risk – Impossible Tasks from Impossible Goals? *Social Policy and Administration*, Vol. 42 (6), 662–675

Lomax, R., Jones, K., Leigh, S., Gay, S. (2010) *Surviving your social work placement*, Basingstoke: Palgrave Macmillan.

Lonne, B., Parton, N., Thompson, J., and Harries, M. (2009) *Reforming Child Protection*, London: Routledge

London Borough of Hillingdon, (1986) Area Review Committee in Child Abuse into the Death of Heidi Koseda.

Lupton, D. (1999) *Risk*, London: Routledge

MacAllister, J., and Lee., W. (2016), Child Neglect and the Development of Communication, in Gardner, R. (2016) (eds) *Tackling Child Neglect*, London: Jessica Kingsley

McCarthy, G. (1999) Attachment style and adult love relationships and friendships: a study of a group of women at risk of experiencing relationship difficulties, *British Journal of Medical Psychology*, Vol. 72(3), pp. 305–321

Madge, N. (2006) *Children These Days*, Bristol: The Policy Press

Macdonald, G., and Macdonald, K. (2010) 'Safeguarding: A Case for Intelligent Risk Management', *British Journal of Social Work*, 40, pp. 1174–1191

Maitland, I (2018) 'Mum and Dad had never been happy. Then he moved his mistress in', *Guardian*,

Mayall, B. (2002) *Towards a Sociology for Childhood: Thinking from Children's Lives*, Buckingham: Open University Press

May-Chahal, C., and Coleman, S. (2003) *Safeguarding Children and Young People*, London: Routledge

Melhuish, E., Belsky, J., Barnes, J, (2010) Evaluation and value of Sure Start, *Archives of Disease in Childhood*, 95 159–161.

Melrose, M., Pearce, J. (2013) (eds) *Critical Perspectives on Child Sexual Exploitation and Related Trafficking*, Basingstoke: Palgrave MacMillan

Merkel-Holguin, L. and Marcynyszyn, L. A. (2015) The Complexity of Measuring System Change: The Case of Family Group Decision-Making, *The British Journal of Social Work*, Vol 45 (2) pp 724–736.

McGaw, S. & Newman, T. (2005) *What Works for Parents with Learning Disabilities?* Essex: Barnardo's

Miller, A. (1990) The Untouched Key: Tracing Childhood Trauma in Creativity and Destructiveness, London: Virago Press

Millet, K. (1977) *Sexual Politics*, London: Virago Press

Milner, J. (2001) *Women and Social Work: Narrative approaches*, Basingstoke: Palgrave Macmillan

Ministry of Justice (2011) *Achieving Best Evidence in Criminal Proceedings: Guidance on interviewing victims and witnesses, and guidance on using special measures*, London: Gov.UK

Morley, C. (2014) *Practicing Critical Reflection to Develop Emancipatory Change: Challenging the legal response to sexual assault*, Surrey: Ashgate

Mulkeen, M. (2013) 'Gendered Process in Child Protection: 'Mother-blaming' and the Erosion of Men's Accountability, *Irish Journal of Applied Social Studies,* Vol. 12 (7) pp. 74–88

Munro, E. (1996) Avoidable and Unavoidable Mistakes in Child Protection Work, *The British Journal of Social Work,* Vol. 26 (6), pp. 793–808

Munro, E. (2005) 'A simpler way to understand the results of risk assessment instruments', *Children and Youth Services Review,* 26, pp. 873–83

Munro, E. (2008) (2nd ed) Effective Child Protection, London: Sage

Munro, E. (2011) The Munro Review of Child Protection. Final Report: A Child-Centred System, London: TSO

National Advisory Committee on Drugs. (2011) *Parental Substance Misuse: Addressing its Impact on Children,* Dublin: SO

National Statistics (2016) Abuse during childhood: Findings from the Crime Survey for England and Wales, year ending March 2016, Office of National Statistics, London.

Nelson, S. (2016) *Tackling child sexual abuse: Radical approaches to prevention, protection and support,* Policy Press: University of Bristol

Newman, T., and Blackburn, S. (2002) *Transitions in the Lives of Children and Young People, Resilience Factors,* Edinburgh, Scottish Executive Education Department

Nutbrown, C., Carter, C. (2010) The Tools of Assessment: Watching and Learning, in Pugh, G., Duffy, B. (2010) (eds) *Contemporary Issues in the Early Years,* London: Sage

Ofsted (2012) *Inspection of local authority arrangements for the protection of children,* Doncaster Metropolitan Borough Council: London: HMI

Oliver, M. & Sapey, B. (2006) *Social Work with Disabled People,* Third Edition, Basingstoke: Palgrave MacMillan

O'Loughlin, M and O'Loughlin, S. (2014) *Effective Observation in Social Work Practice,* Learning Matters/Sage: London

O'Reilly, A. (2004) Between the Baby and the Bathwater: Some Thoughts on a Mother-Centred Theory and Practice of Feminist Mothering, *Journal of the Association for Research on Mothering,* Vol 8 (1), pp. 323–330

Orme, J. (2001) *Gender and Community Care: social work and social care perspectives,* Basingstoke: Palgrave Macmillan

Parton, N. (2014) The Politics of Child Protection: Contemporary Developments and Future Directions, Basingstoke: Palgrave Macmillan

Pennell, J., and Burford, G. (2017) Family Group Decision-Making and Family Violence, in Burford, G., and Hudson, J. *Family Group Conferencing: New Directions in Community-Centred Child and Family Practice,* London: Routledge

Petr, C. G. (1990) Adultcentrism in Practice with Children, *Families in Society,* 73(7), pp 408–416

Peters, S. (2018) *The Silent Guides: Understanding and developing the mind throughout life,* London: Lagom

Phillips, C., R. (2014) 'Seeing the Child' beyond the literal: Considering Dance Choreography and the Body in Child Welfare and Protection, *The British Journal of Social Work,* Vol 44 (8), pp. 2254–2271

Platt, D. (2006) Threshold decisions: How social workers prioritize referrals of child concern, *Child Abuse Review,* 15(1), 4–18.

Portela, M. J. O., Pells, K. (2014) Risks and Protective Factors for Children Experiencing Adverse Events, in Bourdillon, M., Boyden, J. (eds) *Growing up in Poverty*, Palgrave Studies on Children and Development, Basingstoke: Palgrave MacMillan

Pranis, K. (2017) Conferencing and the Community, in Burford, G., and Hudson, J. *Family Group Conferencing: New Directions in Community-Centred Child and Family Practice*, London: Routledge

Pritchard, C. (2004) *The Child Abusers: Research and Controversy*, Maidenhead: Open University Press: McGraw-Hill Education

Provan, S. (2012) *The Uncanny Place of the Bad Mother and the Innocent Child at the Heart of New Zealand's 'Cultural Identity'*, Unpublished PhD thesis, University of Canterbury Christchurch, NZ. Retrieved from http://hdl.handle.net

Public Health England (2016) *The Eatwell Guide: How does it differ to the eatwell plate?* London: Public Health England

Rempel, G., R., Neufield, A., Kushner, K., E. (2007) Interactive use of Genograms and Ecomaps in Family Caregiving Research, *Journal of Family Nursing*, Vol. 13 (4), pp. 403–419

Rennison, G. (1962) *Man on His Own: Social work and industrial society*, Melbourne: Melbourne University Press

Risley-Curtiss, C., and Heffernan, K. (2003) Gender Biases in Child Welfare, *Affilia*, Vol. 18. Pp. 2–15

Rogowski, S. (2013) *Critical social work with children and families: theory, context and practice*, Bristol: Policy Press

Rose, J. (2018) *Mothers: An Essay on Love and Cruelty*, New York: Farrar, Straus and Giroux

Ross, J., W. (2011) *Specialist Communication Skills for Social Workers: Focussing on Service Users' Needs*, Basingstoke: Palgrave MacMillan

Ruch, G., Turney, D., and Ward, A. (2010) *Relationship-Based Social Work: Getting to the Heart of it*, London: Jessica Kingsley

Sabin, M. A., Ford, A., Hunt, L., Jamal, R., Crowne, E., Shield, J.P.H., (2007) Which factors are associated with a successful outcome in a weight management programme for obese children? *Journal of Evaluation in Clinical Practice* Vol. 13 (3), pp. 364–368

Schraer, R. (2014) 85% of social workers were assaulted, harassed or verbally abused in the past year, *Violence Against Social Workers: Community Care*, http://www.communitycare.co.uk/2014/09/16/violence-social-workers-just-part-job-70-incidents-investigated/

SCIE. (2008) *Learning together to safeguard children: developing a multi-agency systems approach for case reviews*, SCIE guide 24, SCIE

Scourfield, J. (2003) *Gender and Child Protection*, Basingstoke: Palgrave MacMillan

Shemmings, D., and Shemmings, Y. (2014) *Assessing Disorganised Attachment Behaviour in Children: An Evidence-Based Model for Understanding and Supporting Families*, London: Jessica Kingsley

Shirani, F., Henwood, K., and Coltart, C. (2012) Meeting the Challenges of Intensive Parenting Culture: Gender, Risk Management and the Moral Parent, *Sociology*, 46, 26–40

Shlonsky, A., and Wagner, D. (2005). The Next Step: Integrating Actuarial Risk Assessment and Clinical Judgment into an Evidence-Based Practice Framework in CPS Case Management. *Children and Youth Services Review*, 27(3), 409–427.

Shoosmith, S. (2016) *Learning from Baby P: the politics of blame, fear and denial,* London: Jessica Kingsley

Sjoberg, L, Moen, B, Rundmo, T. (2004) *Explaining Risk Perception: An evaluation of the psychometric paradigm in risk perception research,* Norwegian University of Science and Technology, Department of Psychology: Trondheim.

Slovic, P. (2002) (eds) *The Perception of Risk,* London: Earthscan

Social Services Committee (1984) *Children in Care,* the Short Report, HC360, London: HMSO

Stanley, T., Du Plessis, R., and Austrin, T. (2010) Making Networks Work: Social Work Action and Children at 'Risk', *Qualitative Social Work,* Vol 10 (1) 49–65

Sternberg, K. J., Lamb, E. , Davies, G. M., Westcott, H. L., (2001) The Memorandum of Good Practice: theory versus practice, *Child Abuse& Neglect,* 25 pp 669–681

Stevens, I., and Cox P. (2007) Complexity Theory: Developing new Understandings of child protection in field settings and residential care, *British Journal of Social Work,* Vol 38 (7) pp 1320–1336

Sumner, W. G. (1906) *Folkways: A study of the sociological importance of usages, manners, customs, mores and morals,* Boston, MA: Gin and Company

Sutton Local Safeguarding Board (2016) *Child D, A Serious Case Review Overview Report,* Sutton LSCB, Davies

Tanner, K. & Turney, D. (2003) 'What do we know about child neglect? A critical review of the literature and its application to social work practice', *Child & Family Social Work,* Vol. 8. PP. 54–34

Tarleton, B., Ward, L. and Howarth, J. (2006) Finding the right support? A review of issues and positive practice in supporting parents with learning disabilities and their children, *The Baring Foundation,* The Norah Fry Research Centre, University of Bristol

Taylor, C. (2013) Critically Reflective Practice, cited in Gray, M. And Webb, A., S. (2013) *The New Politics of Social Work,* London: Palgrave MacMillan

Terr, L., C. (1991) 'Childhood traumas – an outline and overview, *American Journal of Psychiatry,* 148:10–20

Thomas, J., Holland, S. (2010) Representing Children's Identities in Core Assessments, *British Journal of Social Work,* Vol. 40 (8), pp. 2617–2633

Thompson, A., Hollis, C., and Richards, D. (2003) 'Authoritarian parenting attitudes as a risk to conduct problems: result from a British national cohort study', *European Child and Adolescent Psychiatry,* Vol. 12(2), PP. 84–91

The Times (2008) 'Words fail', 13 November

Timms, N. (2018) *Recording in Social Work,* London: Routledge

Trevithick, P. (2000) *Social Work Skills: A Practice Handbook,* Open University Press: Buckingham

Turney, D., Platt, D., Selwyn, J, and Farmer, E. (2011) Social Work Assessment of Child in Need: What Do We Know? Messages from Research, London: TSO

Tyler, I. (2008) 'Chav Mum Chav Scum': Class disgust in contemporary Britain, *Feminist Media Studies,* Vol 8 (1), pp. 17–34

Velleman, R., and Orford, J.(2001), *Adult who were the children of problematic drinkers,* Amsterdam, Harwood Academic Publishers

Wade, C., Llewellyn, G. , and Matthews, J. (2008) Review of Parent Training Interventions for Parents with Intellectual Disability, *Journal of Applied Research in Intellectual Disabilities*, 21, 352–366

Walby, S. (2007) Complexity Theory, Systems Theory, and Multiple Intersecting Social Inequalities, *Philosophy of the Social Sciences*, 37, 449–470

Walter, B. (2000) *Outsiders Inside: Whiteness, place and Irish Women(Gender, Racism and Ethnicity)*, London: Routledge

Warner, J. (2015) The Emotional Politics of Social Work and Child Protection, Bristol: Policy Press

Webb, S. A. (2006) *Social Work in a Risk Society*, London: Palgrave Macmillan

Welbourne, P. (2012) *Social Work with Children and Families (Post- Qualifying Social Work)*, London: Routledge.

Wilkins, D. (2013) Balancing Risk and Protective Factors: How Do Social Workers and Social Work Managers Analyse Referrals that May Indicate Children Are at Risk of Significant Harm, *British Journal of Social Work*, September 1–17

White, R., Carr, P., and Lowe, N. (1990) A Guide To The Children Act 1989, Butterworths: London

White, V. (2006) *The State of Feminist Social Work*, Bristol: Policy Press

Whittaker, J. K., del Valle, J, F., and Holmes, L. (2015) (eds) *Therapeutic Residential Care for Children and Youth: Developing International Evidence-Based Practice*, London: Jessica Kingsley

Williams, C., Soyden, H. (2005) When and How Does Ethnicity Matter? A Cross-National Study of Social Work Responses to Ethnicity in Child Protection Cases, *British Journal of Social Work*, Vol. 35(6), pp. 901–920

Wood, D., D., Dekker, S., Cook, R., Johannesen, L., Sarter, N. (2010) *Behind Human Error*, Surrey: Ashgate

Wrench, K. (2017) *Helping Vulnerable Children and Adolescents to Stay Safe: Creative Ideas and Activities for Building Protective Behaviours*, London: Jessica Kingsley

Wong, B. W. L., and Donahue, M. L. (2002) (eds) *The Social Dimensions of Learning Disabilities*, London: Routledge

Appendix

Question	Tips
What is the purpose of the observation?	Think carefully about what the purpose of child observation is. For example are you assessing risk and or need? Are you assessing the child's development? Are you examining the child's behaviour?
	Tip: Your observation should focus on one of the above. Avoid trying to do too much. Set clear parameters for the observation. One child observation will provide you with a wealth of information.
Who is the child?	Know the child's age, ethnicity, culture, religion, gender, abilities, behaviour, development, education and health.
	Tip: Before carrying out an observation you should review what information you have about the child. The outcome may affect how you go about your observation.
What are the child's individual attributes?	All children are individuals and each is affected by a unique set of circumstances and situations. The child cannot be understood primarily through the eyes and words of adults or categories.
	Tip: Practice the skill of 'tuning-in' to the child's experience (Ross, 2011) and consider how they may try to please or test the social worker and other adults or use their developed coping strategies and mechanisms – such as withdrawing emotionally and physically (hiding, humming, constantly moving, standing or sitting very still, picking at their clothes or furniture).
What is your time frame?	Ask yourself how fast findings from an analysis of your observation are needed.
	Tip: If you need an immediate analysis from the observation you will have to tailor the tools and approach. Carrying out a home visit for the first time you will have to rely on your skills and abilities to see and remember. When you carry out your write up after the observation use memory prompts that focus on the child. For example:
	How did they look?
	How did they behave?
	How did they communicate?
	Where did you see them?
	Who was present with them?
	What did they say?
	What were they doing?

Question	Tips
What legal framework is in place, if any?	Be aware of the legal context and what your analysis will mean to different audiences.
	Tip: Think about the information you have gathered and be confident in your analysis. Remember if you observed the child strapped into a buggy or chair, this is a fact. Your analysis should flow from this.
What will be the impact of the observation?	You may be concerned with carrying out an observation and providing an analysis that meets the needs of different audiences.
	Tip: Think carefully about the impact of the observation and how your findings will have an impact on the child and their future.
What is your relationship to the child?	Depending on your role and responsibilities, you may be entering the world of the child for the first time. Equally, you may have been involved with the child over a period of time.
	Tip: Think carefully about how your role and responsibilities may influence how you approach the child and the observation.
Where will the observation take place?	You may carry out an observation of the child in a range of settings.
	Tip: Think carefully about the setting as the child may have a specific relationship with the space and place. This will influence how the child responds and behaves and how you make an analysis of what you observe.
What are the strengths and limitations of the child's family and social relationships?	You may be observing the child in circumstances where they are surrounded by other adults, siblings or friends.
	Tip: Be aware that whoever is present will influence the child and provide you with additional information to think about and make sense of.
What should I use in my analysis?	The observation will have provided you with some answers and more than likely produced a range of questions.
	Tip: Reflect on what you now know. Set out what you find under basic headings such as:
	1. What you saw (facts)
	2. What you think about what you saw (interpretation)
	3. Why you think this (analysis supported by research)
	4. What should happen next? (recommendations)

Index

Lightning Source UK Ltd.
Milton Keynes UK
UKHW021620040123
414801UK00005B/210